Wicked Practise & Sorcerye
has been published in a
Limited Edition
of which this is

Number

170

FRONT COVER: 1619 woodcut of witches

The monument to the sixth Earl in Bottesford church. (By permission of the Grantham Journal. Photographer Gerry Wright)

Fleming Bridge and St Mary's Church, Bottesford. (VPE)

WICKED PRACTISE
& SORCERYE

The Belvoir Witchcraft case of 1619

Michael Honeybone

BARON
BUCKINGHAM
MMVIII

PUBLISHED in 2008 BY BARON BOOKS of BUCKINGHAM
and PRODUCED by ANTONY ROWE LIMITED
with origination by Academic & Technical Typesetting

© Michael Honeybone 2008

ISBN 978 0 86023 690 0

Published in paperback 2008
ISBN 978 0 86023 689 4

By the same author

The Book of Grantham 1980, 1988
The Book of Bottesford 1989, 2002
The Vale of Belvoir 1987, 2001

CONTENTS

PREFACE *by Rev Stuart J Foster Oblate OSB*

Chaplain to Their Graces the Duke and Duchess of Rutland and Rector of Bottesford

The seventeenth century was a time of social and political upheaval within a climate of significant theological change in English society; people were traumatised by uncertainty and distrust. Following the dissolution of the monasteries, aristocratic households like that at Belvoir Castle were still learning how to handle their new found responsibilities in people and land management. We cannot underestimate the effect all this was having upon the Vale of Belvoir and its people. On top of that came the trial of the Flower sisters. The fact that the Earl of Rutland's family had lost one child and were living with two others who were often ill, would have meant theirs was an emotionally charged household, as the Earl saw his heirs slipping away from their likely inheritance.

Contending with disgruntled members of staff, who appear to have been seeking some form of supernatural retribution against their family, may well have been the straw that broke the camel's back.

Within the Vale of Belvoir the rumour machine would have been working overtime and the efforts of their family Chaplain the Rev Samuel Fleming, and the then Rector of Langar, the Rev Charles Odingsells, was one of damage limitation. They were called to exercise some judicial expediency at a time when people were wondering which way the ecclesiastical pendulum might next swing.

With a Catholic Chaplain ensconced at the Castle and Rev Samuel Fleming in Bottesford, the Rutlands may well have been keeping their options open – or as Michael Honeybone suggests, they may well have been maintaining 'both a private and public religion simultaneously'. As the current Chaplain at Belvoir and Rector of Bottesford I can well imagine the pressure Samuel Fleming might have been under in order to bring this unhappy affair to a swift conclusion and especially so for an Earl and Countess who were presented as benevolent, honourable and kindly disposed towards all their servant and tenants.

That an act of spite could have such major and lasting repercussions, holding people's interest and dividing opinions to this day does not surprise a community like the Vale of Belvoir. To one degree or another, the Castle remains central to the Vale and once again we find ourselves living in a society going through immense social, economic and political change which is reflected in a church undergoing an act of re-forming itself. Which way will the pendulum swing?

8

FOREWORD

by The Duke and Duchess of Rutland

We are happy to introduce readers to Michael Honeybone's book on the Witches of Belvoir, set in the beautiful Vale of Belvoir which is our home. The Tenth Duke of Rutland wrote the Preface to the author's earlier book *The Vale of Belvoir*; in it he emphasised the long and distinguished history of our family. This book develops that theme, showing the important part our family has played in the history of the area and of the country. We at Belvoir have always highlighted the fascinating story of how the Flower family was accused of witchcraft against members of our family. Each year we have a re-enactment of the story here at Belvoir Castle, to give our visitors an insight into this remarkable episode from our past.

We welcome this book because it provides a detailed re-telling of this seventeenth-century story, and also sets it into its context of local and national events of the time. The reader will find out about the history of the Manners family from the First to the Sixth Earl, their children, the doctors who were called in to care for them and the family's famous associates, from King James I to Shakespeare and the Earl of Essex. The book also gives a picture of the lives of the Earl and Countess's household and the villagers who worked in the Vale of Belvoir. We are always pleased to welcome visitors who have read this fascinating story and would like to visit today's Castle to see Belvoir for themselves.

Rutland   *Emma Rutland*

TO THE READER

The purpose of the book is to offer a context for one of the best known stories of Jacobean witchcraft – how the children of the Earl of Rutland suffered from alleged witchcraft. Every child in the Vale of Belvoir in north-east Leicestershire is brought up with this story and they are still fascinated by the accounts of how the Flower family, with Rutterkin their cat terrified the locality with sympathetic magic. Visitors to Belvoir Castle are entertained with the details and all manner of re-enactments are regularly and rightly enjoyed. I am grateful to the present Duke and Duchess of Rutland for access to their archives, from which so much of the material for the book has been collected.

The story has a national appeal, for it involved King James I, of Gunpowder Plot fame, who regularly came to Belvoir for the wonderful hunting across the Vale and whose interest in witchcraft is well known. Shakespeare's ever-popular account of the three witches in *Macbeth* comes to mind, especially as Mr Shakespeare worked for the Rutland family, by creating a Rutland family motto for a Royal tournament in 1613. The original story of the affair, *The Wonderfull Discoverie of the Witchcrafts of Margaret and Phillip Flower,* has been both locally and nationally popular and has indeed been through at least ten editions since it first appeared in 1619, nearly 400 years ago. This book has as an Appendix the eleventh printing and I am particularly grateful to Vance Harvey for graciously allowing us to reprint his 1970 edition.

I hope readers will dip into this Appendix as they read the book, for there they will find the story as it was first offered to a national audience in 1619. Many other historical documents, maps and pictures are reproduced as illustrations to the book in order to further expose the nature of the everyday world of Jacobean England. The central purpose of the book is to recreate the cultural and social world as it appeared to villagers, to gentry, to medical, clerical and legal men and to the Royal court during the first quarter of the seventeenth century. The reader is asked to fit the witchcraft story into that world in order to understand how such tragic events might have happened.

10

I do not favour any one set of causes for the extraordinary events described in the book. Modern witchcraft studies are packed with complex examinations which I have read with enthusiasm and which open up many ideas. The work of Robin Briggs, Stuart Clark and Marion Gibson has perhaps had the greatest influence on me and I very much appreciate their responses to my queries. Anthropological, psychological, mentality and gender studies have all in their turn shed a different light on the complex issues at the heart of witchcraft studies. In the end I would ask readers to make up their own mind about the interaction between the Flower family, the Vale of Belvoir villagers and the Earl of Rutland's family. I trust that, while doing so, they will enjoy this investigation into the world of James I.

It is possible to find the sources for the quotations in the References which are all brought together at the end of the book. Many of the quotations included are taken from documents and published books produced in earlier periods, particularly from the seventeenth century. These have been reproduced in a form as close as possible to the original. Long quotations are indented. Short quotations within the body of the text are placed within single inverted commas. Capital letters and italics used in the original texts have been retained. The spelling of the original texts has been retained; occasionally a modern equivalent of a particularly obscure or obsolete expression has been inserted in square brackets.

The only changes made, for ease of reading and presentation, are in certain features of seventeenth-century printing. If 'u' is printed in the original text where 'v' would be used today, 'v' has been used, *eg* 'Deuil' has been rendered as 'Devil'. If 'i' is used in the original text where today's printing would use 'j', this book uses 'j', *eg* 'iustice' is rendered as 'justice'. Where 'the long 's' is originally printed, it is rendered as 's'. In the seventeenth century in England, the year officially began on 25 March, so that dates in January, February and until 24 March were given what a modern reader would regard as the previous year's date. This book uses the modern dating convention. Consequently, the date of the execution of the Flower sisters is given as 11 March 1619 in this book, whereas in the Bottesford pamphlet it is given as 11 March 1618, following their arrest in December 1618, which a modern reader would find confusing.

This study has been greatly facilitated by the Open University. The Department of History of Science, Technology and

Medicine has assisted me over the past five years with a Visiting Research Fellowship. This has given me access to that outstanding Internet-based research tool, Early English Books Online (EEBO). I am particularly grateful to EEBO for permission to reprint pages from sixteenth- and seventeenth-century printed books. Other on-line databases such as the new Oxford Dictionary of National Biography and Eighteenth-Century Collections Online have also proved extremely valuable.

Over the years I have accumulated many debts of gratitude for help in this communal effort to understand the story. The Rectors and Churchwardens of St Mary's Church, Bottesford have been unfailingly helpful. The members of the Bottesford Local History Society have listened with patience to my developing ideas and its present chairman and secretary, Peter and Peggy Topps, have continuously demonstrated just how thoughtful Bottesford folk really are. Neil Fortey has effectively established the Belvoir Living History Project, which is shedding new light on the village past and present. The book has benefited greatly from continuous discussion with Clare Painting-Stubbs, who has always been willing to share her expertise on Abraham Fleming. Roy Palmer and Judith Havens gave helpful advice on the ballad. For medical understanding I have relied on knowledge learnt during very helpful discussions with Dr John Cleary and Dr Tania Morley. My two biggest debts will be clear as the reader looks at the book. Ted Rayson has produced an outstanding set of photographs. He, a Bottesford man, has shown through his skill and dedication how we can begin to understand the past by looking at its visual sources. For several years my publisher, Clive Birch, has encouraged me to persevere with this study and I am very grateful for his interest and his expertise.

PROLOGUE

On 11 March 1619 Margaret and Philippa Flower, the daughters of Joan Flower, from the Vale of Belvoir on the border between Leicestershire and Lincolnshire, were hanged in Lincoln Castle. They had been tried at Lincoln Assizes and condemned for witchcraft, defined in law as dealing with evil and wicked spirits, aimed against the family of Francis Manners, sixth Earl of Rutland and Lord of Belvoir Castle, contrary to the 1604 Witchcraft Act. The Earl's elder son, Henry Manners, called Lord Roos, had died in 1613; his only sister, Katherine Manners, and his younger brother, Francis Manners, suffered from 'extreame maladies and unusuall fits' (*The Belvoir pamphlet page 11*). The accused witches confessed to having cast spells against the children and to bewitching the Earl and his lady that 'they should have no more children'. The belief that witchcraft was used against his family was so entrenched in the Earl's mind that he still claimed in the inscription which he ordered for his tomb in St Mary's Church, Bottesford, prepared before his death in 1632, that his two sons had 'dyed in their infancy by wicked practise & sorcerye' despite the fact that the younger, Francis, died in 1620 after the execution of the Flower sisters.

This sad story of the aristocratic Manners family and their old-established household servants, the Flower family, can help us understand the strange phenomenon of English witchcraft in Jacobean times, the first quarter of the seventeenth century. The story has at its heart disputes within and between social classes and between the sexes. It highlights the search for scapegoats to explain the apparently inexplicable, and it draws our attention to the psychological and physical distress apparent in Jacobean village communities, struggling with plague and occasional famine. This story of disputes involving the whole local community can perhaps also be used to clarify the power conflicts which the historian Robin Briggs suggests lay at the heart of European witchcraft, by which 'secret and unnatural power' could be attributed 'to those who were formally powerless'. The practice of witchcraft could be a means by which ordinary people asserted themselves against those they saw as injuring them or treating them unjustly.

The Belvoir case, while sharing similarities with many other typical witchcraft accusations and trials, is of particular interest because of its complexity. It involves a leading aristocratic family as its alleged victims, a rare case since most accusations were between neighbours in villages or small towns. It reveals a complicated series of motivations driving both accusers and accused. The examination of the witnesses recorded in the 1619 pamphlet which recounts the story throws light on beliefs of the period concerning witchcraft. The well-preserved family archives of the Manners family are also of value in filling in the background to this case. Another important aspect which the story illustrates is the historian Stuart Clark's perception that witchcraft at the turn of the sixteenth and seventeenth centuries was seen as a punishment from God and a warning to true Christians: that it, like so many other contemporary phenomena, foretold the imminent cataclysm of the World.

England was ruled by James I, who had learnt the role of a crowned King the hard way, having been, as he said, a 'cradle king', King of Scotland from babyhood. In 1603 he was delighted to exchange the straitened circumstances of his court in Edinburgh for London, the largest city in Europe, with a population of around a quarter of a million. James was determined to rule in his own way: he only called four Parliaments during his reign and he made extensive use of Royal proclamations. But ruling England was never going to be easy, as the four million inhabitants of England were widely spread across the nation in small towns and villages, and with a strong sense of local community and identity.

In reality these communities were controlled by the local aristocrats and gentry families, who had profited from the huge market in land freed by the sale of all the monastic lands after the dissolution of the monasteries by Henry VIII in the 1530s. These families married early to ensure heirs who would inherit their ever-increasing landed estates. In contrast, the typical tradesman or agricultural worker could not afford to marry early, generally delaying marriage until his late twenties and having as few children as the rudimentary family planning circumstances of the period allowed. There was not the distinct separation between these groups which had developed by the nineteenth century. The aristocrats and gentry maintained a large staff of servants in their houses and estates, including the upper servants with whom they were in close daily contact, so that any news or rumours current in their area reached their attention easily. Prices were high in England because all easily available land had been brought into farming use and the population was rising, doubling between 1500 and 1620. One apparent effect of an increasing population was a perceived rise in crime, which led to much new legislation to control the poor. Litigation by the rich and lawbreaking by the poor led to large numbers of lawyers and the need for more education; the Protestant emphasis on the need to know the Word of God in the Bible also encouraged widespread literacy. This resulted in the expansion of educational provision at all levels, particularly in the universities of Oxford and Cambridge and the Inns of Court in London, in local grammar schools and in the establishment of parish elementary or 'petty' schools. In consequence a new phenomenon was apparent for the first time – cheap literature, which could be distributed right across the country in the form of pamphlets or chapbooks. The newly-literate population also became more adept at trade, especially in the many small towns across the country.

As King in Britain, James I was determined to work towards a peaceful Europe across which trade could flow more freely and would not be disrupted by religious conflict.

England was to some extent different from the mainstream of European life. Religious differences were more extreme in France and Germany, partly because there were more university towns there than in England, encouraging religious debate, and central control from the capital was harder to impose. Particularly in France, large regional towns such as Lyon and Rouen dominated their local provinces. Life across Europe was, however, essentially rural, controlled by seasonal labour sowing in springtime, harvesting in autumn and sometimes facing shortages in the harder months. Women ruled domestic life, overseeing childbirth and trying to keep their children alive through herbal remedies and by avoiding the ill-will of neighbours. In cases of illness, the rich could use the services of physicians and apothecaries, while the poor used home-made medicines or turned to the services of local 'cunning men' or white witches.

These facts should underpin any examination of the Belvoir witchcraft story. What is also essential is to use the almost overwhelming body of evidence available about the local Vale of Belvoir people and the social contacts of the fifth and sixth Earls of Rutland, who were at the time rebuilding a family fortune of real significance. The first public accounts of the presumed witchcraft were written immediately after the trial, appearing in London in 1619 in two forms: an unusually full pamphlet and an associated popular ballad. Both the Belvoir pamphlet and the ballad are reproduced in this book, generally in their original language. There is no doubt about the provenance of the pamphlet: it contains such a sophisticated intellectual discussion of witchcraft and so many personal details of the Manners family that it must have been produced under the Earl's patronage.

What gives the pamphlet further historical resonance is the number of local families from the Vale of Belvoir who feature in it. Over thirty villagers are mentioned; it is possible to trace nearly all of their families and thus analyse their village networks through parish documents in local archives. All the villagers owed allegiance to the Earl as their lord of the manor, but their own social inter-relationships were equally important in their lives. All the examining magistrates, lay and clerical, are identifiable. In addition there is the huge collection of Manners family documents which open up for us knowledge of doctors and apothecaries, the family servants and the family inter-relationships.

This book is built around that body of evidence. Each chapter examines one factor which contributed to the accusation of witchcraft against the Flower family and which helps us to understand why this case was brought to trial when many other such accusations came to nothing. The first two chapters examine in detail the Vale of Belvoir families and the Manners family to understand the blood relationships and the formal layers of patronage which created English social interactions at the beginning of the seventeenth century. Having presented the *dramatis personae* in Chapters One and Two, the events of the twenty years before the trial are examined in detail in two further chapters. Chapter Three concentrates on the Manners family's medical problems which were to prove so intractable and which led to their willingness, when medical attentions failed, to consider witchcraft as an explanation for their children's illness. The archives of the present Duke of Rutland hold the names of a surprising number of significant English physicians, who treated the fifth and sixth Earls and their families. Their styles of doctoring will be investigated to help understand Jacobean medical knowledge, outlook and treatments.

16

Chapter Four presents both the theological and popular view of witchcraft in the Jacobean period. This involves a discussion of the theological positions held by those local clergy of whom we have any evidence. What emerges from this is a fascinating relationship between the Catholic Manners family and the theoretically Protestant clerics of the locality, which perhaps led to mutual support over the witchcraft question. It points to a local climate of belief which accepted the existence of witchcraft as a cause of otherwise inexplicable misfortune.

Chapter Five brings all this together, by focusing on the trial of Margaret and Phillip (or Philippa) Flower on a charge of encompassing the death of the Earl's elder son by witchcraft. It sums up the story of this case as brought to court, and investigates the evidence given by local women examined by the county magistrates. It concentrates on the law relating to witchcraft and on an account of events associated with the trial itself. The task and function of the magistracy, the justices of the peace and their clerks, can be discussed in detail, since it was the JPs, including the sixth Earl and his brother, who collected the evidence. This evidence, printed in great detail in the Belvoir pamphlet, was presented to the pre-trial hearings at Lincoln Assizes in the first week of March 1619 and led to the apparently inescapable verdict of 'guilty'.

The records of the final trial itself have not survived, since the huge mountain of documentary evidence following the Royal judges around the Midland Circuit became so unwieldy by the beginning of the nineteenth century that cartloads of assize papers were destroyed. The judges, though, were well known: it is significant that the two judges at the Lent Assizes in Lincoln in March 1619 were the Lord Chief Justice of the Common Pleas, Sir Henry Hobart, and Sir Edward Bromley, the latter of whom had sentenced ten women accused of witchcraft to death in the Pendle witchcraft trial held at Lancaster in 1612.

It is important, however, to point out that accused witches were not easily found guilty at this time. Indeed, a central figure in this story, King James, was by 1616 so sceptical about witchcraft prosecutions that he had halted a series of executions in Leicester and dismissed the case, as he argued that it was based on a child's hysterical evidence. The King visited Belvoir Castle six times whilst Francis Manners was sixth Earl; the Earl was attending the King in London at Christmas 1618 when the scandal broke and the Flower family were accused. The judges who tried the two young women at Lincoln were James' own appointments and he would have followed with care their judgements in this case. Accordingly Chapter Five presents an overview of the nature of the accusations and likely process of the trial. This account is derived from the legal examinations taken at the time and on evidence from the few other trials which have been well recorded, notably that at the 1612 Lancaster Assizes.

The Epilogue addresses the issue of the changing attitudes to witchcraft since 1619. Here it is necessary to distinguish between two concepts: the law relating to witchcraft and the belief in witchcraft, both of which changed over time. I am concerned in this book with a specific trial arising from the 1604 statute law which had replaced the first effective English parliamentary law against witchcraft, that of 1563 with its extension in 1581. The 1563 statute made 'invocations or conjurations of wicked and evil spirits... witchcraft, enchantment, charm or sorcery, whereby any person shall happen to be killed or destroyed' a felony, therefore punishable by the 'pains of death'. In 1604, James' first Parliament repealed this statute and enacted that

> 'if any person or persons... shall use practise or exercise any invocation or conjuration of any evil or wicked spirit, or shall consult, covenant with, entertain, employ, feed, or reward any evil and wicked spirit to or for any intent or purpose; or take up any dead man, woman, or child out of his, her, or their grave, or any other place, or child out of his, her, or their grave, or any other place where the dead body resteth, or the skin, bone, or any other part of any dead person, to be employed or used in any manner of witchcraft, sorcery, charm, or enchantment; or shall use, practise, or exercise any witchcraft, enchantment, charm, or sorcery, whereby any person shall be killed, destroyed, wasted, consumed, pined, or lamed in his body, or any part thereof;... shall suffer pains of death.'

The law, clarified by this statute (which survived until 1735/1736), thus imposed the death penalty on any person who confessed to consulting with spirits to cause harm. This harsh statute law had arisen from the sixteenth century reformation of the church in England, which removed the jurisdiction of the Pope and of European canon or church law from England; it made witchcraft a state crime, in addition to being an offence answerable in the mild church courts of the Church of England.

It is relatively easy to specify the legal definition of witchcraft; what is problematic is to offer any generally acceptable view of the common understanding of and belief in witchcraft in 1619. Indeed, the literary scholar Marion Gibson in *Reading Witchcraft* suggests that 'there is no stable thing, called "witchcraft", which lies hidden beneath its various constructions'. Undoubtedly there was in the early seventeenth century a certain stereotype of a witch, and the author of the Belvoir pamphlet (*page 8*) offers such a picture in his account of Mistress Joan Flower:

> 'the Mother was a monstrous malicious woman, full of oathes, curses, and imprecations irreligious, and for any thing they saw by her, a plaine Atheist; besides of late days her very countenance was estranged, her eyes were fiery and hollow, her speech fell and envious, her demeanour strange and exoticke, and her conversation sequestered; so that the whole course of her life gave great suspition she was a notorious witch'

The stereotype had not changed since it was first satirically described by Reginald Scot in 1584: witches were 'women which be commonly old, lame, blear-eied, pale, fowle, and full of wrinkles; poore, sullen, superstitious, and papists; or such as knowe no religion... For alas! What an unapt instrument is a toothles, old, impotent, and unweldie woman to flie in the aier? Trulie, the divell little needs such instruments to bring his purposes to passe'. But this is the Oxford educated gentleman speaking. Most people accepted the concept of witchcraft, holding the view that spirits could be summoned to help in both positive and negative enterprises. Cunning folk offered medical help, using charms and herbal remedies to solve all sorts of problems. The Belvoir pamphlet is sceptical about 'the conceit of wisemen or wise women, they are all meerely coseners and deceivers; so that if they make you believe that by their meanes you shall heare of things lost or stolne, it is either done by Confederacy, or put off by protraction to deceive you of your money' (*page 4*). Indeed the act of 1604 specifically and separately enacted means for the punishment of these confidence tricksters.

The problem lies in the general religious concept of *a spirit*. More specifically, the Protestant reformers had abolished the prayers for the souls of the dead and so the notion of spirits in some way relating to the everyday world was no longer viable. What happened to the ghosts of the dead? They existed in some form in the minds of most people, yet suddenly they had no official place in this Protestant England. Also there was the problem of evil. A credible explanation for its existence in this world was that the chief *spirit* of darkness, the Devil, sought to spread evil by making contact with human beings and this was an accepted theological position of all believers. It appeared to be perfectly reasonable to most people to accept the concept of *maleficium*, which involved making a compact with the Devil to attack someone. The issue of how the Devil actually passed on his evil instructions was apparently solved in what some people would consider to be a particularly English way: by his familiars, the ubiquitous cats and dogs and other common animals of the countryside as they snuggled up to their owners.

A belief in witchcraft was virtually omnipresent in Europe at the beginning of the seventeenth century but it flared up only rarely into vicious accusations in certain areas and these did not always come to trial. Where it did, it was most commonly associated with actions perceived as having their foundation in malice or revenge. Exactly why accusations were launched in the Vale of Belvoir and why these came to court and resulted in execution can only be clarified by a local investigation, to understand the motives of both accused and accusers. This leads us to focus first on the Vale village families, particularly the Flower family who were the accused, and on the Belvoir Castle family, the Manners.

ABOVE: The ford at Bottesford, close by St Mary's Church and BELOW: a house by the ford, close to St Mary's, sometimes incorrectly known as the Witch's House, although the original house here dates from the right period. (Both HER)

21

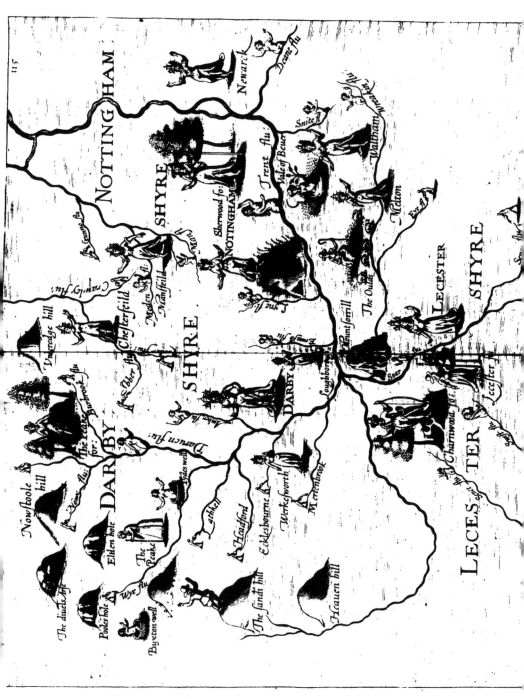

The counties of eastern England in 1622 from Michael Drayton's Poly-Olbion. *(EEBO & HCL)*

22

THE
WONDERFVL
DISCOVERIE OF THE

Witchcrafts of *Margaret* and *Phillip*
Flower, daughters of *Ioan Flower* neere *Beuer*
Caſtle: Executed at Lincolne, *March* 11. 1618.

Who were ſpecially arraigned and condemned before Sir
Henry Hobart, and Sir *Edward Bromley*, Iudges of Aſ-
ſiſe, for confeſſing themſelues actors in the deſtruction
of *Henry* Lord *Roſſe*, with their damnable practiſes againſt
others the Children of the Right Honourable
FRANCIS Earle of *Rutland*.

Together with the ſeuerall Examinations and Confeſſions of *Anne*
Baker, Ioan Willimot, and *Ellen Greene*, Witches in *Leiceſterſhire*

Printed at London by *G. Eld* for *I. Barnes*, dwelling in the long Walke
neere Chriſt-Church. 1619.

Title page of the first edition of the Belvoir Pamphlet, 1619. (BL)

Damnable Practises

Of three Lincolne-ſhire Witches, *Joane Flower*, and her two Daughters, Margret and *Phillip Flower*, againſt *Henry* Lord Roſſe, with others the Children of the Right Honourable the Earle of Rutland, at Beauer Caſtle, who for the ſame were executed at Lincolne the 11. of *March* laſt.
To the tune of the Ladies fall.

OF damned deeds, and deadly dole,
 I make my mournfull ſong,
By Witches done in Lincolne-ſhire,
 where they haue liued long:
And practiſ'd many a wicked deed,
 within that Country there,
Which fills my breſt and boſome full,
 of ſobs, and trembling feare.

The Beauer Caſtle is a place,
 that welcome giues to all,
p which the Earle of Rutland gaines
 the loues of great and ſmall:
A Counteſſe of like friendlineſſe,
 as beare as free a mind,
As ſo from them both rich and poore,
 helps and ſuccour find.

And the reſt were Witches three,
 as to this Caſtle came,
Margaret and Phillip Flower,
 was Joane their Mothers name:
And Women daply found reliefe,
 and were contented well:
And the laſt this Margret was,
 ceiued there to dwell.

She vnto ſuch houſhold charge,
 vnto her belongd,
She poſſeſt with fraud and guile,
 ſo place and office wrongd,
Secretly purloyned things
 and her mother home:
Vnlawfull bowers from thence,
 ſhe nightly goe and com

en the Earle & Count ſhe heard,
 her dealings knew,
ſued much that ſhe ſhould proue,
 ſo vntrue:

And ſo diſcharg'd her of the houſe,
 therein to come no more:
For of her lewd and filching prankes,
 of proofes there were ſome ſtore.

And likewiſe that her Mother was,
 a woman full of wrath,
A ſwearing and blaſpheming wretch,
 foreſpeaking ſodaine death:
And how that neighbours in her lookes,
 malitious ſignes did ſee:
And ſome affirm'd ſhe dealt with Spirits,
 and ſo a Witch might be.

And that her Siſter Phillip was,
 well knowne a Strumpet lewd,
And how ſhe had a young mans loue,
 bewitched and ſubdued:
Which made the young man often ſay,
 he had no power to leaue
Her curſt inticing company,
 that did him ſo deceaue.

When to the Earle and Counteſſe thus,
 theſe iuſt complaints were made,
Their hearts began to breed diſlike,
 and greatly grew affraid:
Commanding that ſhe neuer ſhould,
 returne vnto their ſight,
Nor back into the Caſtle come,
 but be excluded quite.

Whereat the old malitious fiend,
 with theſe her darlings thought:
The Earle and Counteſſe them diſgrac't,
 and their diſcredits wrought:
In turning thus deſpightfully,
 her daughter out of doores,
For which reuengement, in her mind
 ſhe many a miſchiefe ſtores.

Whereat the Diuell made entrance in,
 his Kingdome to inlarge,
And puts his creeping wrath,
 vnto theſe womens charge:
Not caring whom it lighted on,
 the Innocent or no,
And offered them his diligence,
 to flye, to run, and goe.

And to attend in pretto formes,
 of Dog, of Cat, or Rat,
To which they freely gaue conſent,
 and much reioyc't thereat:
And as it ſeemd they ſould their ſoules,
 for ſeruice of ſuch Spirits,
And ſealing it with drops of blood,
 damnation ſo inherits.

Theſe Women thus being Diuels growne
 moſt cunning in their Arts:
With charmes and with inchanting ſpells,
 they plaid moſt damned parts:
They did foreſpeake, and Cattle kild,
 that neighbours could not thriue,
And oftentimes their Children young,
 of life they would depriue.

At length the Counteſſe and her Lord,
 to fits of ſickneſſe grew:
The which they deemd the hand of God,
 and their correction due:
Which croſſes patiently they bore,
 miſdoubting no ſuch deeds,
As from theſe wicked Witches heare,
 malitiouſly proceeds.

Yet ſo their mallice more increaſt,
 that miſchiefe ſet in fote,
To blaſt the branches of that houſe,
 and vndermine the roote:
Their eldeſt ſonne Henry Lord Roſſe,
 poſſeſt with ſickneſſe ſtrange,
Did lingring, lye tormented long,
 till death his life did change.

Their ſecond ſonne Lord Francis next,
 felt like continuing woe:
Both day and night in grieuous ſort,
 yet none the cauſe did know:
And then the Lady Katherin,
 into ſuch torments fell:
By theſe their deuiliſh practiſes,
 as grieues my heart to tell.

That strangly be confum'd away,
vntill the houre he dyed.

And likewife the confeſt how they,
  together all agreed :
Againſt the children of this Earle,
  to practiſe and proceed.
Not leauing them a child aliue,
  and neuer to haue moe :
If witchcraft ſo could doe, becauſe,
  they turn'd them out of doze.

The mother as the daughters told,
  could hardly this deny :
For which they were attached all,
  by Juſtice ſpeedily.
And vnto Lincolne Citty borne,
  therein to lye in Jayle :
Vntill the Judging Size came,
  that death might be their bayle.

But there this hatefull mother witch,
  theſe ſpeeches did recall :
And ſaid that in Lord Roſſes death,
  ſhe had no hand at all.
Whereon ſhe bread and butter tooke,
  God let this ſame (quoth ſhe)
If I be guilty of his death,
  paſſe neuer thorough me.

So mumbling it within her mouth,
  ſhe neuer ſpake moe words :
But fell downe dead, a judgment juſt,
  and wonder of the Lords.
Her Daughters two their tryalls had,
  of which being guilty found,
They dyed in ſhame, by ſtrangling twiſt,
  and layd by ſhame in ground.

Haue mercy Heauen, on ſinners all,
  and grant that neuer like
Be in this Nation knowne or done,
  but Lord in vengeance ſtrike :
Or elſe conuert their wicked liues
  which in bad wayes are ſpent :
The feares of God and loue of heauen,
  ſuch courſes will preuent.

FINIS.

Yet did this noble minded Earle,
  ſo patiently it beare :
As if his childrens puniſhments,
  right natures troubles were :
Suſpecting little, that ſuch meanes,
  againſt them ſhould be wrought,
Untill it pleaſ'd the Lord to haue
  to light theſe miſchiefes brought.

For greatly here the hand of God,
  did worke in iuſtice cauſe :
When he for theſe their practiſes
  them all in queſtion drawes.
And ſo before the Magiſtrates,
  when as the yongeſt came,
Who being guilty of the fact
  confeſt and tould the ſame.

How that her mother and her ſelfe,
  and ſiſter gaue conſent :
To giue the Counteſſe and her Lord,
  occaſions to repeat
That ere they turn'd her out of dores,
  in ſuch a vile diſgrace :
For which, or them as theirs ſhould be,
  brought into heauy caſe.

And how her ſiſter found a time,
  Lord Roſſes gloue to take :
Who gaue it to her mothers hand
  conſuming ſpels to make.
The which ſhe prickt all full of holes,
  and layd it deepe in ground :
Whereas it rotted, ſo ſhould he,
  be quite away conſum'd.

All which her elder ſiſter did,
  acknowledge to be true :
And how that ſhe in boyling blood,
  did oft the ſame imbrew,
And hereupon the yong Lord Roſſe,
  ſuch torments did abide :

There is a booke printed of theſe
Witches, wherein you ſhall know
all their examinations and confeſſions
at large : As alſo the wicked practiſe
of three other moſt Notorious Witches in Leceſter-ſhire with all their
examinations and confeſſions.

Printed by G. Eld for John Barnes, dwelling in the long Walke neere Chriſt-Church
1619.

OPPOSITE: The Belvoir Witchcraft Ballad part 1 and ABOVE: part 2. (Both MCC)

Saxton's map of Leicestershire, showing Bottesford, as printed by William Burton in his Description of Leicestershire *of 1622. (EEBO&CUL)*

BEluoire Priory, standing vpon the vtmost part of the Shire, almost vp-on the very Mere; so that to say, whether it be of Lincolne, or Leice-ster, I cannot directly affirme; this Roll of 5.H.3. heere below vouched, doth shew that it is in the County of Leicester, vpon which ground I haue heere inserted it. The Castle is certainely of Lincolnshire, standing vpon the top of a very lofty hill, containing from the foot to the top, about two hundred steps; yeelding euery way a most delicious & pleasing pro-spect, being accounted one of the best prospects in the land. I haue often viewed this Castle from the place where I dwell at Falde neere Tutbury, in the County of Stafford, with the helpe of a prospectiue glasse, the di-stance of 32. miles. Of this faire prospect it hath this French name of Beluoir, and is commonly called Beuer. This Castle was founded (as M. Camden saith) by Totney a Norman; but (vnder his fauor) I rather think it to be founded by one of the house of Albeney, whose first name might be (perhaps) Totney: my reason is, for that I haue seen ancient Records about the time of King Henry the first, or perhaps elder, proouing the Albanies then here to be resident, who were true Naturalists of this Land, and no Normans or strangers, for I haue found them twice or thrice written with this addition, Willimus de Albiniaco Brito: The heire generall of Albany was married to Ros of Hamlake, whose heire generall was married vnto Mannors, from whom is descended the righ honourable the Earle of Rut-land, now Lord of this Castle.

This Priory, (saith Leland) was founded by Robert de Beluoir, sine Tot-ney, and was dedicated to the Virgin Mary, and was of the Order of black Monkes of S. Albanes, to which house it was a Cell (as Leland saith). The yearly rents of this Priory at the time of the suppression (as he saith) were valued at 135. pound: it is now the inheritance of the right honourable the Earle of Rutland. Prioratus de Belnoir patronus Willimus de Albaniaco. *Leland t.T. Collect. fol. 90. I do verily be-leeue that Tot-ney is mistake for Albaney. Ros 5.H.3. In Decanatu de Framland. Leic.*

BErtsanby or Beselby, in the Hundred of Framland, it is in the parish of Salsby, and in 5.H.3. had a Chappell within it, which was to be ser-ued three daies in the weeke by the Mother Church. Sir Andrew Lutte-rell Knight was Lord of this Mannor, and died 37.E.3.

BIllesdon in the Hundred of Gartrey: In the time of K. Henry the third, William Franceis was seised of certaine lands heere, & conueyed them by deed to one Robert de Diggeby, In 20.E.3. the heire of Diggeby, John de Schirford, and Geffrey de Skeffington were also seized of lands here, held of the Honor of Peuerell, in King Ed.4. (5 .E.4.) granted vnto Sir Walter Deureux Knight, costs and ten yard land heere. *Rot.20.E.3.*

Ecclesia de Billesdon patronus Abbas Leic. habens eam in proprios vsus ab antiquo & habet Capellam * *Goulcby; qua libere est habens capellanum resi-dentem, & omnia iure parochialia sed non soluit synodalia, Item* * *Rolinston qua consueuit de seruiri tribus diebus in ebdomada per matricem ecclesiam, vicarius institutus per Episcopum.* *Rot.5.H.3. *Goulcby. **Rolinston.*

F 2   The

Bottesford, sometimes written *Bottlesford*, in the Hundred of *Framland*: This Mannor was long since the inheritance of *William de Albaney*, Baron of *Belvoire*, and (by marriage) came to the house of *Ros*, and from them to *Manners*, of whom is descended the right honourable *Francis Manners* Earle of *Rutland*, now Lord thereof. King *Edward* the first (27. E.1.) gaue liberty of free Warren here to *Isabell Ros*.

Ecclesia de Bottisford patronus Willimus de Albaniaco persona Radulphus institutus per F. nunc Epum Leic. vicarius institutus per eundem & percipit nomine vicaria sua omnes prouentus alteragÿ & habet capellam de Normaton qua consueuit deseruiri tribus diebus in ebdomada per matricem ecclesiam. Monachi de Beluero percipiunt duas garbas garbarum in villa de Bottisford de Dominicis Willimi de Albaniaco & Willimi de Stodham ab antiquo.

The now Patron of this Rectory is *Francis* Earle of *Rutland*.

This Vicarage is valued in the Kings bookes at 5 1.li. 5.s.

The Church is very faire and large, with an high spire Steeple, into which (at the suppression of the Abbeyes) many ancient Monuments of the *Albanies* and *Rosses* were remoued from the Priory of *Beuer*, by the command of *Thomas* Earle of *Rutland*.

ABOVE: William Burton's description of Bottesford in 1622. (EEBO & CUL) BELOW: Belvoir Castle today. (HER)

THE VALE FAMILIES

The Flower family

The Earls and their family were well known and well-documented, but what do we know about the people of Belvoir and of Bottesford, the large village close to the Castle? It was mainly populated by the Earl's tenants; from there many of the Castle servants were drawn, and it was there that the first rumours of witchcraft will have circulated. What, in particular, do we know about the family of Joan, Margaret and Philippa Flower, and about their relationships with the other local people?

The Flower family served the Earls of Rutland, Lords of Belvoir and of the Manor of Bottesford, the large north Leicestershire parish in the Vale of Belvoir, adjoining the Castle. Consequently they were called servants, but it is important to understand the concept of 'servant' in the Elizabethan and Jacobean sense, when it could denote someone of gentry status, at least in origin. For example, courtiers were servants of the Crown. The Earls of Rutland held court at Belvoir or at one of their other houses such as Garendon and they were served by gentry families, by yeoman families, and by servile families who carried out the most menial roles, such as those in the kitchens and laundry.

The Flower family hovered within these three conditions. In the middle of the sixteenth century, in 1557, an earlier Mistress Flower was a lady's gentlewoman to the Countess of Rutland, receiving a quarterly payment of a mark (13s 4d). In 1603 five shillings was given by the Countess's commandment to Mrs Flower's man. Later, on 16 April 1615, Goodwyfe Flower was given, as a reward, two shillings for bringing a present of '2 hennes'. The documents that survive in the Duke's archives at Belvoir Castle offer enough references to the Flower family in the sixteenth and seventeenth centuries to prove that they were well known to the Manners. They had connections with the Earl and the Countess over two or three generations but, by 1615, they were no longer among their gentry servants. The change from 'Mistress' to 'Goodwyfe' was a distinctive social alteration marking a change in status. Nonetheless, it is clear that the

Flower family was important in the Vale of Belvoir, apart from its association with the Castle. Thomas Flower, for example, was a significant parishioner of Bottesford in 1604, when he was listed as one of only eight men paying the national grant of tax, the lay subsidy, to the Crown.

Other leading Vale families: The Fairbairn family

Evidence also survives of other significant families in the Bottesford area, who play a part in the story as told in the Belvoir pamphlet. Thomas Flower married Elizabeth Fairbairn in Bottesford in December 1598, so Joan Flower was not his wife. Thomas and Elizabeth had three children and, at the time of the birth of Harrye Flower born in 1602, Thomas was listed as a gentleman. It is impossible to be ascertain if Thomas had any closer family relationship with Joan Flower and her two daughters but the Fairbairn family certainly did. Through these connections there emerge the village associations of the three Flower women, through Elizabeth Fairbairn's father Thomas Fairbairn, the Receiver General of the Earl's rents in the area.

Bottesford parish registers, Manners family papers, the Belvoir pamphlet (reproduced here as Appendix I), and records held in the Leicestershire County Record Office or National Archives at Kew expose much about the Fairbairn family and typical village life. The Bottesford registers are extensive, showing both careful maintenance and personal comment (which was, strictly speaking, illegal). When there were 104 burials between February and December 1610, as opposed to a typical average of twenty-four per year during the second half of the sixteenth century, the curate, John Brearcliffe, could not restrain himself. After recording the death of Katherine Hawett in February, 1610, he wrote 'Hanc pestis primo mortifera misit ad umbras innumeros secu[m] cuius contagio traxit' He then translated this into verse:

> 'And here the plague began she dying, poyson'd many.
> The infection was so great wher't came it scarce left any.'

An adult member of the Fairbairn family who died of plague, Anthony Fairbairn, was possibly a son of Thomas Fairbairn the Earl's Receiver, as Thomas and his wife Katherine did have a son Anthony, born in 1568 in Bottesford. William Fairbairn, father of another William and of Thomas, was the churchwarden of Bottesford, listed as guardian in the parish register for 1599. He died in 1618 and his death was unusually fully recorded in Latin: 'Gulielmus Farbarne obiit sexto die maii et sepultus erat septimo eiusdem aetatem 56'. At this time a new curate, John Knowles, had replaced John Brearcliffe and he kept the registers for four years between 1617 and 1620 in Latin. Here we are close to the heart of Jacobean Bottesford and these families of the Earl's Receiver General and of the Bottesford churchwarden, who are both associated with the witchcraft story.

The Fairbairn family was extensive in Bottesford: William Fairbairn, probably the nephew of Thomas, the Earl's Receiver, was married in 1596 to Mary Calcraft. They had at least two sons, Thomas, born in 1597 and William, born in 1598. We have Thomas junior's will which is reproduced on page 44 as a typical Bottesford example. Thomas was a tenant farmer, or husbandman, in Easthorpe, a hamlet in the parish of Bottesford, who died relatively young at 31 in 1628. His bequests reveal both home life and his farming activities. In his will he asked that 'if it please god that my wife be with child my will is that it shall have ten pounds to be paied when it comes to the age of nyne yeares'. He left his wife £25 in money and goods, which his brother-in-law Christopher Farnham held for her; clearly he was handing over responsibility for his wife on his death to her brother.

After several other bequests, Thomas gave 'all the rest of my goods and chattel[s]' to his brother, William, whom he made his executor. Thomas left £3 6s 8d each to his two surviving sisters, Elizabeth and Mary Fairbairn, and both were to receive 'twoo paire of Curtaine sheets'. In addition Mary was given a black heifer cow. He gave his 'Cloke and my best shert' to his uncle Marshall, and his best ewe sheep to Elizabeth Marshall. As befitted a relative of a past church-warden, Thomas gave 3s 4d to the church of Bottesford and 2s 6d to the poor of Easthorpe. This is a typical will of a moderately prosperous husbandman; clearly he was not wealthy but he was connected with the best known families of the village, appointing his uncle Francis Calcraft and William Vincent, significant parish worthies, as the supervisors of his will.

Anne Baker

Thomas's brother William Fairbairn was specified by name in the witchcraft pamphlet as being involved in a fracas with Anne Baker. Anne was a Bottesford spinster, and her judicial examination was to be the first evidence in the witchcraft accusation. Her story is entirely derived from the major record of the witchcraft trial, the Belvoir pamphlet. In the pamphlet two and a half pages were devoted to the examination of Anne by three justices of the peace on 1 and 2 March 1619. The argument between William Fairbairn and Anne Baker, as described in the pamphlet, involved her seeing something she called 'the Blew Planett strike Thomas Fairebairne,the eldest sonne of William Fairebarne of Bottesford aforesaid by the Pinfold there, within the which time the said William Fairebarne did beat her and breake her head, whereuppon the said Thomas Faire-barne, did mend. And being asked who did send that Planet? [Anne Baker] answered it was not I' (*page 14*). This quotation from the examination of Anne Baker in the pamphlet offers an understanding of the common beliefs of the local Bottesford people, and the widespread resort to the supernatural in order to explain and come to terms with everyday problems. It also reveals that the modern Bottesford road, Pinfold Lane, derives from the seventeenth century.

The historian Keith Thomas has explained Anne Baker's attribution of Thomas Fairebairn's problems to 'planets': 'it was common to invoke the planets as a direct cause of a mysterious illness'. It appeared that Anne was associating the influence of the planets with evil spirits. Anne claimed she knew of four planets, or evil spirits: 'she saith, that there are foure colours of Planets, Blacke, Yellow, Greene, and Blew: and that Blacke is always Death' (*page 14*). What is significant is Anne Baker's awareness of contemporary medical analysis and the coming together of two popular, yet rival, explanations of illness: astrology and witchcraft. She was also demonstrating that she belonged to the category of 'ignorant people that desire to be instructed' listed by the famous late-Elizabethan preacher William Perkins. One of the common misconceptions these people held, according to Perkins in his *Foundations of the Christian Religion* (1600) was 'that if any be strangely visited, he is either taken with a Planet, or bewitched'.

It is clear that Anne Baker enjoyed the role in Bottesford of a wise-woman, who could be called upon in cases of illness; proof of this is presented in the Belvoir pamphlet, where she 'confesseth that shee came to Joane Gylles house, her Child being sicke, and that shee [Joan Gylles] intreated this Examinat [Anne Baker] to look on the Child, and to tell her whether it was forspoken [bewitched] or no and this Examinat said it was forspoken' (*page 15*). Here the commonplace acceptance of the existence of witchcraft as an explanation of illness, so crucial to the Flower witchcraft story, becomes clear.

Anne Baker and the Stanage family

Later in the pamphlet, Anne was accused of bewitching a child of Anne Stanage to death. When she was examined by the Earl on this matter, her response was reported:

> 'Anne Stannidge did deliver her Childe into her hands, and that shee did lay it upon her skirt, but did no harme unto it; And being charged by the Mother of the Childe, that upon the burning of the haire and the paring of the nailes of the said Childe, the said Anne Baker came in and set her down, and for one houres space could speake nothing; confesseth she came into the house of the said Anne Stannidge in greate pain, but did not know of the burning of the haire and nailes of the said Childe; but said she was sicke that she did not know whither she went.' (*page 15*)

Therein lies an echo of Deuteronomy 22 verse 12: 'Then thou shalt bring her home to thine house; and she shall shave her head, and pare her nails' It is unlikely that Anne was sufficiently aware of Hebrew customs to consciously cite biblical precedents but Bottesford clerics would know them, particularly the well educated curate John Knowles. This burning of hair and nails was one of the popular methods of gaining power over a witch. It was believed that this could make the witch suffer and return to the victim, to make some form of reparation or offer help in undoing the previous harm, as Robin Briggs points out. Anne seems to have acted in the expected manner, returning to the Stanages' house confused and in pain. Even the well-educated could entertain such beliefs alongside their more rational or theologically acceptable views. This is a case of sympathetic magic, whereby objects taken from a person could be used to do good or harm to that person. A further manner in which early modern people sought to protect themselves against witchcraft was through the use of witch bottles, which were filled 'with varying quantities of bent nails, cloth, human hair, fingernail clippings and urine'.

This is another element of the contemporary perception of witchcraft which, along with medical lore, partly understood theology, widespread folk explanations and mythology, helps clarify why witchcraft accusations were widespread. The Stannidge or Stanage family, well known in Bottesford, clearly felt disturbed by the presence of Anne Baker, so they might have reported their concerns to the constables when the witchcraft accusation was launched against the Flowers. The family is identified by Hugh Stanage's will, dated 26 April 1620. He was an Easthorpe husbandman, a neighbour of Thomas Fairbairn, and he gave 2s 0d to the church of Bottesford, so perhaps he was slightly less well off. As one of the overseers of his will he named his wife Anne's brother, Martin Wormell of Melton, and Martin's job was to ensure that Anne and her four children, John, Hugh, Edward and Anne, were looked after until such time as Anne might marry again, which she did in June 1622. The other supervisor of Hugh's will was Anthony Gill of Bottesford.

Anne Baker and the Gill family

The Gill family was at the centre of Bottesford family life. Anthony was an important yeoman farmer, whose family is well recorded in parish registers and wills. A member of the Gill family was named by Anne Baker in her examination

> 'And being asked concerning Nortley carrying of his child unto his own house, where the said Anne Baker was, shee asked him, who gave the said Childe that loafe, he told her Anthony Gill, to whom this Examinate said, he might have had a Child of his owne if hee would have sought in time for it; which words she confessed shee did speak.' (*page 15*)

This Anthony was not Anthony the mature supervisor of Hugh Stanage's will, but probably a second cousin, (and incidentally the son of a third Anthony Gill), who was born in December1592, married Joan Bower in December 1615 and had a short- lived daughter in 1617. The Latin account of the baby's brief life appears in the 1617 Bottesford registers: 'Anna Gill filia Anthonie Gill obiit Septimo die Septembris et sepulta erat Octavo die mensis aetatis sex menc[?s]ium'. Anne Baker perhaps was referring to the death of Anna in her evidence and it is tempting to view Anne Baker here as having offered help to the Gill family when their new-born child was ill.

Anthony Gill, Hugh Stanage's supervisor, was the son of yet another Anthony Gill, for many years Bottesford church-warden during the reign of Elizabeth. Anthony Gill, friend of husbandman Hugh Stanage, was a yeoman and richer than Hugh. He left ten shillings for Bottesford Church, twenty shillings for the poor of the parish and five shillings for mending the causeway leading to the High Cross. He gave

34

twenty shillings to one servant and five shillings to another, Elisabeth Bower, 'my maide'; she must have been the daughter of the supervisor of his will, William Bower, whose other daughter, Joan Bower, had married the young Anthony Gill. This extreme density of family relationships is the key to understanding this witchcraft affair. These village stories demonstrate what must have been the continuous worry at the heart of family life: would the children live? Alongside this was the belief that children's good health was liable to be destroyed both by natural events and by supernatural happenings. This is seen clearly in the pamphlet, where the wise women called in to treat children are suspected of witchcraft if a child's health mysteriously deteriorates.

Anne Baker and her master

As a wise woman, Anne Baker was involved with other Bottesford families. When she was examined by the Justices of the Peace in March 1619, she told a story of how

> 'shee saw a hand appeare unto her, and shee heard a voice in the ayre said unto her: Anne Baker, save thyselfe, for tomorrow thou and thy maister must be slaine: and the next day her maister and shee were in a Cart together; and suddainly shee saw a flash of fire, and said her prayers, and the fire went away, and shortly after a Crow came and peched upon her cloathes, and shee said her prayers againe, and bad the Crow to go to whom he was sent, and the Crow went unto her Maister, and did beat him to death, and shee with her prayers recovered him to life; but hee was sicke a fortnight after, and saith, that if shee had not had more knowledge then her maister, both he and shee and all the Cattell had been slaine.' (*pages 14–15*)

Emerging from Anne Baker's 'stream of consciousness' account are everyday beliefs which the clergy of the Church, especially important Cambridge preachers such as William Perkins, were so anxious to disentangle from Christian belief. Anne Baker told this story as part of her rambling evidence to the justices examining her regarding witchcraft. She seemed concerned to hold on to her reputation as a wise woman, someone who could be expected to overcome strange events by prayer and by her knowledge of the supernatural world.

Anne Baker's crow story demonstrates this well. For millennia crows have been seen as, at the very least, portents of trouble.

In his *Dictionarium Britannicum* of 1730, Nathan Bailey defines a crow firstly as 'a bird well known' but then goes on: 'a crow hieroglyphically represents a soothsayer, because it is dedicated to Apollo the God of soothsaying and prophecy. When crows are put together, they signify'd discord and war'. The crow episode reveals links between the intellectual appreciation of myth and legend and the commonplace superstitions of Jacobean villagers. This, alongside the earlier account of retaining clippings of hair and nails, demonstrates a vital conjunction between the elite group and the village communities: they both inhabit an allegorical world, where the elements of nature tell at least two different stories.

Anne Baker and the Hough family

Anne Baker was also associated with another significant Bottesford family, the Houghs. During her examination it was suggested to her that

> 'shee bewitched Elizabeth Hough, the wife of William Hough to death, for that she angred her in giving her almes of her second [stale] bread; confesseth that she was angry with her and said she might have given her of her better bread, for she had gone too often on her errands, but more she saith not'. (*page 15*)

This story demonstrates a frequently asserted cause of Jacobean witchcraft: revenge by a poor person for alleged slighting by another. In *Early Modern Witches* Marion Gibson lists eight cases at the heart of English witchcraft accusations at that time, where charity was denied or spurned. Both historians Keith Thomas and Alan Macfarlane accept this as a general cause of trouble ending in witchcraft accusations; indeed, Thomas argues that 'the overwhelming majority of fully documented witch cases fall into this simple pattern'. Robin Briggs suggests that 'at first it did seem as if a more general interpretation of witchcraft could be built around the refusal of charity'. But, he suggests, a deeper analysis indicates that, while charity refusals were significant, 'there was something of a vicious circle; weaker and poorer members of the community made more demands on their neighbours, risked being rejected or treated with less respect by them and could only attempt to defend themselves by displays of aggression'.

The story of Anne Baker and the Hough family can be further clarified by a careful examination of Bottesford records. The

Houghs filled the post of Bottesford churchwarden twice during the reign of James I: William Hough in 1604 and Thomas Hough in 1607. This William died in 1610 at the height of the plague outbreak, but his son William, born in 1595, went on to marry Elizabeth Gill in May 1616. William and Elizabeth Hough had twin children, William and Richard, baptised on 3 December 1616. Both sons died within a month, but in January 1618 William and Elizabeth had a daughter, Agneta or Agnes. Then in May 1618 John Knowles the curate recorded in the register: 'Elizabeth Hough uxor Gulielmi Hough obiit vicessimo septimo die Maii et sepulta erat vicessimo octavo eiusdem'. Given this sad series of events, so similar to the story of the young Anthony Gill and his wife Joan losing their daughter in 1617, it is easy to understand why a suggestion of witchcraft might then have occurred to the village people and been reported to the justices.

Yet there is no evidence that this suggestion of witchcraft by Anne Baker led to Anne's condemnation. What perhaps happened is that gossip spread across the village following the arrest of the Flower family, and inevitably the best known local wise woman became the focus of the judicial examinations, which had, by law, to follow any official accusation of a felony. The justices reported Anne Baker's reaction to their suggestion of witchcraft. But she was seemingly examined as part of the accusation process against the Flower family, not because of an accusation against her. Her own confession of witchcraft seems to have been ignored by the justices, other than for its value as evidence against the Flower family.

There is no record of any proceedings against Anne, which tended to be the fate of most early modern accusations against witches. She was important for her evidence against the Flower family, and that importance is emphasised by her examination being the first in the pamphlet account of the trial and by the fact that her judicial examiners were none other than 'the Right Honourable, Francis Earl of Rutland, Sir George Manners Knight [his brother], two of his Majesties Justices of the peace for the Countie of Lincolne, and Samuel Fleming, one of her Majesties Justices of the peace for the County of Leicester'. (*page 14*)

In her examination before them, Anne mentioned other Bottesford families, those of Nortley and Milles, both of whom can be located in the parish registers. William Nortley married

Hester Vavasour in 1609 and they had a daughter Hester Nortley, born in May 1616, who could be the child referred to in Anne's evidence regarding Anthony Gill. However, the Vavasour family are also significant, for they connect the village and the Castle; the Vavasours were long-term gentry servants of the Manners family as well as friends of the Flower family, for 'Mr Vavasor' had given the Flower family 'a paire of gloves' (*page 22*). Regarding Joan Flower, 'Mr Vavasor abandoned her company, as... suspicious of her lewd life' (*page 9*). This evidence for antagonism from the Vavasours, a family with strong links with both the village and the castle, suggests that the Flower family had begun to suffer from some level of social estrangement, for reasons distinct from witchcraft suspicions before the official accusations began. Robin Briggs uses the phrase 'accumulation of rumours' to sum up the process by which a range of local gossip and stories came together into an accusation of witchcraft. If such an 'accumulation' was building up against the Flower family, local people, as tenants or servants of the Manners family, or otherwise dependent on their goodwill, would know which side to support, especially if the Flower women had already made themselves unpopular in the neighbourhood. The pamphlet writer certainly depicts them as isolated and disliked, accepted only by the Earl and Countess – until their thefts displeased their noble employers and so caused the loss of their only, and most significant supporters (*page 9*).

The accumulation of rumours

The author of the Belvoir pamphlet was determined to blacken the characters of the three Flower women, both in their relationship with the Manners family, and in the perception he offered of the nature of the Bottesford villagers' association with them. He suggested that those who visited them were 'certaine deboist and base company' (*page 9*). Henry Cockeram in his *English Dictionary or Interpreter of Hard English Words* of 1626 defined 'a deboist fellow, A lewd scum of the earth'. The Belvoir pamphlet's author then specified exactly what the Flower sisters were suspected of:

> 'Concerning Phillip[a], that she was lewdly transported with the love of one Th: Simpson, who presumed to say, that shee had bewitched him: for hee had no power to leave, and was as hee supposed marvellously altered both in minde and body, since her acquainted company: these

complaints began many yeares before either their conviction, or publique apprehension' (*page 9*)

Here was a classic explanation for village antagonisms. The 'deboist company' were some men of the area who frequented 'this Joane Flowers house the mother, & especially her youngest Daughter' (*page 9*). With the convenient agreement of a young man anxious to explain away his behaviour, the village gossips were able finally to destroy the reputation of the Flower family and to open the way for a judicial attack which, if successful, would remove them finally and totally from the area.

Perhaps the crucial part of Anne Baker's evidence was that given to Dr Samuel Fleming, the Bottesford rector, on 2 March 1619:

'that about 3. yeares agoe, shee went into Northamptonshire, and that at her coming back againe one Peakes wife and Dennis his wife of Belvoyre told her that my young Lord Henry was dead, and that their was a glove of the said Lord buried inthe ground; and as that glove did rot and wast, so did the liver of the said Lord rot and wast'. (*page 16*)

This evidence is vague and imprecise but central to the witchcraft story. Bottesford spinster Anne Baker left the village for a stay in Northamptonshire, for reasons that she does not mention, in the mid-1610s, perhaps around 1615 or 1616. When she returned, she caught up on local news by gossiping with two women, Mrs Peake, the wife of 'Robert Peake of Belvoir', and Mrs Dennis, possibly the wife of 'William Deynis': both men are mentioned in the Rutland manuscripts. Anne's references to them are of the kind common in a neighbourhood where she expected everyone to know everyone else, and to be aware of local relationships; she is giving evidence to the local rector, whom she can expect to know everyone, so she can simply make allusions to people. The magistrates' clerks had to turn this into the language of legal examination.

These people were Castle servants: Peake and the Flower family were involved in some kind of serious altercation; the cause of this was not specified by Anne, who presumably assumed that it was well-known locally. The Belvoir pamphlet asserted (*page 9*) that the Earl of Rutland supported Peake against Mrs Flower. This animosity was at the heart of the witchcraft accusation and when Anne Baker returned, the gossip was turning nasty. Descriptions of sympathetic magic, such as are contained in this account, were the stuff of local stories. Unfortunately, the dates are problematic, as 'my young lord Henry' had died in 1613.

The pamphlet's author takes the case against the Flower women even further, attempting to blacken them yet more by implying that they were also offenders against their noble employers, the Earl and Countess, and that their punishment was fully justified. In the same way as they are presented as evil corrupters of innocent village neighbours, the pamphlet's author, well aware of his audience and perhaps commissioned by the Earl or looking for patronage, presents them as offenders against the equally innocent Manners family. As Marion Gibson points out, the story as told in the Belvoir pamphlet cuts away the ground from any case for seeing the Flowers' actions as motivated by justified anger at Margaret's dismissal. Instead, those actions are presented as 'a story of "motiveless" attack on well-born innocents'.

The Earl and his Countess are presented as benevolent, honourable and kindly-disposed towards all their servants and tenants. Marion Gibson points out an implicit contradiction in the pamphlet's account. On one hand, they are described as model employers 'neither displacing Tenants [nor] discharging servants' (pp.7–8) and 'relieving' the Flower women and giving them work, particularly Margaret's post in the Castle laundry. On the other hand, when Margaret's behaviour was considered to show 'some undecencies both in her life and neglect of her businesse... [the Countess] discharged her'. Even then, the Countess is shown in a good light, purging the Castle of an ill-behaved servant but giving her money and a gift of bedding. In this way, the Manners family are exonerated of offence and freed from any responsibility for the Flowers' malignity. Marion Gibson comments that such a presentation of the offended party is common in popular witchcraft pamphlets from 1590 onwards. What was in many ways a typical revenge attack is presented as 'motiveless malignity' like that attributed to Iago in *Othello*.

The Belvoir pamphlet's author describes them as 'such base and poore Creatures whom nobody loved but the Earles houshold' (*page 9*). It is, however, possible to read into this a cause for growing resentment and a wish for revenge, among a family now virtually unemployable, in an area dominated by the Manners family and their relations and friends in the aristocracy and gentry.

So much for the 'ordinary' families of the Vale. To move on to the chronology of the Manners' family life and relationships, and a reconstruction of their medical history, will help to pin down the events which led to the accusation of witchcraft.

ABOVE: The Rutland Almshouse, Bottesford, established in the 1590s by the Countess of Rutland and BELOW: Bottesford Market Cross, stocks and whipping post. (Both HER)

41

LEFT: The bellman and the spire, St Mary's Church. RIGHT: The passion of Christ on the west entrance to St Mary's Church, Bottesford; Ralph Calcraft gave 2s 8d to the Guild of Jesus in Bottesford in 1535. (VPE) BELOW: The de Ros family seal from Nichols' History and Antiquities of the County of Leicester *and the de Ros shield on the west entrance to St Mary's Church, Bottesford. (VPE)*

INVENTORY OF THOMAS CALCRAFT, 1556

In the barne

Item whett [wheat] be estimacion iiij quarters	iiijli	[£4]
Item Rye be estimacion iij quarters	iijli	[£3]
Item Barley be estimacion xxti [twenty] quarters	xvli	[£15]
Item pees be estimacion iij quarters	xlijs	[42s]
Item hay be estimacion	xls	[40s]
Item waine [cart] and plowghe yokes and temes [teams] and geres [harness] belonigng to the same	xxxiijs iiijd	[33s 4d]
Item hovels, pallis [posts] with other wode in the yeard [yard]	xxvjs viijd	[26s 8d]

Cattle belonging to the yeard

Frist [first] Oxen iiij	vjli	[£6
Item iiij kye [kine]	iiijli	[£4]
Item ij heffers	xxs	[20s]
Item ij calves	viijs	[8s]
Item ij bey [bay] mares with ij foles	xxs	[20s]
Item i bar mare and j downcolte of v yeers hold	xxxs	[30s]
Item Old Shepe xvj	xxxijs	[32s]
Item lames x	xvjs viijd	[16s 8d]
Item Swyne five	xs	[10s]

Given by Mr. Francis Proberte, the xvj[th] daie of Aprill, 1615, in reward unto Sir Thomas Compton's man that brought a present, viz. one veale and 2 lambs, vs.; unto Mr. Chawoorthe's man of Anesley that brought one kidde, ij*d.* vj*d.*; goodwyfe Flower 2 hennes, ij*s.*; geven John Bucke that broughte troutes, vj*d.*——x*s.*

Gyven, the xxviij[th] of June, 1615, unto one that broughte cherries from the Lady Skippwoorthe, ij*s.*; gyven Mistris Segreave's mayd that brought chickens, ij*s.* vj*d.*——iiij*s.* vj*d.*

ABOVE: A Calcraft family inventory of possessions in 1556. (LRO) BELOW: An entry in the Rutland Manuscripts for 1615, volume IV, page 505, perhaps relating to Joan Flower. (BCA)

In the name of god amen the fourth day of
December in the yeare of the raigne off our
most gracious soveraigne lord kinge Charles
by the grace off god of England Scotland
fraunce and Ireland kinge defender off
the fayth the third I Thomas Fearbarne off
Eastthorp in the pish off Bottesford in the
county off Leicester husband man being
sicke in body but of good and pfet memory
thankes be to allmighty god make this my last
will and testament in maner and forme folow-
inge first I do bequeath my soule into the hands off
allmighty god my maker trustinge to be saved by
the merites off Jesus christ my Redemer and
my body to the earth from whence it came
Item I give unto the Church off Bottesford ijs iijd
Item unto my wife xx li and all the moveables
which is in her brother Christopher and all the people
in one yeare and a halfe after my death
my sister Elizabeth and mary . . .
Item unto the aforsaid Elizabeth and mary . . .
tenn paire off our kine . . .
my sister one blacke heffer . . . Item unto mary
. . . marshall my . . . and my best short ff
Item unto my . . .
horse and if Elizabeth marshall the . . .
child my will is that . . . my wife be with . . .
yeard when it comes to the age off nyne yeares
all the rest off my goods and chattell I give and bequea
unto my brother William Fearbarne which I make my
full executor off this my last will and testament
desiring my . . . frendes Oliver . . . and William
. . . to be supervisors sealed with my seale
and signed with my hand in the presence off

Christofer
[marks/signatures]   Thomas Fearbarn
                                    his mark
. . . vincent
his mark

Thomas Fearbarne's [Fairbairn's] will, 4 December 1628. (LRO)

THE CASTLE FAMILY:
THE EARLS OF RUTLAND

The people of Bottesford looked up the Belvoir ridge to the Castle and its aristocratic family in more ways than one, for the two social organisations were intricately bound up with each other. This helps to clarify the tightly inter-connected social structure of life in the Jacobean Vale of Belvoir and to see how rumours and stories could spread in both directions, from villages to Castle and from the Castle to the villages. It demonstrates the isolation of anyone who, like the Flower family, managed to antagonise both sides of this network, so that an accusation against them would be more easily believed.

An excellent way to begin to understand the complex relationship between the villagers and the castle is to list the administrative duties of those responsible for both. One link between Bottesford and Belvoir Castle was the manor court or court leet, which regulated farming practices and oversaw land tenure, for which the Earl of Rutland, as Lord and owner of the Manor of Bottesford, was responsible through the agency of his stewards. Both Anthony Gill senior and Hugh Stanage senior were members of the jury of twelve men sworn in as members of the manor court annually, to oversee the process whereby parish farming activities were regulated. Crimes were reported by the village constable to the Justice of the Peace, the Rector Samuel Fleming who was also the Earl's official chaplain.

However, there was a potential clash of jurisdictions here, as Belvoir Castle was officially seen to be in Lincolnshire, while Bottesford was in Leicestershire. One result of this topographical anomaly was that the Earl was the Lord Lieutenant of Lincolnshire and on the Justices Roll for that county, whereas Samuel Fleming as Rector of Bottesford was on the Leicestershire Roll of Justices. So it is, technically speaking, strange to find Anne Baker of Bottesford being examined at the same time by magistrates from both Lincolnshire and Leicestershire. Another issue was taxation; this was levied by

Parliament as a lay subsidy on either land or goods, and was paid to the Commissioners of either Lincolnshire or Leicestershire and the Earl was directly responsible to the Privy Council in London for the work of the local Commissioners. The Earl paid his hefty tax bill, as the holder of Belvoir Castle direct from the Crown, to the Commissioner for Lincolnshire: he paid £120 from his lands to the 1621 Lay Subsidy for Lincolnshire, whereas Thomas Flower paid five shillings on goods worth £3 to the 1604 Lay Subsidy for Leicestershire. The Earl as Lord Lieutenant was totally responsible for all the Crown's activities in the County of Lincolnshire, so any problem in Belvoir came under his purview.

Belvoir Castle

The Castle was regarded as in Lincolnshire in 1622 when William Burton wrote his *Description of Leicestershire*. Close by the Castle was the mediæval Benedictine priory of which Burton wrote:

> 'Belvoire Priory, standing upon the utmost part of [Leicester]shire, whether it be in Lincolne or Leicester, I cannot directly affirme; this roll of 5.H. [Henry] 3 heere below vouched, doth shew that it is in the County of Leicester, upon which ground I have heere inserted it. The Castle is certainly of Lincolnshire, standing upon the top of a very lofty hill, containing from the foot to the top, about two hundred steps, yielding every way a most delicious & pleasing prospect, being accounted one of the best prospects in the land.'

Burton's mention of Belvoir Priory in 1622 is significant as it highlights the place which was, up to the dissolution of the monasteries in the 1530s and the 1540s, the centre of welfare in the Vale, to which Bottesford parishioners could go for medical and charitable help. The first known Norman lord of Belvoir, Robert de Tosny (also known as Robert de Pulchro Visu), in agreement with the Abbot of St Albans, had founded the Priory as a cell of the Benedictine abbey of St Albans towards the end of the eleventh century. The small cell of four or five Black Monks provided medical care to the area, as is vouched for by a book held by the Priory at its dissolution: *De virtutibus simplicium Medicinarum*, which described the power and use of medicinal herbs. When the Priory was dissolved in 1536 its extensive lands in Nottinghamshire, Leicestershire and Lincolnshire reverted back to the lineal descendants of the first Lord, its founder, and in Jacobean times we find Francis Manners, the sixth Earl, carrying on the Priory's charitable responsibilities. The author of the Belvoir pamphlet, certainly in the retinue of the sixth Earl, described him as proceeding

> '...so honourably in the course of his life, as neither displacing Tenants, discharging servants, denying the accesse of the poore, welcoming of strangers, and performing all the duties of a noble Lord... so that Beaver Castle was a continuall Pallace of entertainment, and a daily reception for all sorts both rich and poore, especially such auncient people as neighboured the same; amongst whom one Joane Flower, with her Daughters Margaret and Phillip [sic] were not only relieved at first from thence, but quickly entertained as Chair-women.' (*pages 7–8*)

This vision of local society at the beginning of the seventeenth century, encapsulating the ideal of *noblesse oblige*, can be investigated in the published archives of the Manners family. Accounts exist of annual expenditure for many years from 1522 to 1632, which largely covers the period from the first Earl to the sixth Earl. During the early years of Francis, the sixth Earl, Mr Francis Vincent of Bottesford was the Receiver of the Earl's accounts from 1609 to 1616, following Thomas Fairbairn. The Earls contributed continuously towards the welfare of local people. In 1610 £3 6s 2d was paid to look after Elizabeth Marshall during the outbreak of plague in Bottesford, and in 1611 a total of £6 was given on different occasions to the plague-stricken people of Leicester. When the funeral of Roger Manners took place in 1612, his brother Francis, the new sixth Earl, ordered that £30 should be given to the poor people of several villages. In 1612 money was given towards the purchase of a bible for Barkestone Church, in the next-door parish to Bottesford.

These examples illustrate the normal activities of a charitable lord of the manor in Jacobean times. They are part of the replacement of the lost charitable functions of the dissolved monasteries. The main parish organisation for supporting the poor was the newly developing poor law system, by which parish overseers ensured that poor rates were paid by the better off towards relief of the destitute. Unfortunately no records of the Bottesford overseers of the poor or of the constables have survived from the early seventeenth century, so that occasional mentions of charitable activity in the Rutland manuscripts are all there is.

The reference in the witchcraft pamphlet to Belvoir Castle as a 'continuall Pallace of entertainment' is borne out effectively by the Rutland papers. During the time of Francis the sixth Earl, the Manners family was one of the wealthiest in England. This arose to some extent from the increasingly careful management of the extraordinarily extensive family estates. The first Lord of Belvoir held estates in 1086 from the Crown in at least twelve English counties: Bedfordshire, Buckinghamshire, Cambridgeshire, Essex, Hertfordshire, Leicestershire, Lincolnshire, Norfolk, Northamptonshire, Rutland, (listed in Domesday Book under Northamptonshire), Suffolk and Yorkshire. Over the next five hundred years many of these estates changed hands but, by the early modern period, the Manners family had consolidated, and held lordships in seven counties: Derbyshire, Leicestershire, Lincolnshire, Nottinghamshire, Rutland, Warwickshire, and Yorkshire.

This process of amalgamation took place mainly as a result of family heiresses marrying into wealthy dynasties. The marriage around 1120 of Cecilia de Belvoir, granddaughter of Robert de Belvoir, to William d'Aubigné (or Albini), brought together Belvoir and the Albini lands. Approximately one hundred years later, the marriage of Albreda de Albini to Robert de Roos, the father of the first holder of the de Roos barony, brought together the Belvoir lands with extensive estates in Yorkshire, centred on Hamlak or Helmsley Castle and Holderness. The last direct descendent of the Roos family was Eleanor who, in the later fifteenth century, brought the accumulated lands of the Tosny, Albini and Roos families, centred on Belvoir, to those of the Manners family when she married Sir Robert Manners, a landowner in Northumberland, whose possessions included parts of Holy Island. They had a son, George Manners, who became the twelfth Lord Roos. It is difficult to standardise the spelling of 'Roos', a name probably cognate with the Welsh 'rhos' and derived originally from the manor of Roos in the East Riding of Yorkshire. Though various spellings have been used by the Manners family, notably Rosse, Ros, Rose, Ross and Roose, here 'Roos' will suffice.

The survival of the Manners family and its hold on its extensive lands was sometimes precarious. The following account of the family from creation of the Earldom to Earl Francis' accession shows the problems that could be caused by the lack of heirs and by conflicting claims to the family's titles and lands. This helps to underline the concern of Francis, the sixth Earl, over

The tomb of Henry Manners, second Earl of Rutland and his wife Bridget, née Hussey (later Lady Bedford) and INSET: The first Earl, Thomas and his wife Eleanor, née Paston. (Both HER & SMCB)

49

THE RIGHT HONORABLE & NOBLE LORD EDWARDE ERLE OF RVT
LANDE LORD ROSSE OF HAMELAC TRVSBOTE & BELVOYRE LIETH
HERE BVRIED IN Ỹ YEARE 1569 HE WAS SENTE INTO Ỹ NORTHPARTS
IN Ỹ TYME OF THOSE CIVILL TROVBLES THERE MADE LIVETENANTE
TO THOMAS ERLE OF SVSSEX (THEN LORD GENERALL OF HER
MA ARMIE) & ALSO COLLONELL OF Ỹ FOOTEMEN & ONE OF Ỹ
COVNSELL IN THAT SERVICE HE BEINGE TEN BVT 20 YEARES OF AGE
& WARDE TO HER MA HE TRAVAILED INTO FRAVNCE 1570.
HE WAS MADE LIVETENANTE OF Ỹ COVNTY OF LINCOLNE
1582. HE WAS MADE KNIGHT OF Ỹ GARTER 1584. ON
Ỹ 5 DAY OF IVLY 1586, AS CHEIF COMISSIONER FOR
HER MAIESTIE HE CONCLVDED WITH Ỹ SCOTTISH
KINGS COMISSIONERS AT BARWICKE VPON

TWEEDE, A LEAGVE OF AMYTYE BETWENE Ỹ TWO REALMES. ON
Ỹ 14 OF APRILL FOLLOWINGE BEINGE GOOD FRIDAY 1587:
HE DEPARTED THIS LIFE NERE PVDDLE WHARFE IN LONDON FRŌ
WHENCE HIS CORPS WAS HITHER BROVGHT & BVRIED Ỹ 15 DAY OF
MAY NEXT FOLLOWINGE. HE LEFTE YSSVE BY HIS HONORABLE
WIEF ISABEL HOLCROFT DAVGHTER TO S THOMAS HOLCROFT
KNIGHT, ONE DAVGHTER NAMED ELIZABETH THEN OF Ỹ
AGE OF ELEVEN YEARES & ALMOST FOVRE MONYTHES
W DAVGHTER WAS MARIED IN IANVARY 1588 TO WILLIA
CELL ESQVIER ELDEST SONNE TO S THOMAS CICELL KNIGHT
EST SONNE TO Ỹ LORD BVRGHLEY THEN & NOW LORD
H TREASOROR OF ENGLANDE. BY WHOM SHE LEFTE YSSVE ONE
NAMED WILLIĀ & DIED AT LONDON IN APRILL 1591

Edward Manners, third Earl of Rutland and his wife Isabel, née Holcroft and the Earl's memorial inscriptions. (HER & SMCB)

ABOVE: The tomb of John Manners, fourth Earl and his wife Elizabeth née Charlton. LEFT: Roger Manners, the fourth Earl's first surviving son, who became the fifth Earl and RIGHT: Elizabeth Manners, only surviving child and heiress of the third Earl and in consequence Baroness Roos in her own right. In 1587 she married William Cecil (later Earl of Exeter) and had one son who became Lord Roos on her death in 1591. (HER & SCMB)

51

ABOVE: The tomb of Roger Manners, fifth Earl of Rutland and his wife Elizabeth, née Sidney, the daughter of Sir Philip Sidney. Both Roger and Elizabeth died childless in 1612. BELOW: Francis Manners, sixth Earl of Rutland and his two wives Frances, née Knyvett, (died 1608) and Cecilia, née Tufton (died 1653). (All HER & SMCB)

the survival of his two ailing young sons. In addition to any parent's anxiety for the health and survival of a child, especially in those days of comparatively high child mortality, he had the further worry of the future of his lands. The family had already faced the temporary loss of property and its baronial title. If the sixth Earl had no male heir, his daughter would take part of the family's lands, those associated with the barony of Roos, to her husband as heiress in her own right. This throws further light on his fear of witchcraft being used against him and his children and his hope that the removal of the accused women would ensure his second son's healthy survival, securing the title and keeping the family lands intact. A brief survey of the sixth Earl's five predecessors shows the family's changing fortunes.

The First Earl of Rutland

The Manners family were related to Henry VIII as a result of the marriage of Anne St Leger, the daughter of Edward IV's sister Anne Plantagenet, to George Manners, Lord Roos. George was a military commander fighting in the French wars, who died in 1513 and his son Thomas was brought up as an associate of King Henry. The King granted the Earldom of Rutland in 1525 to his close friend Thomas, no doubt with reference to the fifteenth-century Earl of Rutland, killed at the battle of Wakefield. This original Earl was the brother of Edward IV and Anne Plantagenet; thus the Manners family always had strong associations with the English Royal family. This friendship between Henry VIII and Thomas Manners, the first Earl, led to what was to be the greatest single acquisition of lands by the Belvoir family since their initial grants at the time of the Norman Conquest.

Following the dissolution of the monasteries in the 1530s and 1540s, Thomas Manners purchased, exchanged, or was granted by Henry VIII lands and income previously held by the church. His will dated 16 August of the 34th year of Henry VIII (1542) lists lands owned in 50 sites in England, spread from north to south of the country in the counties of Northumberland, Yorkshire, Lincolnshire, Nottinghamshire, Leicestershire, Northamptonshire, Norfolk and Sussex. Amongst this expanse of territory were lands originally belonging to eleven monasteries: Belvoir, Croxton, Rievaulx, Kirkham, Lilleshall, Newstead, Nuneaton, Drax, Oulveston, Garendon, Warter and the Knights Templars' Commandery of Eagle. The lands of the First Earl yielded £1862 1s 8d a year in 1542. The Earl had to pay £552 16s 5¾d tax to the Crown annually, leaving him with a net annual income of £1309 5s 2¼d, an enormous amount when one considers that in 1536 the £20 paid to his Treasurer was the highest annual salary he paid any of his servants at Belvoir Castle and that he paid his shepherds £1 a year. The contemporary worth of the first Earl's wealth can be compared to that of some of the richest men of England – Charles Brandon, a friend of both Henry and Thomas Manners and husband of Henry VIII's sister Mary, and Elizabeth I's first Chancellor of the Exchequer, Sir Walter Mildmay.

Brandon, the first Duke of Suffolk, had an annual income at his death of £3000, and Mildmay an annual income of £500. The aristocrat in favour with the Crown could become extremely rich but, in return for this, he had to raise significant numbers of fighting men and be ready for extremely costly Royal service or ambassadorships, while remaining spotlessly loyal to the Crown.

By the time of the witchcraft affair, Francis Manners as sixth Earl was slowly rebuilding the Manners estates, which had been seriously diminished by the huge expense of aristocratic duties and by the vagaries of fortune at the centre of political life. When Francis succeeded his brother Roger Manners, the fifth Earl, in 1612, the family fortunes were only beginning to recover from a potentially disastrous situation at the beginning of that century. Roger had been sent to the Tower of London accused along with the Earl of Essex, of high treason in 1601; two of his brothers, Francis and George, had been put under arrest. The uncle of these three was horrified. He wrote to his brother George on 16 February 1601:

> 'Good Brother, of this tumult this bearer can tell you more than I have will to write. I wold my three nephews had never byn borne then by so horrible offence offend so gratius a sufferan, to the overthrow of ther howse and name for ever, always before loyall.'

The Second Earl of Rutland
The gracious sovereign was of course Queen Elizabeth I whom the second, third and fourth Earls of Rutland had served with dedication. Henry Manners, the second Earl, although briefly involved with the Lady Jane Grey debacle, had successfully negotiated the problematic years of the reigns of Edward VI and Mary Tudor, holding important military commands under

both. He was one of the military commanders who lost Calais in 1558, but he was easily able to transfer his loyalty to Elizabeth later that year. Three years later Henry was appointed Lord President of the North, responsible for the ever-dangerous border country with Scotland, where a new threat from disgruntled Roman Catholics was just beginning to be felt. He had completed his father's total rebuilding of the Castle, begun in 1528, which had been destroyed during the last years of the Wars of the Roses, 'making it a nobler structure than it was before'.

This sixteenth-century Belvoir Castle, where the Flower family served, is difficult to imagine, for it suffered a second destruction in the seventeenth century. The Tudor Castle was deliberately taken to pieces after the Second Civil War in 1648, following the order by the republican Council of State in April 1649 that 'the Castle of Belvoir be demolished'. A few references to the sixteenth-century castle in the early sixteenth-century Rutland papers show that there were stables, a great chamber, a nursery, guest chambers, a brewhouse and a new hunting park and a warren for rabbits by1539. The 1539 recital of wages lists workers in the kitchens, chambers, cellars, pantry, buttery, ewery (the office where water for guests was kept), hall, and the laundry which employed five women. By 1543 the rebuilding of the Castle must have been well advanced as is shown by the inventory reproduced on pages 344 to 349 of the fourth volume of the Rutland papers. In 1588, on the death of the fourth Earl, there is a reference to 'the keys of the library near the chapel, of a little closet in the old great chamber and of the counting house in Belvoir Castle'. By the 1590s the Countess of Rutland had extensive bee-keeping facilities and fishponds at Belvoir thus completing a splendid residence, although new houses of office (toilets) had to be installed when King James I visited during his triumphal progress south on his accession to the throne in 1603.

The Third Earl of Rutland and Wardship
The second Earl had apparently died during an outbreak of plague in 1563, and so his young son Edward became a ward of court. Henry Manners, who as second Earl had continued his father's work at Belvoir, had increased the Manners income to £2485 annually but, as Lord President of the Council of the North, he had some heavy expenditure. Thus, when his son Edward succeeded, as a minor aged fourteen, spending on

behalf of the Crown on top of the rebuilding of Belvoir Castle generated large debts. The fortunes of the Manners family were frequently to be put at risk during minorities, particularly as both Edward, the third Earl, and Roger, the fifth Earl succeeded as such. Fortunately William Cecil, the Lincolnshire lawyer who had became Chief Secretary to Queen Elizabeth, had acquired the extremely lucrative role of Master of the Wards and so the Rutland affairs became his responsibility during the minorities of Edward and Roger.

Wardship was the technique whereby orphan children were handed over to the care of their social superiors, who looked after the heir's finances until he or she came of age. This happened at all levels of society. In Bottesford the Earl as Lord of the Manor held the wardships of Bottesford and the surrounding manors' orphans. In 1586 Thomas Fairbarne reported to Edward, the third Earl, that 'Richard Marshall of Bottesford, one of your freeholders, died, leaving a wife and six small children, the eldest being 13 years of age. The widow asks to have the wardship of her son'. She needed to have this to be able to benefit from the produce of his land, held directly from the Earl. In 1610 Francis Vincent the fifth Earl's Receiver in Bottesford, 'Received the xxiiij[th] of December, 1610, of Mr William Draper and Thomas Houghe, of Bottsford, in parte of fortie pounds for the wardship and maryage of Richard Houghe, xxli'. In effect Mr Draper and Thomas Hough paid the Earl forty pounds for maintaining the property and receiving the rents of Richard Hough up to his marriage. Both the Bottesford men and the Earl would make a profit from this and the heir's prosperity depended on the honesty of the holders of the wardship.

This concept of guardianship was a feudal right, intended to ensure that estates continued to make profits for the lord while a child was reared. The profits of wardship were maintained by the holder of the wardship until the heir was twenty-one and included the right to arrange the marriage of the heir, again an opportunity for real financial gain if marriage to a rich heiress could be arranged. This understanding of wardship is important to the witchcraft story as it involves the health and survival of children, the central focus of the Belvoir witchcraft scandal.

William Cecil, who was to become Lord Burghley, proved a good guardian to Edward Manners, the third Earl, sending him to

France for his travels and giving him extensive advice on how to behave. Edward wrote from France to Cecil with detailed information about French politics and the disposition of French forts and garrisons. On his return to London, Cecil organised his education in law and learning. The effect of this was not exactly as Cecil had hoped: Edward became a somewhat reclusive intellectual, a young man happy enough to carry out the role of the significant county aristocrat, overseeing the towns in his area, notably Nottingham, Newark and Grantham, but not yet developing a major role in national affairs, although he was well able to undertake the highest office. He did accept one national task, which was to prove of great significance to the Manners family and to this story.

During the 1580s two central issues of English policy were becoming clarified. Firstly the nature of the threat from Spain as a militantly Catholic European nation became abundantly clear and secondly it became clear that the Protestant Queen of England was never going to marry. The effect of this was to focus interest on Mary Stewart, the Catholic ex-Queen of Scotland, deprived of her own throne and yet, as cousin to Elizabeth, the heir to the English throne. She had for many years languished in exile in the East Midlands of England, under the reluctant care of 'the Great Earl', the Earl of Shrewsbury, and his even more reluctant estranged wife, better known today as Bess of Hardwick, both of whom were the neighbours in Derbyshire of a branch of the Manners family. As plots appeared to multiply around the Catholic Mary, so it became clear even to Elizabeth that to maintain the Church of England, she must at least hint who was her preferred Protestant heir to the throne and thus remove the possibility of Mary's succession.

To this end, serious negotiations were set up in 1586 to establish the future relationship of England and Scotland, whose young King, James VI, the only child of Mary Stewart, aged 20 at the time, was clearly next in line to the English throne after Mary. In 1586 Edward Manners, as third Earl of Rutland, was chosen to lead the negotiations and to face, in the border town of Berwick, James VI's cousin and temporary favourite Francis Stewart, Earl of Bothwell. Together the two Earls successfully hammered out a defensive treaty between England and Scotland, aimed against the ever-increasing threat of the naval strength of Spain. What perhaps pleased James most about the final treaty was that it included an appendix, giving James a guaranteed English annuity of £4000, which was regularly paid by the English treasury throughout the rest of Elizabeth's reign (much to James' relief, as he always suffered from financial shortfalls). Certainly James appreciated the work of Edward Manners for, when the third Earl died in the following year in 1587, he was reported to be especially upset.

Edward Manners as third Earl had financial problems at Belvoir which he, like his nephew the sixth Earl, wished to maintain as a 'continuall Pallace of entertainment' but which was heavily indebted. One major expenditure during the last years of his life seems to have been on books: he purchased Camden's *Britannia*, 'King Arthure's book for my lady', an interpretation of Aristotle's *Logic*, Aquinas' *Summa Theologica*, Machiavelli's *Discourses in French*, and volumes of Livy, Matthew Paris and Polydore Vergil. William Cecil's educational efforts were bearing fruit: the flower of the English aristocracy were becoming erudite men of culture. The Rutland accounts are full towards the end of Edward's life, including details of expenditure on Newark Castle and Helmsley as well as Belvoir.

Eventually he was able to recommence adding to the family wealth by purchasing new manors, a process well documented in his will. In a codicil written just before his death in 1587 he said that, for the four previous years, he had 'purchased and obteyned divers other landes rentes and hereditamentes'. Edward had no sons, so he knew that on his death the Rutland estates would be dismantled. The ancient Roos lands would pass to his only child Elizabeth, born in 1576, who was entitled to become the Baroness de Roos of Hamlake or Helmsley in her own right, as this ancient barony, dating from the thirteenth century, could pass through the female line. The Tudor creation of the Rutland earldom was entailed through heirs male and accordingly it would pass to his brother John Manners, the future fourth Earl.

Elizabeth Manners and the Wardships of Roger Manners and William Cecil Lord Roos

On the death of Edward, the third Earl, the Rutland family were thus in an extraordinary and confusing situation. Elizabeth Manners was now Baroness Roos, yet John Manners' eldest son Roger was presumed by some to be entitled to the same honorary title of Lord Roos as the eldest son of John, the fourth Earl of Rutland. Fortunately, Edward the third Earl had foreseen this ambivalence and had appointed as supervisors of his will a galaxy of high-ranking English courtiers, Lord High Treasurer of England William Cecil, now Lord Burghley, Lord Chancellor of England Sir Thomas Bromley, the Queen's Principal Secretary Sir Francis Walsingham, Chief Justice of England Sir Christopher Wray, Chief Justice of Common Pleas Sir Edmund Anderson and finally, and most important for this story, Sir Philip Sidney. Edward's brother John was fourth Earl of Rutland for only one year before he too died in 1588, leaving as his heir and as a ward of the Queen the new fifth Earl Roger Manners, a young boy and budding intellectual like his uncle, aged around thirteen, studying at Cambridge.

In 1588 the Dowager Countess passed on the wardship of her son Roger to Lord Burghley who, twenty-five years previously, as William Cecil, had carried out the role effectively for Edward the third Earl. But this time the wardship was much more fraught as Lord Burghley, looking forward to the future of his family after his own death, had a complex agenda of dynastic marriage in his mind. He arranged for his own grandson, confusingly also called William Cecil, son and heir of Burghley's son Thomas Cecil who was later to be Earl of Exeter, to be married in January 1589 to Elizabeth Manners, the third Earl's only surviving child and the new Baroness Roos, whose wardship was held by the Queen.

Elizabeth Manners' role in this extraordinary story is a short, tragic but vital one. The couple, William Cecil junior and Elizabeth, set up their home in Newark Castle, one of the castles owned by the Manners, which Elizabeth inherited from her father Edward Mannners. The marriage lasted for three short years, during which one child was born in May 1590, baptised in Newark and also named, (confusingly for us) after his father and his great-grandfather, William Cecil. Elizabeth Cecil, Baroness Roos, née Manners, died in May 1591, leaving her infant son to claim absolutely legally the old title of Lord Roos. Lord Burghley was Master of the Queen's Wards and was thus responsible for both claimants to the title of Lord Roos – William Cecil and Roger Manners.

A glance at the pamphlet and the ballad brings us back to 'Lord Rosse'. The Flower sisters were hanged for the murder of Lord Roos, the son of the sixth Earl, but their apparent victim was neither of those cousins being cared for as Royal wards of court in the 1590s. The 'Henry Lord Rosse' of the Jacobean scandal sheets was the eldest son of Francis Manners, younger brother of Earl Roger. Both Earl Roger and William Cecil, the baby son of Elizabeth Cecil née Manners, were initially looked after by the Crown. Roger's mother, Elizabeth Countess of Rutland, widow of the fourth Earl, was granted the oversight of her son's affairs by Lord Burghley, acting for the Queen. His letter of April 1588 to the Countess gives an excellent picture of the responsibilities of wardship:

> 'Though I have had no acquaintance with you yet my love for the house in which you are matched moves me to have respect, in anything meet for my calling, to pleasure you and yours... For the young Earl, I think he should return to Cambridge, where I hear he has an honest and discreet tutor, and I beg that he may remain till the Queen signifies her further pleasure. I will undertake that all reasonable charges be paid for his tutor and his diet and the number of persons that shall be necessary to attend upon him, as of one to learn and follow his book or any other good qualities. I beg some one may repair to me for following his causes at law.'

The Countess was a diligent overseer of the young Earl's affairs and she also continued the charitable activities of the family, for it was she who built and furnished the Men's Hospital in Bottesford in 1592 and 1593 as an almshouse for aged former servants of the family.

It is also possible to follow the wardship of William Cecil, Lord Roos. Lord Burghley on his death was succeeded in his offices by his son Robert Cecil who during the reign of James I became Earl of Salisbury and Master of the King's Wards. Thus it was that the Earl of Salisbury took final responsibility for Baron Roos. There exists in the Salisbury MSS a letter dated January 1608 from Lord Roos's grandfather, the Earl of Exeter, to the Master of the King's Wards:

> There is of late descended to my Lord Rosse, by the death of Mr Roger Mannours, the manor of Lynton in Yorkshire, for which I moved you at my last seeing you at Court that I might become tenant to the King during Lord Rosse's minority, as I am to the rest of his possessions that remain in the King's hands, which you seemed then willing I should have. I therefore renew my suit to grant me your warrant for a particular. I hope you will have some consideration in imposing the fine, the lease being only for three years, when Lord Rosse will be of full age.

What was happening here is a request from the holder of a Royal wardship that he might have the revenues from an estate that the Royal ward, Lord Roos, had just inherited from the brother of the second Earl of Rutland, the old uncle Roger Manners. This was the same Roger who was so distressed when Roger the fifth Earl became involved with the Earl of Essex's conspiracy against Queen Elizabeth. The confusion of two claimants to the title of Lord Roos was eventually resolved by Royal intervention and by a sad event. In 1616 Francis Manners applied to King James for support in his legal claim for the title, and the King intervened in the law case. James correctly supported William Cecil as Lord Roos but he then created a new barony for Earl Francis, that of Baron Roos of Hamlake. The young William Cecil, son of Elizabeth Manners, then died married but childless in 1618; with no direct heirs to his title, it passed back to the Manners family and Francis became the seventeenth Baron de Roos, so holding both titles.

The Fifth Earl of Rutland

Roger the fifth Earl was apparently happy at Cambridge where he had begun residence in 1587 at the age of eleven or twelve, living in residence, first at Queens' College, where he had 'the seeds of Religion' taught him by his tutor, Dr John Jegon, whom he followed to Corpus Christi College until 1595. At this stage Roger's mother died; following this, perhaps the most important influence upon him was the Earl of Essex, who arranged great festivities in Cambridge in February 1595, during which Roger and a galaxy of other noblemen received their Master's degrees. In October 1595 the Queen granted Roger leave to travel abroad, always seen at that time as a hazardous activity, when the possibilities of religious conversion were taken seriously. Roger was to be abroad, particularly in the Netherlands, Germany, Italy and France, for the next two years. He spent some time in Padua, where he matriculated at the University, and suffered some illness. Young English aristocrats were the target of Catholic propaganda and, if they travelled as far as Italy, they were watched carefully and given extensive advice.

It was from the Earl of Essex's secretariat that there appeared a famous letter of moral advice to Roger:

'Your Lordships purpose is to travel; and your study must bee what use to make thereof. The question is ordinary, and there is to it an ordinary answer; that is your Lordship shall see the beauty of many Cities, know the manners of the people of many Countries and learne the languages of many Nations... The last thing I am to speake, is but the first you are to seeke; It is Knowledge... Above all other bookes, bee conversant in Histories, for they will best instruct you in matters Morall, Politicke, and Military...'

Among this correct series of suggestions Roger was encouraged to learn as much as possible about the military establishments he might see. The grand tour at the end of the sixteenth century took place in time of European religious struggles, so young aristocrats were taught to pick up as much information as possible to report on their return. Roger clearly found the tour of value both intellectually and militarily and Essex's advice aimed to ensure that the tour prepared him for his life of service to the Crown.

From this European adventure in the fifth Earl of Rutland's life, some imaginative historians have made of him an extraordinarily intellectually well-endowed and cultured aristocrat, and so brilliant a literary star as to be one of the possible authors of Shakespeare's works. This theory derives from the fortuitous combination of two pieces of evidence. Firstly this advice letter has been widely studied and, one after another, all members of Essex's entourage have been proposed, in particular Francis Bacon.

The second piece of evidence comes from 1613, soon after Roger's death, when Francis Bacon became Attorney General. It appears in the Rutland accounts as a unique payment to William Shakespeare. The entry reads: 'Item, 31 Martii,[1613], to Mr Shakspeare in gold about my Lorde's impresso, xliiijs.; to Richard Burbage for paynting and making yt, in gold xliiijs.— iiijli.viiis.' This payment is associated with the celebrations in London in February and March 1613 of the marriage of King James' daughter Elizabeth with the Elector Palatine Frederick, the ruler of the principality of the Rhineland. During these celebrations, Shakespeare's company performed fourteen plays at court so he was available along with his close friend and fellow actor Richard Burbage, to create an impresso, a heraldic device on the Earl of Rutland's shield, to be used in the court celebrations of the wedding.

Since this evidence was first published in Volume IV of the Rutland Manuscripts in 1905, the literary world had been awash with new candidates for the authorship of Shakespeare's plays.

This latter-day fascination with their authorship arose from the difficulty that some in a class-based society faced in accepting that a tradesman's son from a small Warwickshire town could have produced such marvels of intellectual and imaginative achievement. The conclusion drawn was that Shakespeare was an actor-manager paid by the Manners to claim authorship of plays and poems produced in their literary circle.

Is there any significance in this suggestion and does it have any association with the tragic account of the witchcraft accusations, which have their origin in the year 1613 when Lord Roos died? What is of value is the intimation that Roger the fifth Earl was a dedicated member of the learned and literary circles which proliferated in late Elizabethan and early Jacobean England. It is important to stress his lifelong love of Cambridge and his attachment to the Earl of Essex, an intellectual of real importance, if mainly for his promotion of learning. Essex's *Letter of Instruction* was typical of late sixteenth century learning: it arose from his coterie of secretaries, who were all Oxford and Cambridge tutors, well versed in the new systematic logic of Ramus, which led to endless methodical tables and lists such as Bacon approved, but most of all imbued with the knowledge of classical Greek and Roman literature, notably the rhetoric of Cicero, the stoicism of Seneca and the history of Tacitus. Francis Bacon and Roger Manners were at the heart of this world. The sixteenth-century Earls of Rutland also owned the land in Shoreditch in London on which James Burbage, the father of Richard Burbage, built 'a playing place called "The Theatre"'.

Another element of this intellectual ferment was associated with Walter Raleigh, perhaps the most important rival of the Earl of Essex in the complicated attempts to replace the Cecils as the political masters of England when Burghley should die, as he did in 1598. Raleigh's own intellectual interests were mathematically and chemically inspired, and he was involved with Henry Percy, the Protestant 'wizard' Earl of Northumberland. Both Raleigh and Percy enjoyed dabbling in the mystical world of sixteenth-century chemical medicine, which contrasted with the classical learning of Essex and Rutland. One result of this was that Raleigh was dogged by suspicions that he was too much of a free-thinker to be taken seriously.

This world boiled over on a Sunday morning in February 1601. On Monday the ninth of February the following proclamation was issued from Queen Elizabeth's Palace of Westminster:

> 'Whereas the Earle of Essex, accompanied with the Earles of
> Rutland & Southampton, and divers other their complices,
> Gentlemen of birth and qualities, knowing themselves to be
> discovered in divers treasonable actions, into which they
> have heretofore entred, as well in our Realme of Ireland,
> where some of them had layed plots with the Traitour
> Tirone, as in this our Realme of England, did upon Sunday,
> being the eight of this Moneth, in the morning...
> traitourously issue into our City of London in armes, with
> great numbers, and there breaking out into open action of
> rebellion... continuing still in armes, and killing divers of
> our Subjects, after many Proclamations of rebellion made
> by our King of Heralds.'

Why did Roger Manners, fifth Earl of Rutland, support the Earl of
Essex and the Earl of Southampton in this action, marching sword
in hand at the head of a band of men into London to attempt to
raise the City against the government? Roger's association with
the Earl of Essex was so close that he must have felt it
incumbent upon him to support him. On Roger's return from
Italy and France in 1597 he had joined Essex in the latest naval
expedition against the Spaniards, with Walter Raleigh as an
argumentative second-in-command. This adventure to the
Azores had ended in chaos, with little gain and much
unpopularity with the Queen. It was followed in late 1598 by
her reluctant appointment of Essex to go to Ireland to sort out
the Earl of Tyrone's rebellion. Naturally Roger wanted to go on
this military action and he was given a colonelcy of foot by
Essex. The Queen felt he was too young and he was advised not
to go. Nonetheless he went, became ill and had to creep back
home in a few months time, in disgrace with the Queen.

One reason for Roger's determination to go to Ireland would
have been his perception that here was an opportunity to gain
military glory. A complementary reason was the fact that
several of his fellow officers were relatives: a group of cousins
from the locality of Belvoir was also in Essex's army. Gervase
Markham, Sir Griffin Markham and Francis Markham were
closely connected to the Rutland family sphere. Another cousin,
married into the Markham family, was John Harrington, soon
to be knighted by Essex for his actions in Ireland. The Manners,
the Markhams and the Harringtons were members of the Essex
coterie, looking to the future when Queen Elizabeth would be

no more. However their position in 1599 was regarded with some suspicion by Elizabeth's ministers and, when Essex returned from Ireland without her permission, he fell into deep disgrace. One of the Queen's objections was to his knighting of his officers, particularly the new Sir John Harrington and George Manners, a younger brother of the fifth Earl.

But this did not prevent Roger from deepening his links with Essex. In 1599 he married Elizabeth Sidney, the daughter of the recently-dead Sir Philip Sidney; Sidney's widow had married the Earl of Essex, so that Elizabeth was Essex's step-daughter. It was this link with the Essex family via his new wife, which finally put Roger into the centre of the Essex entourage for good or ill. As a result, when the general call for help was sent out from Essex House on the morning of the eighth of February 1601, Roger had no other course of action than support. He had been schooled in the classical ideals of brotherhood by Essex himself. Fortunately for Roger, the government understood the nature of his relationship with Essex and as a result he was not put on trial for treason.

Why in particular did he link up with the Earl of Southampton on the fateful day? The two Earls had been close friends for some time and in particular they enjoyed the theatre. Roger certainly entertained Southampton at his London house, rented from the Fortescue family, Ivy Bridge, near Covent Garden. Indeed, they were eating together there on Tuesday, 3 February 1601, when earlier that same day the Earl of Essex had met Southampton and his 'most ardent partisans' at one of Essex's houses, Drury House, to plot the uprising. It was arranged that there should be a performance of Shakespeare's play *Richard II*, about the overthrow of King Richard II by Henry Bolingbroke, at the Globe Theatre during that week.

On the evening before the 'open action of rebellion' Roger had dinner at Ivy Bridge with his brothers Francis and George, along with Sir Thomas Fairfax, Sir Griffin Markham and Mr Henry Withegton. Of these six, the three Manners brothers were all involved in the march on Sunday, 8 February from Essex House to try to raise the City in favour of Essex. None of the other three at the Manners' dinner on Saturday 7 February was involved in the plot and so this tends to suggest that the Manners brothers acted on the spur of the moment. Yet there is no doubt that Roger was one of the leaders of the band of over 80 men who, led by Essex, marched along the Strand with drawn swords. Indeed, Roger confessed when he was examined by the Queen's chief ministers that their purpose was to possess the City and to march on the Court in Westminster.

By that evening Roger was incarcerated in the Tower of London, along with Essex and Southampton and several other lords and knights, including Lord Monteagle, Sir Charles Danvers and Sir John Davis, all three of whom had been Roger's dinner guests at Ivy Bridge earlier on 19 January. All were examined and some were tried, in exactly the same way as suspect witches were to be imprisoned, examined and some tried in 1619. Essex, Southampton, Danvers and Davis were all sentenced to death. Southampton and Davis were reprieved but both Essex and Danvers were beheaded on Tower Hill. None of the Manners brothers were tried. Robert Cecil, by now Chief Secretary to the Queen, went to the Tower to inform Roger of his fate, as explained in a contemporary letter dated 14 March 1601.

> 'The right honorable Sir Robert Cycill... Monday last delyvered unto my Lord of Rutland in the Tower Her Majesty's pleasure concernynge hys present estate, viz., That her pleasure was not to bringe his lyffe in questione, and that her will was that he should be restored to his honor and dignytie and to receave possession of his landes and goodes.'

This ensured that they were merely fined. Cecil was granted the fines as a perquisite of office and he arranged matters so that most was never collected. By August 1601 Roger was released and he, with his brothers, returned to normal life. Roger was initially released into the custody of his well-respected courtier-uncle Roger, where he remained until early 1602. By now Earl Roger was 25, having been Earl of Rutland since he was 11. When in 1597 he became 21, he was for a while extremely rich from fines paid by tenants of his land due to him on his majority. He received a 'cash portion of £4000' on his marriage to Elizabeth Sidney in 1599.

What eventually relieved the Rutland estate of further serious financial worries were two processes, one social and one economic. In 1603 the old Queen died and King James entered into his inheritance, happy to acknowledge families such as the Manners, who had rendered him services during the years of waiting for the English throne. Immediately, those who had survived the Essex coup were rewarded: all Roger's debt to the Crown arising from his fine was cancelled and Southampton was released from the Tower and restored to his titles. But perhaps just as significant for his wealth was the manner in which the fifth Earl was able to take real advantage from the first Earl's investments in monastic lands. The iron-works associated with his lands on the former monastic property at Rievaulx became seriously profitable: in 1606 'the sale of a very large quantity of iron to London merchants for £4,200 enabled the Earl to clear off the worst of his debts'.

Thus by the end of the first decade of the seventeenth century the Rutland affairs were in better order than at the beginning. But the Manners family could hardly be called contented as Roger and Elizabeth Manners (née Sidney) had no direct heir. The Rutland accounts are packed with references to payments to physicians, but there is no direct comment on gynaecological affairs concerning the fifth Earl and his Countess. The Countess frequently went to Bath to take the waters but she and the fifth Earl had no heirs, male or female, clearly a considerable disappointment to the family. The fifth Earl's brother Francis likewise had no male heir from his first wife, the heiress Frances Bevill née Knyvett who, after an initial unsuccessful pregnancy in 1603, died in 1605 of smallpox, just having given birth to their daughter Katherine. By 1608 Francis was anxiously wooing another heiress, Cecily Tufton, the rich widow of Sir Edward Hungerford, a matter discussed in great detail by the family steward, Thomas Screven, in a letter to the fifth Earl dated the 26 October 1608.

'This wooing of Sir Francis Manners goeth exceedingly well forward and he applies yt like a good woer. She is come to London, lodged in one house by herself; her father [Sir John Tufton] is here also in his owne howse. Sir Francis Manners hath ben with him – not without the ladies consent – and prayed his good allowance to the match... The Lord Chamberlain was with her yesterday, who deales most nobly herein. It pleased him to tell me this morning – being sent for to him – that he fyndes all well and her affection strong; yet semying willing – though not tyed therto – to geve some satisfaction to her father and frends in the course of bestowing herself. Hereupon his Lordship had her father with him this morning at Whitehall – at what tyme I also there attended – and brake with him at large thereabouts, plainely delivering to him your Lordship's honorable purpose to your brother, all which it pleased his Lordship to imparte to me as soon as the knight [Cecily's father] was gon. In substance – that your Lordship wold settle Sir Francis Manners present estate, with your addition to that which he gave of his owne, to be a thousand markes yearely, [£666] for present maintenance, for her jointure and to the heirs male begotten on her.'

Here is the essence of this book: the problem of a direct male heir to an aristocratic family. Cecily and Francis married as soon as Roger's consent to the marriage settlement was obtained, although the fifth Earl was ill, as Screven mentioned in a later letter of 9 November. He asked for 'a speedy dispatche' of the business as other suitors for Cecily Tufton were making 'greate offres'. The letter could hardly have been more direct; 'if, therefore, your Lordship will vowchsafe this honorable favor for your brother's advancement, to make his whole estate for the present to be yearely 1000 markes, and will assure the same for her jointure, and upon the yssue male, this marriage will be don at the end of this or the begynning of the next monythe'.

Cecily was already known to the Manners family. Her sister Ann Tufton had married Francis Tresham, both an Essex plot and a Gunpowder Plot conspirator, who had warned Lord Monteagle several days before 5 November 1605 not to attend the opening of Parliament and had thus alerted James and his Council to the danger. Like Tresham, Cecily was a Roman Catholic and this was to be of great importance to the succeeding history of the Manners family. The marriage of Cecily and Francis Manners proved both fertile and as far as one can see loving, and as such was in contrast to that of Elizabeth and Roger Manners which was tragically infertile and the source of much gossip, all of which is impossible to verify. That marriage ended with the death of Roger in June 1612 and of Elizabeth in August of the same year.

The Sixth Earl of Rutland

1612 to 1613 was to prove a difficult time for the Manners family. Roger's death in June 1612 led to the succession of his brother Francis as sixth Earl. This event was followed rapidly by a Royal visit: King James came to Belvoir in August, soon after Roger's funeral in July, for the first of six visits in which he was enabled to indulge his love of hunting. This honour, although expensive, would have been welcome to Francis, for it enabled him to reinforce the good relations the Manners family enjoyed with James, following the second Earl's negotiation of James's pension in 1586.

But the visit was to presage a series of sad events; soon after he had accompanied his father to Belvoir, Prince Henry, the Prince of Wales, became ill and died. Then in 1613 Francis Manners, the new sixth Earl, and his wife suffered the loss of their eldest son Henry Lord Roos. In addition, Francis's youngest brother, the Roman Catholic Oliver Manners, died in 1613. This heavy mortality cast a shadow over the new Earl's succession. It is helpful at this stage to consider what remedies existed at the time to try to maintain the health of the family, and to look next at the connection between the family's health and the events leading to the witchcraft accusations of 1619.

Thomas, 1st Earl   Henry, 2nd Earl   Edward, 3rd Earl   John, 4th Earl

Roger, 5th Earl   Francis, 6th Earl   George, 7th Earl   John, 8th Earl

GENEALOGICAL TABLE

Sir Robert Manners, Knt., Sheriff of Northumberland, = Eleanor, Daughter of Lord Ros *d.* 1487
Descendant of Sir Robert Manners, Lord of the manor of
Ethale, Northumberland. (eleventh century)

Sir George Manners, Lord Ros = Ann, daughter of Sir Thomas St. Ledger *d.* 1526
d. 1513

Sir Thomas Manners, Lord Ros *cr.* Earl of Rutland 1526 = Eleanor, daughter of Sir William Paston *d.* 1551
d. 1543

Henry, 2nd Earl = Margaret   Sir John Manners = Dorothy Vernon of Haddon Hall *d.* 1584
d. 1563   daughter of Earl of   *d.* 1611
Westmorland *d.* 1560

Edward, 3rd Earl   John, 4th Earl = Elizabeth Charlton   Sir George Manners = Grace, daughter of Sir Henry Pierpoint
d. 1587   *d.* 1588   *d.* 1623   *d.* 1650

Roger, 5th Earl   Francis, 6th Earl   George, 7th Earl   John, 8th Earl = Frances, daughter of Lord Montagu *d.* 1671
d. 1612   *d.* 1632   *d.* 1641   *d.* 1679

The first eight Earls of Rutland. (BCA)

70

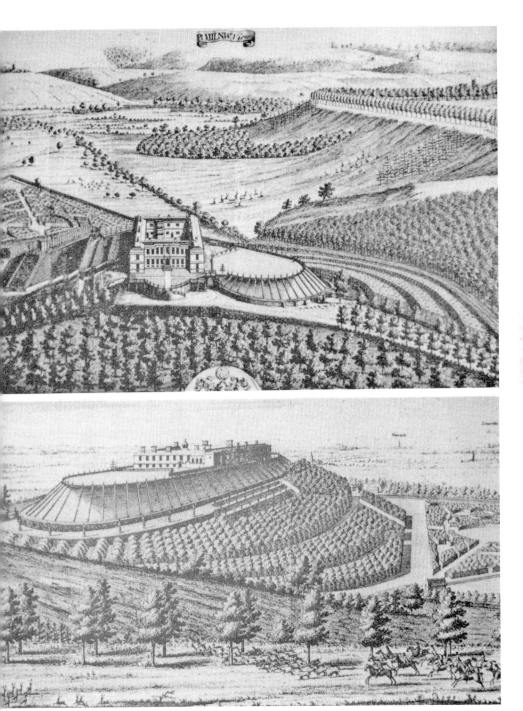

Hunting around Belvoir, recorded a century later. (JN)

ORLANDO

FVRIOSO

IN ENGLISH

HEROICAL VERSE, BY

IOHN HARINGTÕ

Principibus placuiſſe viris non vltima laus eſt.

Horace

Sir John Harrington and his dog Bungay in his translation of Ariosto's Orlando
Furioso. *(OUP & UEAL)*

❧By the Queene.

Hereas the Earle of Essex, accompanied with the Earles of Rutland & South-ampton, and diuers other their complices, Gentlemen of birth and qualitie, knowing themselues to be discouered in diuers treasonable actions, into which they haue heeretofore entred, aswell in our Realme of Ireland, where some of them had layed plots with the Traitour Tirone, as in this our Realme of Eng-land, did vpon Sunday, being the eight of this Moneth, in the morning, not onely imprison our Keeper of our Great Seale of England, our Chiefe Iustice of England, and others both of our Nobilitie and Councell, that were sent in our Name to his house; to perswade the sayd Earle to lay open any his petitions or complaints, with promise (if he would disperse his disordered company in his house) that all his iust requests shoulde bee heard, and graciously considered : but also did (after strait order giuen by him to murder our sayd Counsellers and others, whensoeuer they should offer to stir of London in armes, with great numbers, and there break diuulged base and foolish lies, That their liues were sought ons, to haue drawen our people to their partie, with pur our Person and State, and to expose as it now appeareth) a number of needy and desperate persons their adherents, Subiects, after many Proclamations of rebellion made by

Forasmuch as notwithstanding (God be thanked) they being now all apprehended, and within our Tower of Lon of Essex, Rutland, and Southampton, as diuers others of Subiects of our Citie, and elsewhere, hauing shewed them towards vs, as not any one of them of any note (that we ca associats; Wee haue bene contented, in regard of the comfo loyall disposition of our people (whereof we neuer doubted) of our Citie and elsewhere, in how thankefull part wee doe a stay from following the false perswasions of the Traitours, shall haue cause to shew it, they shall finde vs more carefull o gard of our gracious meaning towards our good people, to sudden, as it cannot yet be throughly looked into, how farre but that it is to bee presumed by the common example of th that it was not without instruments and ministers disper people, to like of their attempts, with calumniating our ministers thereof ; That they shall doe well (and so wee char

conuersation of persons not well knowen for their good behauiour, and to the speaches of any such rumo out slanderous and vndutifull wordes or rumours against vs and our gouernment : And they that be in autho-ritie, to lay holde on such Spreaders of rumours, And such as be not in authority, to aduertise those there-of that haue authoritie, to the end that by the apprehension of such dangerous instruments, both the drift & pur-pose of euill minded persons may be discouered, their desseignes preuented, and our people conserued in such peace and tranquillitie, as heeretofore by Gods fauour, we haue mainteined, and doe hope still to continue amongst them. Giuen at our Palace of Westminster the ninth day of February 1600, in the three and fortieth yeere of our reigne.

God saue the Queene.

❧ Imprinted at London by ROBERT BARKER, Printer
to the Queenes most excellent Maiestie.
1600.

INSET: Henry Wriothesley, Third Earl of Southampton, involved in the Essex rebellion (BC) and Queen Elizabeth's Proclamation, accusing Essex, Rutland and Southampton of treason. (EEBO & OBL)

Prince Henry, the first-born son of James VI & I and Queen Anne, died 1612, from
Michael Drayton's Poly-Olbion *of 1622. (EEBO & OBL)*

THE PHYSICIANS

For the Manners family, as for many landed families at the time, the birth and healthy survival of an heir was crucial to the retention of title and lands. The Manners had already experienced the passing of the title from one brother without a male heir to another, and seen the succession to the barony go to the Cecils. The sixth Earl's first marriage had produced a daughter, who could not inherit the earldom as it could only pass in the male line. Although his second marriage had brought him two sons, when their health began to fail there was more than just parental concern at stake. The Earl was in the fortunate position of being able to draw on the services of the best-known physicians of his time.

What actually caused premature death and infertility? These eternal questions were as widespread in 1612 as now, but the answers then were markedly different to those generally accepted today. The general response then was three-fold. Illness was seen as specifically sent as a warning by God. It was also seen as an aspect of the natural world that could be dealt with by rational action. A third explanation existed in Jacobean times, as Stuart Clark points out: 'the idea that devils could cause disease was a commonplace'. In order to understand illness in the context of the Rutland family and the witchcraft trial of 1619, there follows a discussion of the work of those physicians, surgeons and apothecaries who treated the Manners family during the first twenty years of the seventeenth century. Thus, the natural foundations of Jacobean medical treatment will be examined, along with the non-natural ideas which underpinned many people's concepts of illness. The perceived relationship between the devil and disease becomes clear through an analysis of the extent to which sorcery was seen as a possible cause of illness. Later, this association between disease and the devil can be considered from the theological viewpoint.

Medicine in the early modern period was effectively defined by Isaac Watts as 'distributed into prophylactick, or the art of preserving health; and therapeutick, or the art of restoring health'. A seventeenth century author, Mathias Prideaux, listed the older styles of medicinal practice as derived from the

'Latines, Greekes, Arabians and Jewes' and the newer styles coming from the 'Paracelsians, Galeno-chymicks, Prophylactics and Empiricks'. Around 1600, physicians tended to follow one of these two styles. The former, derived from classical Greek ideas, was generally known as Galenic and put its greatest emphasis on preventive medicine, which meant leading a healthy life-style. Medical historian Andrew Wear gives a neat précis of the Galenic essentials: '(1) air, (2) food and drink, (3) sleep and walking, (4) movement and rest, (5) retention and evacuation, including sexual activity, and (6) the passions of the soul or the emotions'

The newer fashion in early modern doctoring retained the Galenic essentials but responded more to outward appearances; as Roy Porter pointed out, Paracelsus's 'fundamental conviction was that nature was sovereign'. As a result, those physicians and surgeons who tended to the newer medical ideas looked to use forces outside the body, emanating from real natural substances, such as mercury. Practitioners from both styles believed that what was natural was good, but the new philosophy added a dimension of spirituality not present in classical medical practice, which they claimed was irreligious as it was derived from ancient Greek and Roman ideas. Astrology received a new lease of life, since planets, which existed beyond the moon, and which in consequence were devoid of harmful mundane agents, were presumed to influence man in hidden or occult ways. The physician's task was to harness this sympathetic but often occult (*ie:* hidden) interaction, by which the positive qualities of nature could be used to cure illness.

These systems of medical treatment had varying success rates. Even with today's advances in medicine, accurate diagnosis and the selection of an appropriate medicine would be far from easy. The medical practitioners of the early seventeenth century were at a greater disadvantage; further difficulties could arise from the side-effects of some of the methods or medicines used, or from occasions when they were carried to excess by a physician convinced that a particular method was a 'cure-all'. Perhaps the best results were obtained by those who concentrated on prescribing an appropriate diet and pattern of life, or what was described in the early eighteenth century as 'Dr Diet, Dr Quiet and Dr Merryman'.

A good way to understand these different approaches to medicine and doctoring is to look at the variety of medical practitioners by whom the Manners family were treated during the Jacobean period. The fifth Earl of Rutland died on 26 June 1612, aged 35 while undergoing treatment in Cambridge. On 21 May 1612 his illness was reported in a letter as follows:

'My Lord of Rutland, who was taken with a dead palsy and sometime was speechless, recovereth lying at Cambridge under Mr Butler's hand. Yesterday was feared as being the fourteenth day of his falling, the change of the moon and the eclipse of the sun. For the two last causes it was dangerous also to my lo. Treasurer.'

The letter writer, John Thorys, presented a clear report on the Earl's palsy, or paralysis, which can be interpreted today as the results of a stroke by his reference to the Earl being speechless. Thorys opened up two significant elements of the medical attention received by the Manners family which are important to this story. Firstly, the Earl's doctor in 1612 was Dr Butler, a Cambridge physician with a national reputation, who treated King James and was the preferred doctor of the Cecil family. Although fashionable, he was not in the main-stream of London College of Physicians doctors, as he preferred to live and work from Cambridge. Clearly the Earl's long-established love of Cambridge was one reason for this choice of physician, our understanding of which is reinforced by the bequest of £50 to Dr Butler in Roger's short will, written 8 May 1612.

The second aspect of Thorys' letter, which is so valuable, is the manner in which the astronomical references reinforce the date. On 30 May 1612 a solar eclipse took place: it was at its greatest at latitude 63.6N and longitude 1.9W, just north of the Shetland Isles. Putting in the correction necessary because England was still using the Julian Calendar, this eclipse would have taken place on 19 or 20 May 1612. If, in addition to the eclipse, the moon was changing *ie:* waning or going from full to crescent, then physicians would have been wary that it symbolised the possible decline of their patient. This attitude reveals the significance accorded to astrology, an element of the medical process at the centre of every practitioner's activity at that time. Following ideas which had become widespread in the sixteenth century, man was seen to be a miniature image of the universe. When great events happened in the skies, then it was anticipated that similarly significant events would happen to the individual man. An eclipse of the sun could signify the eclipse of a great man and the waning of the moon could foretell the decline of a person's health.

John Thorys wrote on 28 May that 'my lo. of Rutland mends again... my lord treasurer... died Sunday at 1 after midday', thus pointing out that Robert Cecil, Earl of Salisbury and James' chief minister, was dead. 1612 was a sad year, as the eclipse had apparently foretold. Only three months after Roger's funeral on 22 July, Henry, Prince of Wales died, having visited Belvoir Castle with his father King James on 7 August. It is important to be aware of this constant presence of death in the early seventeenth century. Equally it is important to attempt to understand the measures taken to understand illness, which the above quotation opens up effectively.

Medical practitioners

Roger, the fifth Earl, had gone to Cambridge for the best available medical care. This was slightly unusual in the early seventeenth century as those doctors who had the greatest reputations tended to practise in London. Official medical practitioners in Jacobean England belonged to three different groups: physicians, surgeons and apothecaries. Historically the best-known were the acknowledged experts – the physicians, who were well paid, with fees ranging from £1 to £10 per visit. They had to be licensed by the London College of Physicians, and they could only obtain their licence if they held a degree from Oxford or Cambridge. They were subject to the discipline of the College, backed by its Royal charter from Henry VIII. Physicians prescribed treatment with physic for internal disease, that is illness perceived as being caused by an imbalance in the fluids (or humours) in the body, as described by Galen. The treatment delivered by early Jacobean doctors was thus generally Galenic in that they followed Galen's classical Greek duopoly of prescribing mainly herbal remedies and of insisting that correct diet should be at the heart of medical treatment. These methods had become acceptable to Christians by the application of Ecclesiasticus 38 verse 4: 'The Lord hath created medicines of the earth, and hee that is wise, will not abhorre them'.

Superior in numbers but not in status to the physicians, the surgeons had their own professional body, the Barber-Surgeons' Company, controlled by a 1540 Act of Parliament. In contrast to physicians, surgeons endeavoured to cut out those diseases that had external symptoms by use of their knives. Most surgeons accepted the theory of humoural balance, as a result of which their main activity was bleeding the patient, to adjust fluid levels within the body. Their fees were usually around £1 per visit. The process of bleeding was both widespread and controversial. Most patients expected to be bled and indeed for centuries bleeding was looked upon as a restorative of health, necessary in illness or to maintain health. The best-regarded surgeons were well-paid; the two surgeons who operated on the fifth Earl in 1612 were paid £50 for their efforts. They also embalmed corpses; Dr Frederick was paid £30 for embalming the body of Sir Oliver Manners in 1613.

The third recognised branch of the healing professions were the apothecaries who in theory made up the medicines prescribed by physicians, but who largely operated as independent, (if illegal, according to the College) prescribers and sellers of drugs, herbal remedies and other prescriptions. However, they were improving their image during the reign of James as they gained the support of James' queen Anne and were able to gain their Royal charter in 1617. In most towns of England, the apothecaries were the principal medical practitioners, often combining their knowledge of herbal remedies with basic medical treatment. We could perhaps compare them with today's general practitioners, while the physicians were closer to the modern specialist consultants. Apothecaries were well-regarded; while they were not as well-paid as physicians or surgeons, they received sound remuneration. An example of a payment for treating the fifth Earl in 1609 was '25 October, paid to Mr Doctour Percywalle, apothecary for 8 oz of elixar of salt £3 4s; water distilled a quart 6s; pylles 2s 6d – £3 12s 6d'.

In addition to these three official groups there were innumerable irregular practitioners. Perhaps the best known popular type of such medical operators was the 'Emperick or Mountibancking Quacksalver' to use Thomas Decker's phrase. Bailey in his 1730 dictionary defined them as 'Quack Doctors or itinerant Pretenders to Physick and Surgery'. These were hands-on (*ie:* empirical) untrained men and women who often set up a stall in a market place, sold their own cure-all and then left quickly. It was because one of their new cures in the sixteenth century was the chemical mercury, or quicksilver, that they eventually gained the name 'quacksalver' or 'quack'. This usage had not appeared when, around 1585, William Clowes, Royal surgeon to Queen Elizabeth, listed the kind of traders, or charlatans, who might prey upon the unwary:

'tinkers, tooth-drawers, peddlars, ostlers, carters, porters, horse-gelders, and horse-leeches, idiots, apple-squires, broom-men, bawds, witches, conjurers, soothsayers, and sow-gelders, rogues, rat-catchers, runagates and proctors of Spittlehouses.'

Among the local cunning men, there could be included wise women and white witches who were reliant on herbal medicines and astrology, both aspects of doctoring totally at the centre of every medical practitioner's activity in the early seventeenth century. Perhaps Anne Baker was Bottesford's representative. These people could sometimes achieve a measure of success in a case where illness was attributed by the patient or the patient's family to witchcraft. By identifying someone as a witch and in some cases causing her, or him, to suffer in return, visit the sufferer and take off the alleged enchantment, a measure of mental relief could be produced which was effective in making the ill person feel better.

As relatively few people could afford the services of physicians, in reality most medical treatment took place in the home, and was administered by the housewife. It was perceived as a central role of motherhood to have the skills necessary to provide a good diet and to be able to offer treatment for everyday illnesses. One popular text was available in the sixteenth century for general readers: the medieval Latin medical verse *Regimen Sanitatis Salerni* had been translated by a monk from Lincolnshire, Thomas Paynell, in 1528 as *The Regimen Sanitatis Salerni: this Boke Techynge al People to Governe them in Helthe*. A new translation appeared in 1617, where the translator Philemon Holland in his preface pointed to 'the three essential parts of Physicke, to wit Dyet, Medicine and Chyrurgy'. An epitome of all of this could best be seen in *The English House-Wife* by Gervase Markham, a cousin of Sir Griffin Markham, one of Roger's dinner guests on the night before the Essex rebellion. Markham published this successful work in 1616 and the extensive first chapter was devoted to treatments and recipes for the full range of diseases, including the palsy, which was to be treated as follows:

'For the Apoplexie or palsie, the strong sent or smell of a Foxe is exceeding soveraigne, or to drinke every morning half a pint of the decoction of Lavendar, and to rub the head every morning and evening exceeding hard with a clean course cloath, whereby the humours may be dissolved and disperst into the outward parts of the body; by all meanes for this infirmity keep your feet safe from cold or wet, and also the nape of your neck, for from those parts it first getteth the strength of evill and unavoidable pains.'

Markham's book shows the extraordinary learning available to any literate gentlewoman or housewife, as it offers treatment for all known diseases from the toothache to jaundice, from the bloody flux to the stone. A second quotation from *The English House-Wife*, offering treatment for epilepsy, known then as the falling sickness, opens up the astrological and herbal activity at the centre of contemporary practice:

> 'Although the falling-sicknes be seldome or never to be cured, yet if the party which is troubled with the same, wil but morning and evening, during the wane of the moone, or when she is in the sign of Virgo, eat the berries of the hearb Asterion [aster or starwort], or beare the hearbs about him next to his bare skin, it is likely he shal find much ease and fal very seldome, although this medicine be somewhat doubtful.'

Markham's detailed remedies for both the palsy and the falling sickness are typical of the treatments readily available to members of the Manners family who suffered from these two illnesses during the second decade of the seventeenth century.

The extensive references to physicians, surgeons, apothecaries, nurses and midwives in the Rutland MSS offer some understanding of the medical problems of the aristocratic house of Manners, which culminated in their conclusion that witchcraft and not least the actions of the Flower women, were responsible for their suffering. Their feelings, as illness followed illness, were described in the words of the ballad, written immediately after the witchcraft trial:

> 'At length the Countesse and her Lord,
> to fits of sicknesse grew:
> The which they deemd the hand of God,
> and their corrections due:
> Which crosses patiently they bore,
> misdoubting no such deeds,
> As from these wicked Witches heere,
> malitiously proceeds.
>
> Yet so their malice more increast,
> that mischiefe set in foote,
> To blast the branches of that house,
> and undermine the roote:

Their eldest sonne Henry Lord Rosse,
possest with sicknesse strange,
Did lingring, lye tormented long,
till death his life did change.'

The ballad expresses the acknowledged first reaction to illness in the early seventeenth century, that it was sent by God to try the patience of the faithful, in order to allow them the opportunity to show the depth of their religion by rising above earthly suffering. But it was also widely accepted that help from the medical profession was a natural process, approved by God in the life of the gospel writer and evangelist St Luke, perceived as the patron saint of doctors.

The medical practitioners of the Earls of Rutland
Who then treated the Manners family? Throughout his life Roger, the fifth Earl, (who was excused attendance at the session of Parliament in 1610, probably because of illness), sought expensive treatment and looked for the most up- to-date cures. Early on, as he came into his majority, he spent hugely, paying £6 for two bezoar stones in 1598. These were stones from India, voided by goats, which were 'A stone of excellent virtue against poison, very costly and of great account in Physick'. In the same year his agent 'paid to the apothecary for almond mylke for 15 days together 25/8d'. This was imported spiced milk specifically prepared for delicate digestive systems. When Roger went to Ireland with Essex in 1599, he was attended by Dr Marbeck, (his personal physician who was also a Royal physician), and furnished with 'waters and physicall things'. He did not stay long in Ireland and, on his return to England, he went to Bath, where he received surgical treatment from 'Mr Goodrous, [William Gooderus] her Majeste's serjeant chirurgian, whom she sent to my Lord'. The financial accounts give few intimate details of medical treatment, but it is clear that the fifth Earl was often a sick man. We can conjecture concerning his condition by studying the careers of his medical men, in particular his later surgeon Mr Frederick and his physician Mr Butler, who together treated him for his palsy in the last months of his life.

The fifth Earl's continuous ill-health seemed to come to a climax in November 1611, when he was surgically treated for the gout: 10 shillings was paid 'for a plaister for the gowt for my Lord'. The symptoms of gout were swelling and inflammation. These were perceived to be signs of humoural imbalance by the early

Jacobean practitioners but, as the symptoms appeared on the external surface of the skin, the gout could be treated by surgeons. This is apparently what happened to Roger. The Rutland MSS contain for January 1612 the tantalising entry: 'for ii litle silver plates with buckles to cover my Lord's issues, with 6s. for making them, sent to Belvoyre,10s'. An 'issue' was 'a small artificial Aperture, made in some fleshy Part of the Body, to drain off superfluous Moisture, or to give vent to some noxious Humour'. Clearly Roger was undergoing surgery, possibly carried out by Mr Frederick and his colleague Mr Guilliam who, on 19 July after Roger's death, were paid £50 for 'the incision made'.

Sir Walter Raleigh

In between these two payments, there occurs, in 1612, one of the most medically detailed yet mystifying of all the Rutland MSS entries:

> 'For extracte of awmber for plaisters, 10 oz. 3£., for chimical oyle of awmber, 11 oz, 3£. 6s., the one half hereof carried to Cambridge by Mr Marks, the other sent thither by me 29 June, and bothe directed by Sir Walter Raleigh, 6£. 6s.'

The mention of Raleigh's name suggests that this was a remedy sent to Thomas Screven, Roger's steward at Belvoir, as a last hope by an acknowledged expert on chemical medicines, Sir Walter Raleigh. Raleigh was imprisoned in the Tower for treasonable activities against King James, but he was allowed to maintain there a chemical laboratory or 'stilhous' and work on chemical remedies. In 1606 Raleigh had treated Roger with 'a water for the collicque'. He was well known for his medical preparations, particularly a cordial offered to Prince Henry's doctors during the prince's last days and much used by the Manners family.

What is interesting about the MSS entry is the content of Raleigh's medical prescription. It was not a herbal prescription. It was in fact a prime example of the external remedies being developed, partly as a result of the popular sixteenth century medical work of Paracelsus. The novelty of Paracelsus' work was, in contrast to Galenism, his idea that disease could be caused by external agents and could be cured by exploiting the hidden powers of external substances. Raleigh's remedy was to appropriate the qualities of the semi-precious and highly valued amber into an ointment or oil by chemical reduction. The use of amber in medicine also owes much to its traditional reputation for having magical, protective and healing properties. A cure using valuable substances such as amber appeared to be caused by the positive qualities of the substance being transferred to the patient, an idea at the root of much early modern medicine. It was suggested that Raleigh prescribed pills for Roger's wife, the Countess Elizabeth, in her last days in the summer of 1612 and the Manners family continued to use Raleigh's cordial during the seventeenth and eighteenth centuries.

Mr Frederick

It was Roger's surgeons and physicians who were applying these novel remedies, in particular Mr Frederick, the surgeon of the Belvoir household and a Royal surgeon. He was also an expert embalmer: he was recorded as embalming the bodies of Roger, of his younger brother Sir Oliver Manners in 1614 and, possibly, in 1625, the body of King James. Frederick was James's sergeant-surgeon from 1609 to 1623. We know that he treated James for 'a broken collar bone, renal stones and hemorrhoids'. He attended the fifth Earl's funeral, where he was listed as a servant, so clearly he had a strong attachment to the Earl. The fact that he embalmed Roger's body opens up the whole question of surgical autopsies which, following the well publicised autopsy after the murder of the French King Henri IV in 1610, were beginning to become possible in England for the first time. Obviously an autopsy would have involved surgical intervention, as did the autopsy carried out on Prince Henry's body in November 1612. This aimed to find out exactly what was the cause of his death, a subject of much controversy involving six doctors, one of whom was Roger's physician, Dr Butler.

Dr Butler

This physician specified in Roger's will, Dr Butler, was one of the most unusual doctors of that period. John Aubrey called him 'the greatest Physitian of his time'. His advice was 'Health is preserved by a knowledge of one's body'. He was particularly concerned to prescribe the use of cardiacs, or cordials for the heart, 'because they nurture, increase and preserve that life-giving nectar of blood, the whole life production of the original moisture and the flower of the spirits'. Another element of his prescribing work was new milk, so it was possibly he who encouraged Roger to consume almond milk. The Galenic theory of physiology stated that the one material essential for life, food, nurtured 'chyle' in the stomach, which was made into the life-giving fluid, blood, by the liver. From the liver, blood flowed to the heart, where air and heat gave it spiritual goodness which arterial veins distributed all around the body.

Butler agreed with this but was a little doubtful about the most common treatment of all: bleeding. The theory behind this was to rid the body of dangerous humours *via* blood-letting, but to Butler this was not necessarily totally efficacious, given the significance of 'that life giving nectar of blood'. In the tragic case of the death of 'England's hope', eighteen-year-old Henry, Prince of Wales in November 1612, there was considerable and well-documented argument between six physicians attending him, including Dr Butler, about the necessity of bleeding the prince. Butler for a time tried to stop his fellow physicians from bleeding the prince, but gave in after several days. Butler preferred in certain cases to use medication such as 'bezoardica', exactly the remedy that Roger was purchasing in 1598. Was Roger's survival until 1612 the result of effective treatment by this most original of doctors, Dr Butler? This is difficult to prove, and unfortunately the printed Rutland documents do not include any references to him.

Dr Atkins

One of the other doctors attending Prince Henry was Dr Henry Atkins. On the ninth day of Henry's illness, Atkins, 'a physitian of London, famous for his practice, honestie & learning, was sent for by his majestie to assiste the reste in the care'. Both Dr Butler and Dr Atkins signed the post mortem report on Prince Henry. Dr Atkins 'opinyon, as they said, was that highness [sic] disease was a corrupt, putrid feaver, the seate whereof was under the lyver'. Twentieth-century analysis of the illness as typhoid fever suggests that both Butler and Atkins had valuable understanding of disease, a standing which was recognised at the time, as they were both employed by the King and by the Manners family.

Henry Atkins, several times president of the Royal College of Physicians, was not only a Royal physician, but also a physician to Robert Cecil, later Earl of Salisbury and Lord Treasurer of England, whose final illness coincided with that of Roger, the fifth Earl. The response of Dr Atkins to Cecil's last days is recorded. 'Mr Doctor Atkins then began, & desired (being phisicion) this religious conference, & so to temper it, that, as my lord was resolved to die, soe he might not neglect the blessed meanes of Godes providence to live'. What Dr Atkins was saying to Cecil was that he accepted Cecil's understanding that his principal purpose in the extremity of illness should be to make peace with his God, but meanwhile he could continue to take advice from his doctor about diet, in case God's providence should be such as to allow him some more time on this earth.

After Roger's death Dr Atkins continued to treat the Manners family. His other patients had included the King's son Prince Charles (whom he was responsible for bringing from Scotland), the family of the Countess of Derby, the Cecil family and Sir Thomas Bodley, the founder of the Bodleian Library in Oxford. He was involved in several autopsies; he became well known as president of the College of Physicians on seven occasions and he encouraged the Apothecaries as they sought and obtained their charter in 1617. Unlike Butler, he was a London-based physician, in the parish of 'Christ Church where I have lived many yeares' as he said when bequeathing forty pounds to the parish poor in his will. He treated the Manners family when they were in London and was consulted at a distance when in September 1616, Francis Manners, the second son and surviving male heir of the sixth Earl, was ill at Belvoir. With this event, for the first time we are able to come close to the medical care of one of the Earl's sons, for Dr Atkins wrote a letter in response to the Countess which has survived

Henry Manners, known by the family as Lord Roos, the first son of Francis and Cecily Manners, sixth Earl and Countess, had died in 1613. The Bottesford registers record: 'September 1613 Henry Manners Lord Roos the eldest sonne of the Right Hon: Lord Francis Earle of Rutland was buryed the 26th day'. The Rutland Manuscripts refer to his death: 'Delyverd, the xxvii of September, 1613, to Mr Jepheson by Mr Sutton to defraye the chardges of my late Lord Rosse's funeral, viii £'. This payment of £8 contrasts with payments for the fifth Earl's funeral in the previous year of over £84. Following Henry's death, Francis the second son became the heir and was given by the Manners family the title of Lord Roos. Thereafter the pages of the Rutland Manuscripts frequently mention doctors, so it is possible to build up a picture of Jacobean health care. There is in the Belvoir archives a letter from Dr Atkins to the Countess about Francis Lord Roos's health. Henry Atkins' letter was revealing, particularly in its concern to be reassuring. He wrote suggesting the 'the matter is not great that y[ou]r L[adyship] rigt of yt because I find not by y[ou]r le[tter] that the little lord hath any convulsions or fits that take away his sence or his motions but onely a jumping of his mouth by reason of some physicke gathering in his mouth & jawes or throte... making him sometime move his mouth some times a little more than ordinary'.

It is possible for a twenty-first-century physician* to analyse this description of medical symptoms. The condition known today as Partial Motor Epilepsy has a well recognised if uncommon variant, that affects one side of the mouth and is associated with difficulty in swallowing and speaking but without loss of consciousness. There are physical effects which parents would notice and it is possible that the twitches or 'jumping of the mouth' which the Countess has written to Dr Atkins about were indeed the early symptoms of epilepsy. We know today that epilepsy can be caused by a progressive tumour or abscess on the brain and that this also might result in unusual behavioural patterns. If this was in fact the case then it is not difficult to understand the increasing worry felt by the Earl and Countess. What is clear is that their determination to find a cure led them to consult the widest possible range of practitioners, and sometimes to go beyond the conventional skills of Dr Atkins and Dr Butler to consider the recommendations of many different physicians, some on the boundary between medicine and magic.

While considering these Manners family physicians, it is also possible to list the times during the second decade of the seventeenth century when the 'little lord' Francis, the heir following his elder brother's death in 1613, was ill. Doctors were continuously attending him from October to December 1614. Doctors were paid in September 1615 and in August and September 1616. Following this there was Dr Atkins' consultation in December 1616. In his letter, Dr Atkins referred to 'Mr Athil a physician of yr Country unknown to me'. This was Dr Athall, a Peterborough physician, who was paid £6 for his medical services in January 1617. The next payments were in January 1618, but it is clear from the record that Francis had been seriously ill late in 1617. There was, it appears, no continuous period in the young Francis' childhood when he was free from illness.

*Dr John Cleary, a retired consultant physician from Peterborough Hospital, has kindly offered this diagnosis.

Dr Ridgley

It is clear from the Rutland accounts that the family was particularly happy to employ a doctor from the locality: Dr Thomas Ridgley. He was consulted by the family between 1607 and 1616 and so was involved in treating the young Francis. He was paid £7 for 'vi daies beeinge at Belvoyre with my Lord Roasse' on 13 November 1614. Then on 19 September 1615 Francis Vincent, the Belvoir Receiver, 'Payd to Doctor Ridgley, of Newarke, by my Ladie's comandement, beeing at Garradon with my Lord Roosse when he was not well; payd to him for vi daies, in goulde, vi £. xiis' The final recorded transaction was 'Paid, the 24th of August, 1616, to Doctor Ridgsley, for mynistringe phisicq to my Lord Roosse at Belvoir, the som of 3 £'. Perhaps Ridgley was popular with the Manners because he, unlike most physicians at the time, could boast that he was descended from an 'old and prominent gentry family'. He married Anne Odingsells, the daughter of Gabriel Odingsells Esquire, of Bulcote in Nottinghamshire, whose first wife was Catherine Markham, the daughter of John Markham, High Sheriff of Lincolnshire during the reign of Elizabeth. The extended Markham gentry family had close connections with the Manners and there is a heartfelt letter in the Rutland archives which testifies to this. On 11 September 1617 Richard Markham wrote to Sir George Manners, the only surviving brother of the sixth Earl, recalling all the past Earls and looking hopefully to the future:

> 'My father was much bounden to the Earls of Rutland all his days and I myself can remember all these Earls resident at Belvoir – first Lord Thomas, then Lord Henry, then, by an interim the Earl of Bedford, then Lord Edward, Lord John, Lord Roger, and now Lord Francis, who long may live and after him his sweet young heir Lord Roos.'

The Markhams, like the Manners' family physicians, were in effect clients of the aristocratic family, relying upon their support for employment. Dr Ridgley, in marrying into the Markham family, was reinforcing his membership of the gentry and thereby smoothing his relationships with the sixth Earl. When he wished to rise in his chosen profession he felt he needed the patronage first of the Earl and then of the King and this was possible because James was a frequent visitor to Belvoir, where he adored the opportunities for hunting. As a result of these connections Dr Ridgley was able eventually to join the College of Physicians and, after moving to London, to become during the 1620s and 1630s one of the best known physicians in England.

He badly needed such high-ranking patronage because of his new style of medical activity which was the result of his being a good practical chemist. He is described as attacking

> 'Those Puritane Alchymists that talk so muche of separating the impure part from the pure cannot with all their art separate or extract anie thing out of Mercury... it being a simple homogeneous body never to be resolved into diverse natures.'

Clearly he made his own medical preparations, using the latest analytical chemistry. Eventually, when he was in London, he installed his own furnace in order to create his own medicines, but we unfortunately have no record of precisely how he treated the young Francis. Francis remained alive during the several years he was being treated by Ridgley; maybe that is the only testimonial he could have.

Dr Napier, *alias* Dr Sandie

Towards the end of 1614, the Rutland MSS record several instances of medical expenditure on behalf of Francis Lord Roos in addition to the payments to Dr Ridgley. At the same time as Dr Ridgley was being consulted, the Manners family was using the different skills of another doctor, Dr Richard Napier, also referred to as 'Dr Sandie'. Owing to the survival of his patient case records, we know a great deal about Dr Napier from Buckinghamshire, the 'astrological physician and Church of England clergyman'. We do not know exactly how Dr Napier treated Lord Francis in October 1614 as Napier's case records for the last months of 1614 are incomplete. But we do know what he was paid : 'Delyverd, the xii[th] day of October,1614 to Doctor Sandie, that came from my Lord Morden to my Lord Roasse, being not well. iiii £'. In addition there was another payment on 'the vi[th] day of November, 1614, for William Chappman's chardges rydinge unto Newporrte Panell for a doctor for my Lord Rosse when he was sick, xviiis. vid.' From this evidence emerge the circumstances of Napier's visit to Belvoir and the style of his consultations.

Dr Napier, a fellow of Exeter College, Oxford from 1580 to 1590, was appointed Rector of Great Linford, immediately to the east of Newport Pagnell, where he remained until his death in 1634. He found preaching difficult and, from his earliest days as rector, he employed curates to undertake his parochial work. This left him free to develop his consuming passion – astrological medicine – by which he diagnosed patients' conditions and then offered prescriptions. The extensive archive of his papers has survived and recently been much studied. Medical historian Michael MacDonald suggested that 'Napier lived during the last era in which a prestigious medical practitioner could reconcile his beliefs in astrology, magic, religion and science'. What is important to stress is that, in spite of not being a member of the College of Physicians, Napier was highly regarded, particularly by the poor, whom he charged low fees, and the Midland aristocracy and gentry who consulted him in great numbers.

Napier was a mixture of practical and spiritual doctor and, his work provides an extraordinary insight into how Jacobean practitioners actually functioned. Using his case notes, it is possible to draw up an approximate idea of Napier's work during 1614 when he was paid by the Earl's receiver the fee of £4. In September he appears to have had nearly one hundred patients and for these he cast fifty-one horoscopes. During October 1614, an extremely rainy month, Napier treated and kept records for over fifty patients and cast horoscopes for twenty- seven, but not apparently for any member of the Manners family. During that month, however, he noted that he 'was instructed to goe... to the Lord of Rutl[and]'. Earlier in the year he treated a female patient with the falling sickness: in July he 'twice let blood in her foot'. On 31 October he noted a prescription for the falling sickness. It is tempting to speculate that he was known for his treatment of what we now know as epilepsy, but the present state of Napier studies does not yet allow us to draw any statistical conclusions about his conventional medical work. An example of his normal treatment can be seen in that which he gave to Elizabeth Jermyn, possibly a relative of an old colleague from Oxford:

'Hor.10.20 August 6th 1614
ill this 3 weeks. Troubled
wth wind & vomiteth her
meat that she eateth
R Tabul stib 5^{d}
 conserv. Absynth
   Garyophil[lum]
 Elect Dyascordii'
 Misc

He dated the time of the consultation so that he could draw up her horoscope if necessary, but he appears to have prescribed a straightforward herbal remedy, possibly taken from the *Materia Medica* of the classical Greek medical author Dioscorides. The plants in English were wormwood and gillyflower; this prescription is a normal Galenic physician's treatment.

Napier's astrological and spiritual concerns led him to offer treatment derived from casting horoscopes and from divination. A medical horoscope involved working out the position of the most significant stars and the planets visible at the time of birth, and at the time of the consultation, and then relating this information to the site in the body of the patient where illness or disease was obviously causing suffering. This was normally done by reference to charts which illustrated 'planetary influence over the organs of the body and their maladies'. Doctors such as Napier Christianised this use of the zodiac by associating star signs with angels and he particularly favoured Raphael and Michael, whom he specified in October 1614 as being the first two angels 'that attend on God'. By emphasising this strongly spiritual approach Napier, as a physician licensed by his local archdeacon of the Church of England, was perceived to be acceptable by local families even though he was never licensed by the College of Physicians. He was not officially disciplined for his style of medicine by the College, as he never practised in London.

Napier was certainly frequently consulted over illness which was perceived to be caused by witchcraft. By the Jacobean period conventional London physicians were generally reluctant to accept witchcraft as an explanation of illness. Michael MacDonald suggested that 'it is easy to see why arguments that banished Satan and witches from the chambers of the sick in all but the most baffling cases appealed to classical physicians', such as Dr John Cotta, the Northampton doctor who wrote extensively on the subject of witchcraft. We do not know the details of exactly how Napier was consulted by the Manners family in 1614, and it is not suggested that he was summoned because witchcraft was suspected as a cause of the young Lord Francis's illness. On the contrary, the visit to Belvoir took place four years before the Flower family became suspect. Napier was summoned because he was well known in the Midlands and because he was seen by aristocratic families as having the right background to treat their family. However, it is worth investigating his approach to medicine, since it provides the proper context to investigate the circumstances of the Manners' eventual recourse to the law concerning witchcraft.

Dr John Cotta

Why did the Manners not appeal to that other famous Midland doctor, John Cotta, who was well known by this time for his writings against quacks and who lived locally? He, unlike Napier, was reluctant to look to witchcraft as a cause of illness, but he would consider it in the last resort. However, he attacked any physician who used astrology and for this reason there was clearly no love lost between Napier and Cotta. In his famous text *The Triall of Witchcraft* Cotta wrote:

> 'as it is not obscure, that some men under the colour of Astrology have practised Magicke and Sorcery; so it is no lesse evident, that many others, under the pretense of advising and counselling in Physicke of curation or prognostification of disease, have likewise exercised the same divellish practice'.

We can distinguish two modes of medical practice by contrasting Napier and Cotta as they had distinct and contrasting sets of gentry patients. Napier's aristocratic patients were often Catholic in orientation, particularly three families, the Fortescues, the family of the young Lord Mordaunt and the Villiers and these were close associates of the Manners who, as the second decade of the seventeenth century went by, were being recognised widely as Catholic. Cotta's patients came from the Puritan gentry families: for example the Hales of Coventry and the family of Sir William Tate of Delapré Abbey. Cotta was prepared to enter into theological dispute, a position inimical to that of the London College of Physicians which endeavoured to steer clear of theology. In the 'Epistle Dedicatorie' to his *Triall of Witchcraft* Cotta wrote:

> 'The envious haply may cavil, that a physician out of his owne supposed precincts should rush into sacred lists or enter upon so high points of Divinitie, as by an unavoidable intercurrence do necessarily insert themselves into this proposed subject. Divinitie it selfe doth herein answere them. In the theory of Theology, it is the duty and praise of every man, to bee without curiositie fruitfully exercised.'

This was the Puritan position and it is intriguing to speculate about its conjunction with that of Napier, in spite of Cotta's strictures against astrologers. Napier believed in the power of angels when appealing for God's help in his consultation. Indeed his approach fitted more closely the generally-held views about the possibility that supernatural spirits were responsible for illness. Both Napier and Cotta accepted the possibility of the intervention of the devil as a possible cause. Michael MacDonald sums up, in sentences which are remarkably reminiscent of the condition of the young Lord Francis:

> 'Occasionally Napier remarked that the symptoms of a sick patient were like the torment experienced by a person who was haunted or bewitched. Most of the clients he described with this comparison suffered from plucking sensations or convulsions that made them look as if they were being manipulated by invisible creatures.'

Dr Francis Anthony

We do not know any more about the effect of the Manners consultation with Napier, but their continuing anxiety for the health of their son showed itself in 1618 in contacting one of the most controversial of all Jacobean physicians, Dr Francis Anthony. Anthony was a well known Paracelsian physician continuously in trouble with the College of Physicians, for his insistence on using an alchemical remedy based on gold. His recipe involved working with 'an ounce of pure refined Gold (which costs £3.13s.4d.) cast into a Wedge and File it into small Dust with a fine file'. After extensive chemical reduction, the liquid gold was dissolved into a menstruum made of vinegar and then further refined to produce a tincture. Then 'take an ounce of this Tincture, and put it into a pint of Canary Sack [wine] and so when it is clear you may drink of it, which will be about a day and a half'.

This was the 'essence of gold' with which the sixth Earl hoped to cure the young lord Francis in January 1618. Two payments are recorded to Dr Anthony in the Rutland MSS. On 15 January he was paid £6 for a 'dram of the essenc [sic] of gold' and then later in February £3 for '30 graines of gold essence'. Clearly Dr Anthony was making money out of the transaction as a dram was 'a small weight, the eight part of an ounce'.

A grain was 'the smallest Weight used in England, taken from the Weight of a Grain of Wheat, taken out of the Middle of an Ear of Corne dry'd', and one hundred made up an ounce. Dr Anthony had argued in both Latin and English texts in favour of his panacea. His principal book, published in 1616, was entitled:

> 'The Apologie, or Defence of a verity heretofore published concerning a medicine called Aurum Potabile, that is, the pure substance of Gold, prepared, and made Potable and Medicinable without corrosives, helpfully given for the health of Man in most Diseases, but especially available for the strenghning [sic] and comforting of the Heart and vitall Spirits the performers of health; as an Universall Medicine.'

This book consisted of twenty-three pages of what he called 'rational' argument in favour of the remedy and 77 pages of 'Experiments and Oculare Testimonies, a few drawn out of a great number, by which the Wonderfull virtues of this my Potable gold in the Curing of Diseases are fully shewed, perhibited [sic: exhibited] and avouched, by oculare and sensible testimonies, free from all future challenge and question'. In other words, he based his arguments on 'what may be proved by reason' and 'experiment'. He listed five arguments: the first was that because some medicines had 'many uses' why was it not possible 'by the help of Art, a Medicine may be made much more comprehensive of efficacie upon diseases?' The second argument insisted that gold was the perfect body, 'endowed with an exact temperament and equalitie of the compounding Elements' and thus was best able to reconcile the conflicting humours of the body. His third reason was that gold was so noble that it would naturally cure the noblest part of the body, the heart and 'if golde administred doe restore integritie of temperament to the Heart, the other parts and members of the bodie shall also receive comfort'. Anthony then argued that treating the heart first was like feeding a pack animal as it walked along: it received the strength necessary for its journey. The final and fifth reason was that 'there is in nature a universall Medicine: which whether it be made of gold or gold made of it it mattereth not much, for either way it sufficiently proveth, the excellent properties of gold most agreeable to mans nature'.

These circular arguments are typical of Renaissance thinking and derive from the hierarchical interpretation of the universe, where gold was seen to be the perfect metal which all other metals aspired to become. Gold to the alchemical doctor was quite clearly the ideal medicine. What Anthony meant by 'experiment' was not the twenty-first century scientific concept, but to experience or 'to find by triall'. Experimental proof lay in bringing together experiences and so he listed the cases of well over a hundred named patients, from families in all branches of society. Four families mentioned in Anthony's case histories in particular were probably close to the sixth Earl: the Cary family (Carew or Carey are alternative spellings of this extended family name), the family of Sir Francis Leake the Derbyshire landowner, that of Sir Francis Fortescue, the Buckinghamshire landowner and the family of Sir Lewis Lewkner. Members of these families were related to the Manners either by blood or marriage.

Dr Anthony wrote at length about Sir Lewis Lewkner, who was possibly the Mr Lewkner mentioned in the Rutland MSS as being amongst the friends of the fifth Earl in his dinner parties, just before the Essex revolt. In 1611 Sir Lewis was stricken by the plague; the same outbreak was recorded in Leicester in the Rutland MSS for that year. Dr Anthony's account of his treatment of this associate of the Manners family helps us understand why they themselves eventually employed him in 1618.

> 'The patient every day waxed worse & worse; at the last an Apostheme [a swelling] appeared in his groyne, a true token in such a disease, of a pestilent and contagious infection.... I was sent for, not knowing the disease, which could not long hide itself, having such manifest tokens... And therefore resolved (by the grace of God) with some powerfull and strong Antidote, to expel the poyson from his heart, and afterwards to proceede for his further recoverie, as occasion should be ministred. To which purpose, I first gave him six grains of my Essence of gold, mixed appropriately... and so every day for 4 daies more I gave againe the same Medicine, in the same quantity, which caused abundant sweating, whereby both the malignitie of the fever and the unnaturall heate was exceedingly abated... Thus he was cured of this mortall and contagious disease.'

Dr Anthony's understanding of what happened was that the gold, as the essence of natural perfection, was applied to the over-heated heart of the patient and calmed it down. The renewed and healthy heart then pumped out from the swelling all opposing unnatural humours or fluids which could not remain in the vicinity of such an ideal natural manifestation of goodness as gold. In consequence the plague swelling 'did daily decrease, and at last quite vanished'. Dr Anthony became rich as the result of his potable gold, particularly after he was supported by the King in actions taken against him by the College of Physicians. With his apparent success, the new chemical medicine became more acceptable to the College, although alchemical medicine struggled and finally failed later in the seventeenth century.

What is important is the continued reference to God as the underlying foundation of medical understanding, a foundation which, as has been shown, was not undermined by the chemical prescriptions of Sir Walter Raleigh and Dr Anthony or by the astrological approach of Dr Napier. Dr Ridgley's own somewhat conservative style of chemical prescription led him to attack the claimed aphrodisiac benefits both of mercury and aurum potabile, a view perhaps derived from his religious principles. Dr Atkins is best remembered for his great support of herbal medicinal practice through his active encouragement of the London apothecaries and his patronage of the College of Physicians' *London Pharmacopoeia* in 1618.

Taking a general view of all the Manners family medical practitioners in the first twenty years of the seventeenth century, it is possible to sum up that, while they were generally mainstream fellows of the London College of Physicians, the sixth Earl in particular was driven to consult doctors on the periphery of acceptability. Why was this? Was it the Earl's religious leanings which apparently prevented him from employing the skills of a Puritan doctor such as Dr Cotta? The College of Physicians tended not to offer specifically theological medical advice. Was this the reason why the sixth Earl went outside the College's membership to employ Dr Napier? He was a beneficed cleric of the Church of England, and as such not really approved of as a medical practitioner by the College. Certainly the Manners family had tried every available medical remedy by 1618 so it is understandable that they might be driven to consider another root cause of the young Lord Francis's condition: witchcraft. It is therefore appropriate to turn to the religious ambiance in which the Manners thrived, in order to better understand the witchcraft accusations.

THE FOUR HUMOURS

Body fluid	Qualities	Temperament	Element	Season	Age
Blood	Wet and Hot	Sanguine	Air	Spring	Childhood
Yellow Bile	Dry and Hot	Choleric	Fire	Summer	Youth
Black Bile	Dry and Cold	Melancholy	Earth	Autumn	Adulthood
Phlegm	Wet and Cold	Phlegmatic	Water	Winter	Old Age

LEFT: Dr Richard Napier, alias Dr Sandie. (OAM), RIGHT: Dr William Butler. (NPG) BELOW: The Four Humours: in order to prescribe treatment, Jacobean physicians attempted to correlate the physical and psychological condition of the patient with many other variables, such as the time of year, age and the astrological situation. In addition diet was seen as central. (MH)

Title page of John Gerard's Herball, *edition of 1636. (EEBO&UI)*

CHAP. 70. *Of Starre-wort.*

¶ The Description.

1 THe first kind of *Aster* or *Inguinalis* hath large broad leaves like *Verbascum Salvifolium* or the great *Conyza*; amongst which riseth up a stalke foure or five handfulls high, hard, rough, and hairy, beset with leaves like Rose Campions, of a darke greene colour. At the top of the said stalks come forth floures of a shining and glistering golden colour.

¶ The Place.

The kindes of Starwort grow upon mountaines and hilly places, and somtimes in woods & medowes lying by rivers sides.

The first kinds grow upon Hampsted heath foure miles from London, in Kent upon Southfleet Downes, and in many other such downy places.

‡ I could never yet find nor heare of any of these Star-floures to grow wilde in this kingdom, but have often seene the Italian Starwort growing in gardens. These kindes that our Author mentions to grow on Hampsted heath and in Kent, are no other than *Hieracia* or Hawkeweeds, which are much differing from these. ‡

LIB. 2.   Of the Historie of Plants.   117

¶ The Names.

This herb is called in Latine, *Aster Atticus*, *Bubonium*, and *Inguinalis*: in French, *Estrille*, and *Asper goutte menne*: in English, Starwort, and Sharewort.

1 *Aster Atticus.*
Starwort.

¶ The Temperature.

That with the blew or purple floure is thought to be that which is of *Virgil* called *Flos Amellus*: of which he maketh mention, *lib.* 4. of his Georgicks: in English thus:

In Medes there is a floure *Amello* nam'd,
By him that seeks it easie to be found,
For that it seems by many branches fram'd
Into a little wood: like gold the ground
Thereof appeares; but leaves that it beset
Shine in the colour of the Violet.

¶ The Vertues.

The leaves of *Aster* or *Inguinalis* stamped, and applied unto botches and bubones, which for the most part happen in *Inguine*, that is, the flanke or share, do mightily maturate them, whereof this herb *Aster* tooke the name *Inguinalis*.

The floures are good to be given unto children against the squinancie and falling sicknesse.

The account of aster or starwort in Gerard's Herball *in the 1927 edition by Marcus Woodward, published by Gerald Howe. (UEAL)*

THE ENGLISH
HOVSE-WIFE,

Containing the inward and outward
Vertues which ought to be in a
complcate Woman.

As her skill in Phyfick, Surgery, Cookery,
Extraction of Oyles, Banquetting ftuffe, Ordering of
great Feafts, Preferving of all forts of Wines, Conceited Secrets, Diftilations, Perfumes, ordering of Wooll, Hempe, Flax,
making Cloth, and Dying : the knowledge of Dayries, Office of
Malting, of Oates, their excellent ufes in a Family, of
Brewing, Baking, and all other things belonging
to an Houfhold.

A Worke generally approved, and now the fifth time much
augmented, purged and made moft profitable and neceffary for
all men, and the generall good of this Kingdome.

By G. M.

LONDON,
Printed by *Anne Griffin* for *Iohn Harrifon*, at the Golden
Vnicorne in Pater-nofter-row. 1657.

Gervase Markham's The English Housewife, *edition of 1656. (EEBO & OBL)*

DAEMONOLO-
GIE, IN FORME
of a Dialogue,

Diuided into three Bookes.

IN MY DEFENCE GOD ME DEFEND.

EDINBVRGH

Printed by Robert Walde-graue

Printer to the Kings Majeſtie. An. 1597.

Cum Privilegio Regio.

Title page of James VI Daemonologie, *published in Edinburgh in 1597.*
(EEBO & HL)

102

PERCEPTIONS OF WITCHCRAFT

How was 'witchcraft' defined in Jacobean times? How were witches thought to gain their power, what were they claimed to be able to do with it, and for what reasons? The main narrative in the Belvoir pamphlet (*pages 7–12*) speaks only in general terms about what the Flowers were said to have done. They appear to have gone through the traditionally accepted standard practices; their malicious dispositions attract the attention of the Devil, who sees them as potential 'instruments to enlarge his Kingdome' (*page 10*). He appears and 'in plaine tearmes' offers them the usual contract; they will '(as it should seeme) give away their Soules' (*page 10*) in return for the service of familiar spirits supplied by the Devil, but here spoken of in general terms rather than specific references, 'in such prety forms of Dog, Cat or Rat' (*page 10*). They perform various kinds of unspecified mischief, 'kill what Cattle they list' (*page 10*) and eventually cause 'sicknesse and extraordinary convulsions' to the Manners family. Another of the contradictions in the pamphlet's account occurs when the author states that the Earl and Countess 'submit with quietnesse to his [God's] mercy, and study nothing more, then to... beare his crosses on earth' (*page 10*) when their household records show many visits from physicians.

The witches then attacked the children, causing 'Henry Lord Rosse' to die and 'a strange sicknesse' (*page 11*) to attack the second son who is now 'named Francis Lord Rosse' and the Lady Katherine and even prevented the Earl and Countess from having more children. No details are given at this stage about how this is achieved. However, it is helpful to sum up the other evidence presented during the examinations. Three local Vale of Belvoir women, associates of the Flower family, told their stories to the pre-trial examining magistrates. Anne Baker confessed that she had heard from two Bottesford women that Lord Henry's death had been caused by the burial of one of his gloves in the ground, 'and as that glove did rot and wast, so did the liver of the said Lord rot and wast' (*page 16*). This is a clear accusation of sympathetic magic, harming or destroying an item belonging to someone so that the same effect would happen to them. Joan Willimot claimed that at Joan Flower's house she saw 'two Spirits one like a Rat, and the other like an Owle' (*page 19*) and watched Joan attack the Earl's son by mixing her spittle with earth and putting it into her purse. The use of bodily fluids in creating harmful spells was well documented in similar cases.

What is extraordinary to twenty-first century readers is that the Flower sisters corroborated the story of the glove. According to Philippa, Margaret had 'brought from the Castle the right hand glove' of Lord Henry (*page 21*); Margaret added that it was one 'which she found on the rushes in the Nurcery' (*page 24*). It was rubbed on the back of another familiar spirit, the cat Rutterkin, then plunged into boiling water and pricked 'often with her [Joan's] knife' (*page 24*) and then buried. Rutterkin is sent to do some successful 'mischief' to Lord Henry; a similar process with Lady Katherine's handkerchief does not have the same effect, as Rutterkin 'whined and cryed Mew' (*page 23*); Joan interprets the cat's objection as showing that he has no power to harm her. Margaret described the creation of a curse to invoke childlessness on the Earl and Countess by boiling together wool from the mattress given to her by the Countess, gloves which were a present from Mr Vavasor and blood. The wool and gloves were then rubbed on the belly of the long-suffering Rutterkin (*page 22*). Philippa's account claimed that Joan 'would boyle feathers and blood together, using many Divellish speeches and strange gestures' (*page 21*).

These examinations reveal the commonly-held notions of what witches in Jacobean England were expected to do. They are the stuff of popular witchcraft stories; each single incident, the use of personal items: girdles, a mattress, gloves and handkerchiefs, the appearance of familiar animals, illness, death, all are related to popular perceptions of witchcraft. Did the events described actually happen? Certainly, in the imagination of Jacobean people, stoked by reading or listening to the popular witchcraft tales, these events were real, so much so that Margaret and Philippa, their minds equally impregnated by popular stories, ultimately confessed to these actions.

There follows a discussion of the popular and the theological understandings of witchcraft prevailing in Jacobean times

104

which can be traced in the preface of the Belvoir witchcraft pamphlet. The precisely theological view, presented first, had been fully developed towards the end of the fifteenth century: God tested people's faith, in particular by allowing the Devil to make contracts with witches so that the victim might be proved to be one of God's people through suffering. The witches' contract with the devil was central to this theological concept. The old popular view, commonplace for centuries, presented later, was that witches could, of their own volition, do good or create evil, thus helping or harming people. Witches could be seen either as beneficial or as one of the causes of much of the misery of everyday life. At the heart of this contrast between two not necessarily conflicting views was the perception of the Devil: that either he could adopt a material existence and therefore appear to witches in person, or that he was exclusively spiritual.

To what extent did these two views, theological and popular, prevail in Belvoir and in Bottesford in the Jacobean period? It is possible to better understand the treatment of the Flower family by considering the religious position of those involved – the villagers, the local clerics and the gentry families – and by a study of the books and pamphlets they read. The Belvoir pamphlet attempted to marry both the old popular and the new theological views of witches. The standpoint of two clerics in the Vale of Belvoir, the Rectors of Bottesford and of nearby Langar, is evident from their careers and sermons and it is possible also to open up more fully the theological standpoints of the people of the Vale of Belvoir, both Protestant and Catholic, particularly as the majority of the Manners family of Belvoir in the Jacobean period were Catholic.

The Theological View of Witchcraft

'... the really crucial decision in witchcraft matters–whether to allow the devils a presence in the physical world or exclude them from it–had to be initiated not on natural philosophical grounds, but on religious and moral ones.'

Stuart Clark has pointed out that ancient Greek medicine 'denied that it is possible for any disease to be brought upon man by demons', but this was not the widely accepted Christian view in the sixteenth and early seventeenth centuries, because of the newly intertwined views of the natural and the supernatural widely promoted at the time. That period, known today as the Renaissance, was famous for investigations into the natural

105

world such as those of Paracelsus, Cornelius Agrippa, Giambattista Della Porta and Francis Bacon. They believed that, while the natural world could be investigated by experiencing material reality, there remained beyond that vast areas of unknown, or occult knowledge, which might yield to understanding by using the techniques of enquiry derived from natural magic, perhaps the best known of which was alchemy.

These ideas went alongside supernatural, divine explanation accessible through the Bible, which could be investigated through notions of the nature of spirit, central to Christian theology. The *Oxford Dictionary of the Christian Church* offers four manifestations of the idea of spirit. The first is the human soul, that intelligent and immaterial part of man which departs from the body at the time of death. Beyond mankind there is being that is superhuman, not subject to the limits of time, space or a bodily frame; in this sense, God is spirit. Thirdly, there are the other lesser creatures belonging to this order of spirits, whether good or evil, e.g. angels or demons. Finally, in the theology of Christianity there is the third person of the Trinity, the Holy Spirit. In considering Jacobean concepts of witchcraft in terms of spirit, there follows, through a reading of the preface, *ie* the first five pages of the Belvoir pamphlet, a study of both the theological views of contemporary preachers and popular views of witchcraft held by village people such as those living in the Vale of Belvoir.

There were writers in Elizabethan England who argued against the material objective reality of spirits; the best known was Reginald Scot. He expressed his view in his *Discoverie of Witchcraft* published in 1594. Scot wrote: 'in what place soever it be found or read in the scriptures, a spirit or divell is to be understood sprituallie, and is neither a corporall nor a visible thing'. In David Wootton's interpretation 'Scot believed in the reality of the devil and the Holy Ghost, but located them entirely inside the self' This view was to some extent in conflict with the officially held Catholic and Protestant position which was that devilish spirits existed outside the individual and could be actually seen and talked to by groups of witches in meetings, known as Sabbaths or 'sabbats'. This theological standpoint had been developed during the century before Scot wrote and was accepted across Europe and authoritatively reinforced by the French author Jean Bodin, in his influential book on witchcraft of 1580.

According to the 1604 English parliamentary statute against witchcraft, it was a capital offence to 'consult, covenant with, entertain, employ, feed, or reward any evil and wicked spirit to or for any intent or purpose'. One purpose of the statute was to pre-empt the best-known evil-creating spirit, the Devil, by preventing his access to gullible people through sabbaths or contracts, and thus to limit the amount of evil in the world. Also underlying the act of Parliament was the wish to eradicate confidence tricksters who profited from the common beliefs in 'witchcraft, enchantment, charm or sorcery,' by selling charms for finding lost or stolen treasure or goods or with 'intent to provoke any person to unlawful love'. The stated purpose of the Act was 'that all manner of practise, use, or exercise of witchcraft, enchantment, charm or sorcery, should be utterly avoided, abolished and taken away'. At the heart of the 1604 Act lay the widespread conviction that angelic and devilish spirits could exist in some form in this world and that, for devils to bring about evil, some kind of assistance from human beings could be helpful, if not actually necessary.

By the sixteenth century the question had arisen as to who was responsible for terrestrial attempts to control or eliminate the evil caused by the Devil. In England during Henry VIII's reign certain processes, which had in the past been undertaken by church authorities, were now officially made the state's responsibility through acts of Parliament. Charitable work, previously largely carried out by monastic institutions, by religiously inspired corporations and by individual testamentary wills, was now set on to a statutory footing with parochial officers, who were overseen by centrally-organised justices of the peace, doling out relief in parishes. If the 1604 Witchcraft Act is seen in the same light, as a central government initiative locally administered by secular justices of the peace, it is possible to understand it as an attempt by the state simply to abolish the practice of witchcraft, as the Act says.

The theological understanding of natural magic

In order to come fully to terms with the case of the Belvoir witches, it is necessary to clarify in even more detail the word *spirit*, given its centrality to this story. During the sixteenth century the belief was that good and bad hidden (*ie:* occult) elements of this world of nature and its inhabitants could be approached through the use of two complementary understandings of the meaning of magic: those of *natural magic*

107

and those of *demonic magic*. Only slowly since 1600 has the word *magic* become associated with superstition, conjuring, sleight of hand and deceiving people. This later meaning was becoming acceptable as the seventeenth century wore on, but earlier it is best to use the first definition of *magic* offered by John Bullokar in his *English Expositor* of 1616: 'at first this word signified great learning or knowledge in the nature of things; now it is most commonly taken for inchantment or sorcerie'. Both natural and demonic magic were perceived as being valid explanatory systems of a world open to intervention by spirits.

Some people thought that medicine was a significant area of natural magic. However, it was commonplace at the time to warn people against confusing natural illness with devil-inspired witchcraft, *ie:* to distinguish between conditions that had causes that were natural to humans and conditions that had demonic causes. William Perkins put it as follows:

> 'it falleth out oftentimes, that straunge diseases doe seaze up men, arising from corrupt humours in the bodie; yea men and women may have straunge passions upon naturall causes extraordinarie effects in them, which the art of Physicke neither can search out, nor cure: and yet they are neither acts of witchcraft, nor real possessions.'

These 'naturall causes unknowne' were called occult, that is hidden from view. Francisco Torreblanca in 1623 explained that 'anyone with the least smattering of philosophy knows that there are occult virtues in nature by which marvels might be worked, if they were well known and adapted to practical use'. We now come closer to the sixteenth and early seventeenth century concept of nature and magic as we see the words 'virtues' and 'marvels' in use. Another essential notion was the concept of powers, immaterial spiritual beings which governed the daily life of the universe, particularly angels. Today Francis Bacon's famous aphorism that 'knowledge is power' has been slightly misinterpreted. What he meant was that it was by knowledge that the world system actually worked, knowledge derived from God by spirits, known also as powers. It was natural for man to attempt to understand these powers and thus this natural magic, and many doctors such as Dr Napier were attempting to find ways of accessing these powers to help mankind. Equally certainly, men thought that some were attempting to use the demonic variant of these powers to hurt, and this was demonic magic, an example of which was witchcraft.

The theological interpretation of demonic magic

According to the Church, it was possible that spirits such as devils caused 'affliction or distresse' by 'satanical molestation'. The popular Church of England preacher William Perkins defined this as a process 'whereby both persons and places of mansion, or abode, are either possessed, or otherwise molested by the malice of the Devill'. If it was certain that witchcraft was operating then Perkins' advice was 'First, men must not consort together, and abide there, where it is certenly knowne, that the Lord hath given the Devill power and libertie'.

The point of this advice is the teaching 'that Satan's power is determined by God... who hath the Devil bound up (as it were) in chaines, will not suffer his power to be inlarged against his owne children, to their destruction and confusion: but so farre forth alone, as shall be expedient for their good and salvation' This was the new theological understanding: God tried the faith of his people by sending the devil to test their capacity to withstand evil.

This theological belief became widespread among clerics in England at the end of Elizabeth's reign and during the first twenty years of James's reign; it reflects the official view of the established Church of England under the archbishops Whitgift, Bancroft and Abbott and of King James himself. They held firmly to the Calvinist view of predestination, that God, before the establishment of Adam and Eve in the Garden of Eden, had chosen some men and women to eternal life and sentenced the rest of humanity to eternal damnation. Witchcraft was sent by God to test the faith of the believer and it could be interpreted as a sign of the certainty of one's own eternal salvation, to be able to undergo such torment and yet emerge with one's faith intact. 'If God sees it to be good for his children to be tried by possessions or witchcraft' wrote Perkins, the response should be to 'flie to God by praier, and to draw neere unto him in their hearts'.

The theology of witchcraft in the Belvoir pamphlet: King James I

The best way to understand the theology expounded in the Belvoir pamphlet is to study the other contemporary witchcraft accounts cited in the pamphlet's preface on pages 2 to 7. The author of the pamphlet grounded his explanation of witchcraft in six works published around the first two decades of the seventeenth century, which also offer us a taste of popular

109

reading matter on witchcraft at that time. He addressed his public directly as he introduced the first of these: 'you may overlooke [look at] if you please that learned Discourse of *Daemonologie*, composed in forme of a Dialogue, by the High and Mighty Prince, JAMES by the grace of God, King of *England, Scotland, France* and *Ireland*, etc and printed (as I take it) according to the coppy of Edinburgh 1603'. S. R. Gardiner's Victorian reaction to James was: 'The belief in the reality of witchcraft was strongly rooted in the minds of the population. James I, in his book on Demonology, had only echoed opinions which were accepted freely by the multitude, and were tacitly admitted without inquiry by the first intellects of the day'.

Two London printing firms welcomed James to the English throne in 1603 by reprinting the original 1598 Edinburgh edition of *Daemonologie*. James himself comes across positively in his *Daemonologie* hoping 'this Treatise (beloved Reader) to be effectual, in arming all them that reads the same, against these above mentioned errours, and recommending my good will to thy friendly acceptation, I bid thee heartily farewell'. In the preface, James attacked Reginald Scot's denial 'that there can be such a thing as Witchcraft'. But he went further than simply attacking Scot for denying witchcraft; he asserted, as Stuart Clark has explained, that 'there can be no better way to know God than by the contrarie' *ie:* knowing the Devil. One explanation for this position is the dominant Renaissance style of argument defined by Robin Briggs as 'polarized binary classification', that is, arguing by comparison of opposites (central to James's interpretation of witchcraft). This understanding of the significance of the Devil in clarifying the nature of God led to the widespread study of demonology, and the consequent strength of the contemporary intellectual interest in witchcraft.

A careful reading of *Daemonologie* reveals James's view of the manner in which the compact with the Devil could arise. James asked how 'the Devill allures persones' and answered that there were three techniques: 'Even by these strange passions that are within ourselves: Curiositie in great ingines [contrivances]: thirst of revenge for some tortes [wrongs] deeply apprehended: or greedy appetite of geare, [possessions] caused through great poverty'. He then described how witches actually met with the Devil 'which is by being carried by the force of the Spirite which is their conducter, either above the earth or above the Sea swiftlie'. This led to the compact with the Devil, contrary to

110

statute law. At this stage James had to admit that proof of the compact was not easy to come by: 'For who but Witches can be proves [proofs] and so witnesses of the doings of witches'. James's absolute belief in the existence of the Devil enabled him to overcome this problem of proof. He asked: 'what if [witches] accuse folke to have bene present at their Imaginar[y] conventiones in the spirite, when their bodies lyes senceless?'

The reply James gave to his own query was 'I think they [the accused] are not a haire the less guiltie: For the Devill durst never have borrowed their shaddow or similitudes to that turne, if their consent had not bene at it. And the consent in these turnes is death of the law'. James was happy to treat the Devil as 'God's hangman' because he saw witchcraft as 'a matter of treason against the Prince, bairnes or wives'. James's interest in witchcraft derived from an episode in his own life. In 1590 on returning from six months in Denmark when he had married his wife Anne of Denmark, the Royal fleet met terrible storms, which his Danish associates put down to witchcraft. His new brother-in-law, King Christian of Denmark, was deeply involved in attacking witchcraft and James initiated a similar campaign on hearing the rumours that Scottish witches were attempting to kill him, a divinely appointed monarch. By the time he arrived on the English throne in 1603, James was actually becoming less certain about the proofs of witchcraft and he was always concerned that witchcraft trials were properly conducted, reserving to himself as King by divine permission the right to intervene in trials.

The theology of witchcraft in the Belvoir pamphlet: Alexander Roberts

The second treatise recommended by the author of the Belvoir pamphlet was *A Treatise of Witchcraft* by 'Alexander Roberts, BD and Preacher of Gods Word at Kings-Linne in NorFolke'. In similar terms to James's comment about 'the consummation of the worlde and our deliverance drawing near', so Roberts began his preface 'in these last days and perilous times'. The widespread seventeenth-century view that the world would soon come to an end was reiterated in innumerable pamphlets. Roberts, like James and the author of the Belvoir chapbook, listed the different types of practitioners of magic. The two principal titles given by James and Roberts to the people carrying out what the Belvoir chapbook called 'exoticke

111

practises of loathsome Artes and Sciences' (*page 4*) were 'magicians' and 'necromancers'. Roberts added 'Inchanters, Wisards, Haggs, Fortune Tellers, Diviners, Witches, Cunning Men and Women'. Like James, Roberts asked the question 'whether there be any witches' and both argued for the existence of witches from biblical and classical accounts and from the existence of national laws aimed to destroy witchcraft. As a 'preacher of God's Word' at King's Lynn, Alexander Roberts had no doubt as to the essence of the theology of witchcraft,

> 'So then to conclude, in every Magicall action, there must be a concurrence of these three. First, the permitting will of God. Secondly, the suggestion of the Divell, and his power cooperating. Thirdly, the desire and consent of the Sorcerer, and if any of these be wanting, no trick of witchcraft can be performed.'

If all these actions coincide, then there is witchcraft, according to Roberts. Wrong-doers will perish through their association with the Devil and thus evil will be removed.

The choice of Alexander Roberts' text for citation by the Belvoir author is helpful towards our understanding of the Belvoir situation as it was published in London in 1616, three years before the appearance of the pamphlet and ballad on the Manners/Flowers tragedy. Roberts was the King's Lynn grammar school master in the early 1590s and thereafter in Lynn a 'preacher of God's word'. His *Treatise* was sermonic in style; he not only lists his fellow-preachers but also gives Biblical citations for his personal conclusions. There is a distinct contrast in style between the preface of the Belvoir pamphlet and that of Roberts; Marion Gibson suggests that the Belvoir author is 'giving an impression of scholarly and gentlemanly erudition rather than pastoral authority' and, unlike Roberts' writing, it has 'no ... sermonic circumlocution'.

The Belvoir author ends his preface with a famous tag from the Vulgate version of the Apocrypha, 'Magna est veritas & prevalebit' (*page 7*) or 'Great is truth and strong above all things'. A second Latin tag is used as an endpiece to the first edition of the pamphlet, 'Utinam tam facile vera invenire possem quam falsa convincere' (*page 26*)], a quotation from Cicero's *De Natura Deorum*. The phrase can be translated as 'If only I could discover the truth as easily as I can expose what is false'. The Belvoir author was as well grounded in classical

112

learning as he was in theology, but his style was less didactic than the sermonic style of Alexander Roberts. Roberts' pamphlet was eighty pages long, of which all but fifteen pages were an erudite discussion of the nature of witchcraft, derived from classical biblical and scholastic sources, and was in no way a popular text. The relatively short popular part of Roberts' work will be presented later among the popular witchcraft tales.

The theology of witchcraft in the Belvoir pamphlet: George Gifford

After citing Roberts, the Belvoir author mentions as another source one of the best known witchcraft writers of Jacobean England, the author of *A Dialogue concerning Witches and Witchcraft*, George Gifford, 'Minister of God's word in Maldon 1603'. Gifford's work may have been well known to the Belvoir author as they both use what Marion Gibson helpfully identifies as a quotation from Virgil: 'Flectere si nequeam Superos, Acheronta movebo'. The Belvoir preface's author brings Virgil's phrase into the Jacobean world, by associating the classical underworld with the sixteenth and seventeenth century concept of the Devil, using a contemporary verse translation,

> 'If Art doe faile to move the Gods
>   consent unto my minde:
> I will the Divells raise, to doe
>   what they can in their kinde.' (*page 4*)

In his *Dialogue*, Gifford used the 'heathen' Virgil's line and translated it as 'If I cannot intreat the goddes, I will downe among the devils'.

The Belvoir author presents Gifford's view of demonology, stating that in Gifford's book 'the cunning of the Divell is discovered, both concerning the deceiving of Witches, and the seducing of others into many great errors' (*page 6*). It is probable that the Belvoir author was strongly influenced by Gifford's view of witchcraft, as his précis of Gifford's ideas clearly refers back to the title-page of the *Dialogue*: 'In which is laid open how craftily the Divell deceiveth not only the Witches, but many other and so leadeth them awrie into many great errours'. Gifford stressed, as does the Belvoir author, that

> 'The high providence of God Almighty and soveraigne rule over all, is set forth so unto us in the Scripture, as that without him a Sparrow can not fall upon the ground. All

the haires of our head are numbred. The Devils would hurt and destroy with bodily harmes both men and beastes and other creatures: but all the Divels in Hell are so chained up and bridled by this high providence that they can not plucke the wing from one poore little Wrenne, without special leave given them from the ruler of the whole earth.'

Here Gifford refers to Providence, the seventeenth century term for God's will, a term which was to dominate seventeenth and eighteenth century religious understanding in England

Gifford was a little sceptical about the details of witchcraft. The Belvoir author believed that without doubt there did exist such a phenomenon as witchcraft, and that it was a technique by which the Devil appeared to expand his influence over humanity. The Belvoir author explicitly condemned 'the particular opinion of some men, who suppose there bee none [*ie:* witches] at all, or at least that they do not personally or truely effect such things as are imputed unto them' (*page 6*). Alexander Roberts in 1616 also condemned the opinion 'that there be no Witches at all: but a sort of melancolique, aged, and ignorant Women, deluded in their imagination'. These words were similar to the Belvoir author's description of witches:

> 'there be certaine men and women growne in years, and over growne with Melancholy and Atheisme, who out of a malitious disposition against their betters or others thriving by them; but most times from a heart-burning desire of revenge, having entertained some impression of displeasure and unkindness, study nothing but mischiefe, and exotique practices of loathsome Arts and Sciences.' (*page 4*).

Gifford was sufficiently sceptical to suggest that the situation concerning witchcraft was likely to produce false accusations: 'these things taking root in the hearts of the people, and so making them afraide of Witches, and raising up suspitions and rumors of sundry innocent persons, many giltles'. His understanding of the nature of witchcraft was sophisticated and based on a thoughtful appreciation of demonic theology and the psychology of everyday people.

Gifford could be called a Puritan, contrasting with the known Catholicism of the Manners family. The nature of his Puritanism is worth discussing, as he gained a national

114

reputation for his writings, in spite of his continuous difficulties with the Church of England's hierarchy of bishops. Alan Macfarlane points out that Gifford's full-scale book on witchcraft was only the 'second work in English on witchcraft and the first in that language based mainly on English evidence'. The central purpose behind Gifford's books was to counter the popular view that witches upheld demonic evil in a manner directly contrary to Christian belief. Gifford, as a Puritan, Calvinist theologian, 'really feared a form of Manichean heresy in which evil powers [eg: witchcraft] had somehow become autonomous. For the [popular] conception of witches had revived the ideal always present throughout the Middle Ages, that pain and suffering are the result of forces outside the Christian God'. The Belvoir author is clearly in sympathy with Gifford's insistence that pain and suffering came totally from God, not from any dualistic view of the world which posited the existence in the world of independent and directly opposed powers of good and evil.

Gifford was certain that witches as independent individuals could not cause harm unless the witch made a compact with the Devil. He wrote 'Look not upon the witch, lay not the cause where it is not'. This belief that suffering and pain was not actually caused by the witch, or even by the Devil, but by God, was taken to heart by the Belvoir author when he wrote of the horrors of evil 'that neither Witch or Divell could doe these things' (*page 26*). Towards the end of the Belvoir pamphlet he stated 'that the Divell is the meere servant and agent of God' (*page 25*) which is the idea at the very heart of Gifford's work. Gifford explained God's reasons for sending misfortunes by witchcraft: 'to trie their faith and patience' or to punish them 'with the rodds and scourges of his wrath'. What we see, then, in the 1619 pamphlet is the sophisticated intellectual view of witchcraft in contrast to the popular view of witches as independent actors, able to cause good or misery in the local community by their own personal actions.

This complexity of explanations takes us to the heart of the Jacobean witchcraft controversy and allows us to focus again on the concept of spirit: we might re-emphasise the two distinct notions, the material and the spiritual, regarding demonic witchcraft which pertained in the early seventeenth century. The popular material English view expressed in the pamphlet, originating from pre-Reformation times, was that 'caitiffs' or wretches existed who wished for revenge and 'then steppeth forth the Divell, and not only sheweth them the way, but prescribeth the manner of effecting the same, with facility and easinesse, assuring [them] that hee himself [the Devil] will attend them in some familiar shape of Rat, Cat, Toade, Birde, Cricket, etc: yea effectuate whatsoever they shall demand or desire, and for their better assurance and corroboration of their credulity, they shall have palpable and forcible touches of sucking, pinching, kissing, closing, colling and such like.' (*page 5*)

This material process was evidence for the 'physical devil depicted in popular literature and folklore' as Darren Oldridge points out. The other concept of the Devil was a spiritual one, existing on earth in the mind of the 'caitiff' and defined extensively by Protestant theologians. From Luther onwards, the Protestant divines believed that it was the Devil's 'ceaseless mission to tempt people into heresy by infecting their minds with superstitious thoughts'. The Belvoir pamphlet author explained that 'the monstrous subtility of the Divell... poison[s] the inward conceite or apprehension' (*page 5*) of the witch. In other words, the Belvoir author offered both the popular material view and the recent theological definition of the Devil. He began the chapbook by saying, 'My meaning is not to make any contentious argument about the discourses, distinction or definition of Witchcraft' (*page 3*) but he also adopted the new view, expressed by Gifford, that witches only acted 'by permission of God, so that the actors of the same have carried away the opinion of the world, to doe that which they did by Witchcraft, or at least to be esteemed Witches, for bringing such and such things to passe' (*page 3*).

The theology of witchcraft in the Belvoir pamphlet: John Cotta

In addition to King James, Alexander Roberts and George Gifford, the Belvoir author was influenced by a fourth author, 'John Cotta, Docter of Physicke in Northampton' (*page 6*). Cotta wrote a general work on 'ignorant and unconsiderate practisers of Physicke' in England, published in 1612 and it is this work which the Belvoir author refers to as 'a Certaine Discovery' (*page 6*). We can be certain that the Belvoir writer actually had this book to hand as he partly repeats its contents page. On page 6 of the Belvoir pamphlet, the author lists unlicensed amateur medical practitioners as 'Empericks, woemen about sicke persons: Quacksalvers, and fugitives which seeme to worke juggling [fraudulent] wonders, Surgeons, Apothecaries, practisers by Spells, the true discovery of Witch-craft, especially in the Sicke,... Wisards, and servants, of Phisitions... the Methodian learned deceiver, or hereticke Phisitions, Astrologers, *Ephemerides*-maisters, conjectures by urine, Travellers'. These correspond completely to the contents page of *A Short Discoverie* with one possibly significant omission, 'Beneficed Practisers'. This might hint that the Belvoir author is anxious not to upset the beneficed clergy or was even a beneficed clergyman himself.

Like Gifford, John Cotta was balanced in his discussion of witchcraft. He certainly believed in the 'subject of Witch-craft, which common sense doth not onely justifie (as in all other subjects) but the word of undoubted truth'. Yet he also states that 'It is true, that in this case of Witch-craft many things are very difficult, hidden and infolded in mists and clouds, over-shadowing our reason and best understanding'. Cotta presented a clear refutation of popular and traditional methods of discovering the truth in witchcraft accusations. He dismissed as ignorant, superstitious and wrong the traditional 'tryalls' of witches, writing

'First that the tryall of Witches by water, is not naturall or according to any reason in nature. Secondly, if it be extraordinary and a miracle, that it is in greater likelihood and probability a miracle of the Divells to insnare, then [than] any manifest miracle of God to glorifie his name, which is the true end of right miracles. Concerning the other imagined trials of Witches, as by beating, scratching, drawing blood from supposed or suspected Witches, whereby it is sayd that the fits or diseases of the bewitched doe cease miraculously; as also concerning the burning of bewitched cattell, whereby it is sayd, that the Witch is miraculously compelled to present her selfe. These and the like, I thinke it vain and needlesse, particularly or singly to confute, because... first they are excluded out of the number of things naturall: secondly... they will also bee rather justly judged miracles of the Divel, then of God, by the former reasons, which have stripped the supposed miraculous detection of witches by the water, of any hopeful opinion that they can be of God.'

Cotta also discussed searching witches to 'reveale secret markes in his or her body' or 'when a supposed Witch required by the bewitched doth touch him or her... he or she immediately are delivered from the present fit or agonie'. He argued in favour of events such as this which he had 'sometimes myselfe heard and seen proved true'. He explained this as follows: 'those supernaturall workes, are onely to be imputed unto men which the Divell, according unto contract or Covenant which those men do practise and produce'. In other words, he justified the condemnation of witches only in so far as the witch confessed to making a contract with the devil, the capital crime of the 1604 statute. This central question of confessions comes later, in considering the accusation and trial of the Flower sisters.

In some manner, Cotta diminished witchcraft; he was anxious to move the origin of witchcraft away from the witch as the unhappy focus of village gossip and scandal. Like Gifford, his concern was to concentrate on 'the cunning of the Divell' (*page 6*) which was responsible for 'the deceiving of witches and the seducing of others into many great errors' (*page 6*). Cotta's conclusion in *The Triall of Witchcraft* would considerably diminish the number of witchcraft condemnations as he pointed out that in his book 'all superstitious and also... all miraculous ways of detection of Witches and Witch-craft [have] been... generally unmasked... being by the same rule and reason compelled unto the golden tryall of sincere religion and affection'. What we can see gradually happening in serious witchcraft studies being read during the Jacobean period is a determination to sideline earlier popular beliefs.

Cotta laid down exactly how an accusation of witchcraft should proceed: 'in the inquisition of Witch-craft, when we have truely first detected an act, done by a spirituall and supernaturall force (because it is in all lawes injurious, to accuse of any act, before it is certainely known the act hath been committed) then, and not before, wee ought [to] indevour directly and necessarily to prove the contract, consent, and affection of the person suspected, unto, or in that supernatural act, that being no lesse essentiall, to detect and discover the true and undoubted Witch, then the supernaturall act, being certainely apparent, doth undoubtedly prove the Divell, and his power therein'. It is through these words of a successful physician and thoughtful author that the whole Belvoir story can be understood.

The historian Peter Elmer has explained that Cotta believed absolutely in witchcraft, but was concerned to apply reason and to bring the detection of witchcraft out of the realm of superstition and into the 'boundaries of contemporary scientific and philosophical thinking'. Cotta, however, was not a London-based member of the College of Physicians. He did not become involved with the College, perhaps because he wished to be free to develop an approach to witchcraft based both on his rejection of medical charlatans and his 'staunch puritanism'. In *A Short Discoverie* Cotta described in great detail the apparent fits of the daughter of a Warwickshire gentleman. He became convinced that the cause of her suffering was natural, not demonic. Her recovery, Cotta argued, was due 'unto God and truth'. He went on, 'It farther confirmeth the negative of witchcraft ... that ... the parents of this gentlewoman at no time in the height of their daughters affliction, or a good space after, could resolve upon whom with any just shew of reason to cast the suspition of bewitching'. Thus the question arises again as to why the Manners family did not apparently use the services of Cotta when their children were afflicted by fits. It is tempting to suggest that Cotta's strong Puritanism militated against him. It is important also to appreciate that Cotta attacked both Dr Napier and Dr Anthony, as physicians who based their medical activities respectively on astrological and chemical foundations, of which Cotta, as a keen Galenical physician, would have been wary.

The popular view of witchcraft: Thomas Potts and the pamphlet printers

In addition to King James, Roberts, Gifford and Cotta, there is a detailed reference in the Belvoir preface to a further popular Jacobean work on witchcraft (*page 6*). In 1612 Thomas Potts produced his full and detailed account of the famous trial of the women from Pendle in Lancashire accused of witchcraft. Potts was the clerk of the court 'imploied in the arraignement and trial' of the nine women and one man executed for witchcraft at the Lent Assizes at Lancaster in April 1612.

Potts' account of the 1612 trial was published in London for the printer William Stansby by John Barnes, son of Joseph Barnes the principal printer for Oxford University in late Elizabethan and early Jacobean times. It was John Barnes who sold the Belvoir chapbook, which was printed by George Eld. William Stansby and George Eld were competing London printers of major significance. Stansby ran 'probably the second largest press in London after the royal printing house'. Well over 350 titles are known to have been printed by Eld, of which 157 were on religious topics, 127 on literary subjects and 124 on historical topics. Both Eld and Stansby printed works by the best-known literary figures of Jacobean England; Eld printed the first edition of Shakespeare's sonnets in 1609 and Stansby was well known for his 1616 edition of Ben Jonson's *Works*.

Printers were often publishers in the Jacobean period and Eld was no exception. He was also somewhat sceptical regarding the absolute truth contained in books. In a rare note 'The Printer to the Reader' in one of his historical productions *Admirable and Memorable Histories containing the wonders of our time* by Goulart, translated from the French by Edmund Grimestone in 1607, Eld showed a lively sense of humour. 'If any thinke these Histories strange, he may see the very title says as much: and it is good for an author to bee as good as his title: And this being a translation, it must be strange. If any thinke that by the name of Histories, all should be true, he may knowe Historiographers confesse they write as they list... And if these be but tales, yet either hee is Maister, or he cites you his tales-maister, (more than most men will do)'. George Eld printed through the Belvoir pamphlet a thoughtful analysis of witchcraft in line with his more academic books.

Potts' book is a legalistic account of the Pendle trial and it does not contain the kind of theological discussion which is central to the Preface of the Belvoir author. But what Potts wrote was a popular account concentrating on the detail of the confessions of the witches. In addition to drawing attention to Potts's extraordinarily thorough account of the trials of the Lancashire witches, the Belvoir author refers in his preface to three contemporary popular stories: the first was Alexander Roberts' account in his book of Mary Smith from King's Lynn, in his book referred to above, and the second was 'an ancient discourse of the fearful practises of foure notorious French witches, with the manner of their strange execution' (*page 6*). The third story taken from the Belvoir author's preface is 'the several and damnable practises of Mother Sutton of Milton Milles in the county of Bedford, and Mary Sutton her daughter who were arraigned, and condemned and executed for the same' (*page 6*). In the second edition of the Belvoir pamphlet, published in 1621, an epilogue was added from this Bedford story, relating in detail one of the best known popular methods of trying witches, the water test. These three stories give the modern reader perfect examples of popular Jacobean witchcraft stories and so will serve as contrasts with the serious work of the theologians, anxious to preach how witchcraft was

ABOVE: Devil-cat: the Devil bringing plague to Job in a late sixteenth century Flemish painted glass. (SGS) The Flowers died because it was held that they brought the Devil's plague upon LEFT: Henry Manners, Lord Roos, the elder son of the sixth Earl and his second wife – he died in 1613 and his burial is recorded in the Bottesford parish registers – and RIGHT: Francis Manners, also Lord Roos, their second son, who died in 1620. They and their ancestors lie at rest in the chancel of St Mary's Church, Bottesford. (Both HER & SMCB)

King James I was much exercised by the impact and nature of witchcraft; here his arms were recorded in the early seventeenth century in Flemish painted glass with his motto Beati Pacifici – from John Macdonald's Windows of Norwich Cathedral *2006. (JM)*

LEFT: Francis Manners, the fourth Earl's second surviving son, who became the sixth Earl and RIGHT: Katherine Manners, only daughter of Francis Manners, who became the sixth Earl, and his first wife, Frances Knyvett. In 1620 she married George Villiers and in consequence became Duchess of Buckingham in 1623. She died a strong Catholic in 1649. (Both HER & SCMB)

THE RIGHT HON:^BLE &
NOBLE LORD FRANCIS EARLE
OF RVTLAND, LORD ROOS OF HAMLACK
TRESBVT, & BELVOIR OF Y:^E MOST NOBLE
ORDER OF Y:^E GARTER KNIGHT, LYETH HERE
INTERRED : ATT 18 YEARES OF AGE HE
WENT TO TRAVAILE IN Y:^E YEARE 1598 :
IN FRANCE, LORAYNE & DIVERS STATES OF ITALYE;
HE WAS HONORABLY RECEIVED BY Y:^E PRINCES THEM=
=SELVES, & NOBLY ENTERTAINED IN THEIR COVRTS :
IN HIS RETVRNE THROVGH GERMANY HE HAD LIKE
HONOR DONE HIM BY FERDINAND ARCHDVKE OF AVSTRIA,
AT HIS COVRT IN GRATZ : BY Y:^E EMPEROR MATHIAS, &
HIS COVRT IN VIENNA : BY COVNT SWARTZEMBOVRG
LEIVETENANT OF IAVARIN IN HVNGARY : BY COVNT
ROSSEMBOVRG AT PRAGVE IN BOHEME : BY Y:^E MARQVIS
OF BRANDENBOVRG, Y:^E DVKES OF SAXONY & OTHER GER=
=MAINE PRINCES IN Y:^E COVRT AT BERLIN : IN 1604 HE
WAS MADE KNIGHT OF Y:^E BATH & MARRIED Y:^E LADY
FRANCIS BEVILL ONE OF Y:^E DAVGHT:^R & COHEIRS OF Y:^E
HON:^BLE KNIGHT S:^R HENRY KNYVETT, BY WHOM HE HAD
ISSVE, ONE ONLY DAVGHT:^R Y:^E MOST VERTVOVS & THRICE
NOBLE PRINCESSE KATHERINE NOW DVTCH:^SS OF BVCKINGH:
IN 1608. HE MARRIED Y:^E LADY CECILIA HVNGERF:^D DAVGHT:
TO Y:^E HON:^BLE KNIGHT S:^R IOHN TVFTON BY WHOM HE HAD
TWO SONNES, BOTH W:^CH DYED IN THEIR INFANCY BY WICKED
PRACTISE & SORCERYE : IN 1612. HE WAS MADE LORD
LEIVETENANT OF LINCOLNESH:^R & AFTER IVSTICE IN EYRE
OF AIL Y:^E KINGS FORRESTS & CHASES ON Y:^E NORTH OF
TRENT : IN 1616. HE WAS MADE KNIGHT OF Y:^E MOST
NOBLE ORDER OF Y:^E GARTER : IN Y:^E YEARE 1616 HE
WAS ONE OF Y:^E LORDS WHO ATTENDED KING IAMES BY
HIS MA:^TS SPECIALL APPOINTM:^T IN HIS IOVRNEY INTO SCOTLAN:^D
IN 1623. HE WAS BY Y:^E SAME KING IAMES MADE ADMIR:^ALL
OF A NAVYE OF HIS M:^TS GREAT SHIPPS & PYNNACES TO
RETVRNE PRINCE CHARLES, NOW OVR DREAD SOVERAIGN:^D
LORD KING OF ENGL:^D OVT OF SPAYNE, W:^CH HE HAPPILY PFOR:^MD

The memorial inscription of Francis Manners, the sixth Earl. After the details of his grand tour and of his marriages there follows the famous inscription regarding his two sons 'both wch dyed in their infancy by wicked practise & sorcerye'. (HER & SMCB)

sent by God to confirm the faith of the true Christian. These are the kind of stories, perhaps read in Bottesford and across the Vale, full of intimate details of everyday life, as were the examinations in the Belvoir pamphlet.

The Accusation of Mary Smith of King's Lynn

The fifteen pages on the Kings Lynn witchcraft case were written in a narrative style by Alexander Roberts to account for what he saw as the wicked practice of Mary Smith, executed for witchcraft on 12 January, 1616. The four examples of the alleged witchcraft for which she was tried offer an excellent view of how commonplace interpersonal relationships and their breakdown could lead to witchcraft accusations. Mary Smith, the wife of Henry Smith, dealt in buying and selling and had a local reputation as a quarrelsome woman. She cursed the hand of John Orkton who had chastised her son by striking him. According to John Orkton, he thereupon lost his fingers. In a second quarrel Mary Smith was accused of stealing and she cursed the Scot family responsible for this accusation. They then suffered illness and anguish so much so that they attacked and killed (with some difficulty) Mary's 'great cat'.

'Not long after this, the witch came forth with a Birchin broome, and threatned to lay it upon the head of Elizabeth Scot and defiled her cloathes therewith, as she swept the street before her shop doore, and that in the sight of [Elizabeth Scot's] husband, who not digesting this indignity offered unto his wife, threatened that if she had any such fitts as she had endured being a Widow before marriage, hee would hang her. At this she clapped her hands, and said he killed her Cat. And within two or three days after this interchange of words betweene them, his wife was perplexed with the like paine and griefe at her heart, as formerly she had beene; and that for two dayes and a night: wherefore her husband went to this wrathfull and malicious person, assuring that if his wife did not amend, hee would accuse her to the Magistrate, and cause the rigor of the law to be executed upon her, which is due to such malefactors.'

The third accusation developed from a quarrel with Cecily Balye,

'who sweeping the street before her maisters doore upon a Saturday in the evening, Mary Smith began to pick a quarrel about the manner of sweeping, and said unto her she was a great fat-tail'd sow, but that fatnesse should shortly be pulled downe and abated. And the next night being Sunday immediatly following, a Cat came unto her [Cecily], sate upon her breast, with which she was grievously tormented, and so oppressed, that she could not without great difficulty draw her breath, and at the same instant did perfectly see the said Mary in the chamber where she lay, who (as she conceived) set that cat upon her, and immediatly after fell sicke, languished and grew exceeding leane.'

Roberts commented at this stage 'thus every light trifle (for what can be lesse than sweeping a little dust awry?) can minister matter to set on fire a wrathfull indignation, and inflame it unto desired revenge'. He then went on to describe how

'the fourth endammaged by this hagge, was one Edmund Newton: the discontentment did arise from this ground; Because he had bought severall bargaines of Holland cheese, and sold them againe, by which she thought her benefit to be somewhat impaired, using the like kinds of trading. The manner of her dealing with him was in this sort. At every severall time of buying Cheese he was grievously afflicted, being thrice, and at the last, either she or a spirit in her likenesse did appeare unto him, and whisked about his face (as he lay in bed) a wet cloath of very loathsome savour; after which he did see one cloathed in russet with a little bush beard, who told him hee was sent to looke upon his sore leg and would heale it; but rising to shew the same, perceiving hee had cloven feet, refused that offer... After this she sent her impes, a Toad, and Crabs crawling about the house... where the servants (hee being a shooe-maker) did worke: one of which tooke that toad, put it into the fire, where it made a groaning noyse for one quarter of an houre before it was consumed; during which time Mary Smith who sent it, did endure (as was reported) torturing paines, testifying the felt grief by her out-cryes then made.'

For these actions, Mary Smith was tried for witchcraft and executed for having personally confessed 'the trueth and number of her owne words' to the Rev Alexander Roberts, that she had made a compact with the Devil to achieve her revenge. Roberts used the story of Mary Smith's actions in his treatise as an illustration of how tragedy could arise from petty revenge.

126

In doing so he has left us, within his serious treatise, a typical popular account of an English witchcraft accusation; the Belvoir story includes all these elements of revenge, which appear to be central to many stories of English witchcraft.

The Foure Notorious French Witches

The popular tale of 'foure notorious French witches' was printed in England as the second part of a 1612 pamphlet of which the first part was *The life and Death of Lewis Gaufredy, a most notorious magician* who was burnt in April 1611 in Aix-en-Provence for murder and sorcery. The story of the four French witches, who were from Le Havre, was thus presented to the English public as an epilogue to the story of a southern French cleric from Marseilles. Louis Gaufredi 'after no long debatement between the Divell and himself, covenanted (wofull covenant!) that for the space of fortie yeares he might enjoy the full fruition of his detested ambition... that he might have power and meanes to know carnally all women or maids whatsoever'. Of course this story would have resonated across England as it echoes so strongly Christopher Marlowe's successful retelling of the Faust legend in his 1590s play, *Dr Faustus*. It was one of a group of widely-publicised French cases which included a sexual element, no doubt seized upon by the printers of pamphlets for their sensational value. This was not true in all cases, however; as Robin Briggs points out, the majority of French witchcraft accusations were on the same pattern as the English ones, arising from everyday quarrels between neighbours.

The 1612 pamphlet was a classic French witchcraft story, of some significance to the history of English witchcraft, as it contains not only the account of how Gaufredi gave his soul to the Devil by a legal agreement, but also his confession that he went to a sabbath where he was marked with a devil's mark, at which 'one shall feele a little piercing heate: and there where he toucheth, the flesh remaines somewhat sunck and hollow'. The notion of a witches' coven meeting at a sabbath was a novelty in English witchcraft stories, being rare, maybe even unknown, before the story of the Pendle witches became widespread. What is worth noting towards our understanding of the Belvoir story is that there was in the 1619 Belvoir chapbook a hint of a sabbath, or meeting of witches. One of the witnesses, Joan Willimot, 'saith, that Joane Flower, Margaret Flower and shee, did meet about a weeke before Joan Flowers apprehension, in Black-borrow-hill, and went from thence home to the said Joan Flowers house, and there she saw two Spirits, one like a Rat, and the other like an Owle: and one of them did suck under her right eare, as she thought: and the said Joan told her, that her spirits did say that shee should neyther be hanged nor burnt' (*page 19*).

Gaufredi was accused of 'deflowering witches at sabbats' as Stuart Clark puts it though there are no hints of sexual malpractice at the meeting of the Belvoir women on Blackborrow Hill, just behind Belvoir Castle (*page 19*). But the four French women from Le Havre executed in 1612 were certainly condemned as a result of some form of sexual evil-doing. The leading French woman was accused of procuring a ten-year-old maid by witchcraft and selling 'her virginity to an ouglie Ruffian'. She was then accused along with three other women of cutting the child to pieces and burning her body in an oven. For this she was 'condemned to be drawn upon an hurdle through the Towne, holding a Torche, and the knife in her hand: and then the same being cutt off... with hote pincers. And lastly her bodie was throwne alive into the fire'. The account of Gaufredi's trial reveals similarities between English and French witchcraft trials which are significant. It appears that similar numbers were executed for witchcraft in the kingdoms of England and France in the first quarter of the seventeenth century, although due to the loss of the majority of historical records of the period, we will never know the true statistics. Civil trials for witchcraft took place in both kingdoms at the regional centre: in France all condemned witches had the right of appeal to the local regional Parliament by 1624 and in England witchcraft as a capital crime was tried at the county assizes.

This account of Father Gaufredi with its tailpiece on the four French witches also allows us to distinguish to some extent between English and French witchcraft and highlights the nature of the Belvoir case. James Sharpe points out that 'English witches were rarely held to have interfered with sex and procreation as witches in some other lands were supposed to have done' [p. 67]. Father Gaufredi was accused of 'many most abhominable Sorceries, but chiefly upon two very faire young Gentlewomen'. The four witches 'caused the young Maide to be defloured'. The Belvoir story contains no salacious details, only tentative hints, never followed up.

Perhaps the best-known of all French witchcraft cases was in 1634 where the nuns of Loudun accused Father Urbain Grandier of interfering with them. It was given publicity in the mid-twentieth century by Aldous Huxley in his book *The Devils of Loudun*. It does appear as though promiscuity was sometimes associated with the popular conceptions of the devil gathering with witches at a sabbath or sabbat. There is, however, only a minor hint of sexual bewitching in the Belvoir case. It was reported that the younger of the two Flower sisters, Philippa, 'was lewdly transported with the love of one Th. Simpson, who presumed to say, that she had bewitched him: for he had no power to leave, and was as he supposed marvellously altered both in minde and body, since her acquainted company' (*page 9*). The Belvoir pamphlet writer knew these French cases and he built in hints of a sabbath meeting and sexual bewitchment. But they were relatively insignificant in the Belvoir case, which was presented as a case of witches searching for revenge.

Mother Sutton of Bedford

This limited element of seduction is apparent in the third popular account of witchcraft hinted at by the Belvoir author: 'the several and damnable practices of Mother Sutton of Milton Miles in the county of Bedford' (*page 6*) in 1612–13. The story of Mrs Sutton and her daughter Mary Sutton provided William Stansby, the printer of the account of the Pendle Witches by Thomas Potts, with an opportunity to produce the narrative of a revenge story, spiced with innuendo and amusing detail, called *Witches Apprehended*. There is a lively account of how a bewitched sow caused a horse-drawn cart carrying sacks of corn to split in half, so that the horses broke away and 'left the wheeles and Axeltree behind them'. 'At last this Tragicke-Comedie drawing to an end, this made a stand, when the servant bringing them backe, and finding their Axeltree pinnes and all things unbroken, took up their corne, made fit their Cart againe, & the horses drew as formally as could be'. According to *Witches Apprehended*, the servant suffered this and other indignities because he had criticised and given 'a little blow or two on the eare' to the illegitimate son of Mary Sutton for dirtying a mill-pond. The poor servant continued to suffer a series of physical attacks until 'his friends were as desirous to see death ridde him from his extremitie, as a woman greate with childe is ever musing upon the time of her deliverie'.

At the next stage in the story, the servant

'in bed and awake, espied Mary Sutton (the daughter) in a Mooneshine night come in at a window in her accustomed

129

and personall habite, and shape, with her knitting worke in her hands, and sitting downe at his beds feete, sometimes working, and knitting with her needles, and sometimes gazing, and staring him in the face, as his griefe was thereby redoubled and increased. Not long after she drewe neerer unto him and sate by his bedde side (yet all this while he had neyther power to stirre or speake) and told him if hee would consent she should come to bedde to him, hee should be restored to his former health and prosperitie. Thus the Divell strives to enlarge his Kingdome, and upon the necke of one wickedness to heape another.'

The servant withstood Mary's demands and had 'by divine assistance free power and libertie to give repulse to her assault, and denial to her filthie and detested motion: and to upbraide her of her abhominable life and behaviour having had three bastards and never married'. Mary 'vanished and departed the same way shee came' and the servant told the tale to his master, the local miller Master Enger. The story now reached its climax as Master Enger investigated and forced Mary Sutton to come to the servant's bedside, where the servant could scratch her, the popular way of identifying a witch. The servant succeeded in this but 'her assiduitie and continuall exercise in doing mischiefe, did so prevail with her to doe this fellow further hurt, that watching but advantage, and opportunitie to touche his necke againe with her finger: It was no sooner done, and she departed, but he fell into as greate or farre worse vexation than he had done before'.

This apparent continuation of the bewitching of his servant led to reports of the Suttons' activities being 'carried up and downe all Bedfordshire'. Master Enger's son picked up the rumours and 'after espying old Mother Sutton going to the Mill to grinde corne, and remembering what speeches he had heard past of her and her daughter followed the old woman, flinging stones at her and calling her Witch'. Details such as this are realistic: we are here at the heart of the popular understanding of witchcraft in Jacobean England. The printer of the Belvoir witchcraft chapbook was so impressed by the popular appeal of the Bedford story that details of the Enger/Sutton case were added as a form of epilogue in the second edition of the Belvoir pamphlet, printed in 1621.

The reason for this addition was to include a popular account of discovering witches, thus extending the appeal of the title of the

130

Belvoir pamphlet, *The Wonderfull Discoverie of the witchcrafts of Margaret and Phillip[a] Flower*. Presumably the Belvoir author saw some similarity between Mrs Flower and Mother Sutton, and between the daughters Margaret and Philippa Flower and Mary Sutton. The Bedfordshire pamphlet was illustrated by a picture which has become iconic in modern witchcraft studies, of 'a strange and most true triall how to know whether a woman be a witch or not'. The picture of the process of swimming an accused witch encapsulates the whole story. After Master Enger's son had been shouting and throwing stones at Mother Sutton, he became ill and died five days later. Master Enger then accused the Suttons of murdering his son by witchcraft and had Mary Sutton swum for witchcraft; the process was described in considerable detail and illustrated with a lively woodcut.

The Belvoir witches were not swum and the first edition of the Belvoir pamphlet has no reference to swimming a witch as a method of establishing innocence or guilt. But the later editions of 1621 and 1635 have an additional epilogue 'The triall of a Witch', which gives a very full discussion of swimming a witch, along with other popular techniques of discovering witches. The picture is an excellent illustration of a commonplace of local seventeenth-century life. A ducking-stool was still in place in the town of Grantham, close to Belvoir, in 1793 as is shown by Claude Nattes' drawing of that date. The common notion of the purifying effects of water is a good example of the old-established, pre-Reformation world of judicial ordeals. Another example of a judicial ordeal in the Belvoir pamphlet is the account of how Joan Flower died. On her way to Lincoln for imprisonment and trial as a suspected witch, she

> '(as they say) called for Bread and Butter, and wished it might never goe through if she were guilty of that, whereupon she was examined: so mumbling it in her mouth, never spake more wordes after, but fell donne and dyed as she was carryed to Lincolne Goale, with a horrible excruciation of soule and body, and was buried at Ancaster.' (*page 11*)

The Theology of Witchcraft in the Vale of Belvoir: the Manners family

Such survivals were popularly accepted, and it is worth noting the unity created in the Belvoir pamphlet between popular cultural actions and theological ideas. To understand this synthesis of the popular commonplace and the theologically rarefied, it is necessary to study the religious atmosphere prevailing in the Vale of Belvoir at the time. The new theological understanding of the nature and purpose of witchcraft is best expressed by Stuart Clark. He explained that

> 'Everywhere, the categories of 'good' and 'evil' behaviour were reversed. Witches traditionally assumed by villagers to be harmful in matter-of-fact physical ways (*maleficium*) were now said to be, in some higher theological sense, vehicles of spiritual benefits brought by a better understanding of providence and sin.'

In other words, as mentioned earlier, some significant preachers were adopting the paradoxical view that God deliberately sent the Devil to test the depth of an individual's faith. The witch was merely the agent of the Devil and thus was in no way an independent healer capable of doing any good. The actions of the witch were perceived by the author of the Belvoir pamphlet as 'Chasticements [*sic*] of the Godly' (*page 2*). Indeed, the author suggested that, while the Earl of Rutland 'had sufficient grief for the losse of his Children; yet no doubt it was the greater to consider the matter, and how it pleased God to inflict on him such a fashion of visitation'. This widespread theological view partly derived from a reading of Paul's Epistle to the Romans, Chapter 5 verses 3 and 4: 'we glory in tribulations also: knowing that tribulation worketh patience; And patience, experience; and experience hope'.

Can we today understand where the sixth Earl of Rutland stood in this continuum from the popular to the theological, which led him, among others, to examine Margaret and Philippa Flower and to leave 'them to judiciall triall, desiring of God, mercy for their soules'? (*page 25*) Unfortunately, no precise statement of his faith has survived but in the year of his death he had had prepared the theological preamble to his will, and he made a clear statement of his wishes while on his death-bed in an inn in Bishop's Stortford. The religious preamble to his will, dated 30 November 1632, is relatively neutral but deeply religious: he bequeathed his soul 'into the handes of Allmightie God, the father the sonne and the holyghoste three p[er]sones and one eternall God hoping thorough the merits and passion of our Lord and Saviour Jesus Christ that my sinnes shalbe forgiven and that my soule shall inherit life everlasting'. This shows neither an extreme Protestant reliance on Christ nor his own place as one of the Elect; nor does it call upon the Virgin Mary and the Saints to intercede as a fervent Catholic might. But his wife Cecily's will uses almost exactly the same language, and her Catholicism was lifelong and well attested. The only conclusion possible is that the Earl and his wife used conventional formulæ for their wills.

In his deathbed speech and in his will, the Earl refers to the church in Bottesford where 'I have caused my Tombe to be erected'. The inscription on his tomb in St Mary's Church clearly states the Earl's belief in the 'wicked practise and sorcerye' which caused his sons to die 'in their infancy'. We can be certain that this was his belief, as in his deathbed speech he stated 'that my toombe is allredy made'. Beyond the statements in the will and on the tomb, it is not possible to offer evidence of his religious position from the Earl's own lips or pen. There is, however, little doubt that at heart the Earl had Catholic sympathies. During the 1620s there was a Catholic chaplain at Belvoir Castle, Richard Broughton, also known as Richard Rous. There are several letters dated 1622–28 surviving at Belvoir Castle of which he was the recipient. There was little harsh persecution of Catholics or even of Catholic priests in the later years of James I. Richard Broughton was able to minister to Catholics in the Midlands of England and write controversial devotional and historical works. He argued strongly for Catholic bishoprics in England and in 1633 wrote *The Ecclesiastical Historie of Great Britaine* which he dedicated to the Earl's wife and daughter, Catherine; in it he stated categorically that the sixth Earl was one of the 'constant supporters of the holy Catholike Religion'.

Broughton's security at Belvoir Castle owed everything to the manner in which a great nobleman in Jacobean England could maintain both a private and a public religion simultaneously. The sixth Earl, as a member of the House of Lords, a Privy Councillor and Lord Lieutenant of Lincolnshire, took the Protestant oath of allegiance to the Crown. His religious views were not officially queried until 1624, when in a House of Lords 'List of reported recusants and Non-communicants who are in places of trust' he was the first named, it being asserted 'that he and his Wife are suspected Popish Recusants', though nothing came of this. It can safely be suggested then that the Earl accepted the Catholic view of witchcraft. But Stuart Clark asserts that 'there does seem to be little to distinguish the Protestant from the Catholic formulation' regarding witchcraft.

One view common to both sects was that witchcraft, along with other manifestations of change such as plague, was part of the widespread eschatological belief during the period that the world was shortly about to end, an ending they believed was foretold in the Bible which was to be foreshadowed by disaster. The only distinction between Catholics and Protestants which might be considered relevant here is a greater belief by the Catholics in the actions of spirits and, of course, in the earthly authority of the Pope and canon law. Witchcraft was perceived as the inverse of true religion and thus both Catholic and Protestant preachers attacked it as evidence for heresy in the opposing sect. But both would agree with the theological conclusion of the first edition of the Belvoir pamphlet:

> 'O then you sonnes of men, take warning by these examples, and eyther divert your steps from the broad way of destruction and irrecoverable gulph of damnation, or with Josuahs counsell to Achan, blesse God for the discovery of wickednesse and take thy death patiently as the prevention [warning] of thy future judgement, and saving innocents from punishment, who otherwise may be suspected without cause.' (*page 26*)

The Latin tag from Cicero which is the pamphlet's final line: 'If only I could discover the truth as easily as I can prove falsehood' (*page 26*) chimes in well with King James's determination to ensure that witch trials were as fair as possible.

Dr Samuel Fleming and his brother Abraham Fleming
Although there was a Catholic chaplain at the Castle in the 1620s, the Earl's official religious chaplain was the Rev Dr Samuel Fleming, rector of Bottesford and of Cottenham near Cambridge from 1581 to his death in 1620. We are aware of Samuel today mostly because he was the half-brother of a significant Elizabethan literary figure, Abraham Fleming, the author of a popular 1577 pamphlet on the Black Dog of Bungay, among many other works. Abraham was deeply involved in the later Elizabethan publishing world, but he was eventually ordained in 1588, becoming in 1597 the rector of a church in the City of London. The two brothers were

clearly close to each other, as ultimately Abraham died when visiting Bottesford in 1607 and his epitaph, written by himself before his death, still survives in the chancel of the church there.

Abraham worked with Reginald Scot on his *Discoverie of Witchcraft* for which he provided in 1584 English translations of Latin poems; amusingly, as David Wootton points out, Abraham appears in the list of authors used by Reginald Scot as 'Grimelf Maharba'. Does the fact that Abraham contributed translations to Scot's sceptical work on witchcraft imply that Abraham held similar views? Abraham, it is suggested, inclined to the Family of Love, a sect which was outwardly conformist but spiritually inwardly-looking to an inner light as the source of religious certainty. In his *Discoverie* Scot extensively used classical poetry, especially Ovid and a stanza from one of Abraham's translations used by Scot demonstrates the view that witchcraft using charms to bring about sexual attraction was wrong:

> 'If any think that evill herbs
> In Haemon land which be,
> Or witchcraft able is to helpe,
> Let him make proofe and see.'

Scot's comment after this verse was 'These verses precedent do show, that Ovid knew that those beggarly sorceries might rather kill one, or make him stark mad, than do him good.' In other words: apply the rules of reason and the law and you will see that witchcraft was useless. Scot's work is not mentioned in the Belvoir pamphlet where the author, referring to the sceptical view of witchcraft, condemns 'the particular opinion of some men, who suppose there bee [no witches] at all, or at least that they do not personally or truly effect such things as are imputed to them' (*page 6*).

Abraham was well known in Elizabethan and Jacobean times as the author of devotional works such as *The Diamond of Devotion* in1581 and *The Footpath to Felicitie* in1586. As a literary man employed by printers, he spent several years collecting, editing and collating historical and literary manuscripts. The manuscripts were accounts of significant events, in particular the events surrounding the Treaty of Berwick, the trial and the execution of Mary Queen of Scots. Samuel Fleming was involved in these activities as the chaplain to the third Earl of

Rutland. Edward Manners, the third Earl, was the 'man of honor' *ie:* the guarantor of the Treaty of Berwick of July 1586, where his actions greatly impressed the young King of Scots, James VI. Immediately afterwards, the Earl went to Fotheringay for the trial of Mary Queen of Scots in October 1586. In the February of the following year Mary was executed, and in August 1587 she was buried in Peterborough Cathedral, with John the fourth Earl of Rutland as a chief mourner. It is probable that Samuel Fleming attended as Henry's chaplain. What is certain is that Edward the third Earl was deeply involved in the trial of Mary Queen of Scots and that Henry the fourth Earl was present at her funeral in Peterborough, at a time when Samuel Fleming was the official chaplain of the Earls.

Both Fleming brothers were intellectuals involved in literary activity. Samuel wrote, but never published, a now-lost account of Mary Tudor, and Abraham collected many historical documents connected with Mary Queen of Scots. Their interest in these two Catholic queens reflected the Elizabethan theological dilemma: how to maintain a coherent religious stance between the perceived extremes of the ultra-Reformed Puritan position and the papist, Jesuitical Roman Catholic one. Samuel led a conventional life with no known hint of dispute to conventional religious views. He edited a version of Foxe's strongly Protestant *Actes and monuments of these latter and perilous dayes*, popularly known as the 'Book of Martyrs'. Both brothers were chaplains to significant aristocratic families. During nearly forty years Samuel was chaplain to four successive Earls of Rutland, being first appointed chaplain to Edward the third Earl in 1582.

Abraham became chaplain, probably in the 1590s, to Catherine Countess of Nottingham and to her husband Lord Howard of Effingham, the admiral of the English fleet against the Spanish Armada, who was created Earl of Nottingham in 1597. Abraham's clerical patron was the Archbishop of Canterbury, John Whitgift, and it was he who appointed Abraham to the small City of London living of St Pancras, Soper Lane (not today's more familiar parish next to the railway station of that name). Abraham's reputation today rests on his extensive editorial work on Holinshed's *Chronicles of England, Scotland and Ireland*, particularly the 1587 edition. Samuel's modern reputation derives almost exclusively from his involvement in the Belvoir witchcraft affair of 1619.

136

Rev Charles Odingsells, Rector of Langar

No sermons by Samuel have survived but we have two sermons actually preached in the Vale of Belvoir in 1619 by his contemporary and neighbouring cleric, Charles Odingsells, Rector of Langar, nearby in the Vale of Belvoir. All three clerics, the two Flemings and Odingsells, were bachelors, a celibate state which Queen Elizabeth preferred in her priests. Odingsells was related to the Markham family through his mother Catherine Markham, and to Dr Thomas Ridgley, who married his sister Anne Odingsells. Like the Flemings, Odingsells was a chaplain to a significant aristocrat: his patron was Emanuel Scrope, later Earl of Sunderland, who had estates at Langar. Scrope, like the sixth Earl of Rutland, was a closet Catholic and this is significant to our understanding of events in the Vale of Belvoir around 1618–19, when the witchcraft accusations were made.

James I's state policy was pro-Spanish because he was anxious to preserve peace with Spain, a major element of his foreign policy throughout his reign. In 1618 war had broken out in continental Europe between the new Holy Roman Emperor Ferdinand II, strongly Catholic and allied to Spain, and James's son-in law Frederick, the Protestant Elector of the Palatinate. James continued his policy of supporting Spain, although this became increasingly unpopular. At the same time in 1618 James had supported the strongly Calvinist Protestants at the Synod of Dort, rejecting the High Church Arminianism which was to dominate the Church of England under Archbishop Laud in the next two decades. This extraordinary conjunction of war and religious controversy created a hectic atmosphere in England in 1618–19, which was conducive to extreme reactions to disturbances, rather than carefully considered responses. The Belvoir witchcraft case was exactly contemporaneous with these events.

Fortunately for our understanding of Jacobean witchcraft beliefs in the Vale of Belvoir, Odingsells delivered his two sermons on the subject to his Vale parishioners and then had them printed in 1619-20. He highlighted witchcraft as symptomatic of the disturbed state of the country's religious equilibrium. One of his particular theological interests was prophecy, which fitted in well with the widespread eschatological preoccupation with the 'last things' prevalent at that time. The first of his two sermons was on 'Prophesying and casting out of Devils', dated at Langar,

4 July 1619, and dedicated to his patron 'Emanuel Lord Scrope, Baron of Bolton... and President of his Majesties Councill in the North'. Scrope, who had a house in Langar, was appointed Lord President in January 1619 in place of a major persecutor of Catholics, clearly one of James's appointments aimed at diminishing active persecution of Catholics as part of his pacifying policies.

The text of the sermon was from St Paul's first letter to the Corinthians, chapter 13, verse 2, which is quoted on the title-page of the printed version: 'Though I have the gift of prophecying, and understand all mysteries and all knowledge, yea, if I have all faith, so that I could remove Mountaynes, and have no charitie, I am nothing'. The sermon discussed the nature of prophecy and attacked false prophets, particularly those 'seduced by an evil spirit'. He went on: 'Evill and ungodly men and women, may foreshew things to come, but *in spiritu Diaboli*, by the spirit of Satan'. Odingsells concentrated much of his sermon against prophecy as witchcraft: 'By this means the Witch of Endor using Necromancy raysed up the Devill in the habit of Samuel'. He explained how devils could move as if by magic: 'and the evill angell did by celeritie and swiftnesse of motion; for both the good and evill Angels can doe much, *quoad motum localem, by local motion,* gliding presently [immediately] from East to West like the lightning'.

The absolute power of God over spirits was explained: 'by the same soveraigne power and authoritie, hee [God] commandeth Devils to enter into men, and they willingly obey; againe, hee commands them to come forth, and they cannot but obey'. Odingsells attacked exorcism, or 'charging of uncleane spirits to come out of men possessed' which has 'now ceased'. He concluded this sermon by stating that this 'gift of prophecying and the power of casting out of Devils, are not infallible markes of a right Catholike, doe not necessarily argue the child of God'. In this sermon preached to his parishioners in the Vale of Belvoir, Odingsells attacked and denied any truth in those who were involved in any way with ideas of foretelling the future or curing illness by appearing to be dealing with devils.

His second sermon was a discourse on miracles, which he approached in the same way as he had discussed prophecy, glorying in the prophecies of Jesus's miracles but insisting that the days of prophecy and miracles were ended after the earthly life of Jesus, a strongly Protestant view. His text was Jesus's words in St Matthew's Gospel chapter 7, verses 22 and 23: 'Many will say unto mee in that day, Lord, Lord, have we not prophecyed in thy name? and in thy name have cast out Devils? and in thy name done many wonderful workes? And then will I professe unto them, I never knew you. Depart from me, ye that worke iniquitie'.

Odingsells admitted: 'It is a matter of some difficultie to discerne true Miracles from false'. He allowed that Satan

> 'can by Gods permission, moove and trouble the spirits, the bloud and humors of mans bodie, and so cause strange imaginations and phantasmes in the phantasie; whereby it comes to passe that men and women thinke they see many strange & uncouth things which indeed they see not. For hee [Satan] will so strongly delude the inward phantasie, as that hee will even palpably deceive the outward sense.'

In these words Odingsells epitomised the early seventeenth-century intellectual view of witchcraft. Any action apparently inspired by the Devil was in the view of theologians of the time always primarily initiated by God. Odingsells insisted on this:

> '[The Devil] may by Gods permission, either assume a true body, or make of the Ayre and other Elements, fayned, counterfeited bodies, as of Men or Women, of Birds, or Beasts, and other living Creatures, so *per fascinum* [by witchcraft] hee hides and clokes that thing which is present, and makes another thing seeme to be there, which indeed is not present.'

He cited a quotation from Psalm 72 as proof: 'Blessed be the Lord God, even the God of Israel, which onely doth wondrous works'.

During this long explanation of witchcraft Odingsells introduced a clear appeal to his listeners. In a rare moment of personal feeling he said: 'I have heretofore disswaded you of this Parish of Langar, from running to them that use charmes, and are *good at words* (as they call them here in the Valley). I have forbidden you to resort to such. But how comes it to passe, that you wil not obey?' He then resorts again to biblical injunctions, citing Deuteronomy chapter 18: 'Let none bee found among you that useth witchcraft, or a Regarder of times, or a Marker of flying of Fowles, or a Sorcerer, or a Charmer, or that counselleth with a Spirit, or a Soothsayer'. He could hardly have been more direct in his condemnation of local dabbling in witchcraft.

Charles Odingsells could represent the standard Anglican priest during the Jacobean period. He steered a careful passage between the covert Catholicism of his patron and the extreme Protestantism of such men as the famous late Elizabethan separatist prophet, the pseudo-messiah William Hacket. Historian Alexandra Walsham explains that, while Hacket was regarded by some as 'the zealous puritan 'mechanic preacher' and popular prophet, in the eyes of others he bore more resemblance to a cunning man, sorcerer, white wizard or witch'. Historians today are studying this association between populist extreme Protestantism and witchcraft. 'Some of [Hacket's] exploits as a popular prophet bear an uncanny resemblance to the activities of the part-time healers, diviners and white wizards who inhabited almost every rural community in Elizabethan England: others bring him closer to the world of black magic and malevolent witchcraft' as Walsham explains.

What Odingsells was concerned to prevent was any involvement at all by his parishioners in witchcraft. He was concerned to eradicate the use of witchcraft by extreme Puritans and he argued by the use of Biblical texts, a method he knew would upset Puritan extremists. He did not deny the possibility of witchcraft; he simply forbade its use. It is possible that he had in mind the tragic use of sympathetic magic that the Flower family had been involved in and which led to the sisters' execution.

The theological background to the Belvoir trial is fraught with complexity. A mixture of opinions from the old Catholic faith and from mystical Protestant prophesyings found a receptive audience among the villagers of the Vale of Belvoir. We are fortunate to be able to locate in the Belvoir pamphlet evidence for the parallel views of witchcraft endemic in Jacobean times. The intermingling of these two features of current attitudes reinforced a widespread belief in the demonic powers of ubiquitous spirits. The Belvoir author cleverly incorporated elements of the popular pre-Reformation folk belief in witchcraft into his account.

He also insisted on building in the contemporary theological view of both Catholic and Protestant divines that God used the Devil and the Devil's servants, witches, to test the depth of people's faith. Samuel Fleming and Charles Odingsells, both Vale of Belvoir rectors, were well aware of the potential dangers of the deep beliefs in witchcraft held by their parishioners. So when a case of witchcraft appeared in Belvoir in 1618, the local priests took action. Samuel Fleming as a justice of the peace investigated it and Charles Odingsells preached against it.

LEFT: James VI of Scotland and RIGHT: Queen Anne, both 1595, and painted by Adrian Vanson. (Both SNPG) BELOW: Duckingstool in Grantham: Claude Nattes, 1793. (LLS)

In the firſt Booke.

In the ſecond booke.

In the third Booke.

The Printer to the Reader.

IF any thinke theſe Hiſtories ſtrange, he may ſee the very title
ſayes as much : And it is good for an author to bee as good
as his title : And this being a tranſlation, it muſt be ſtrange. If
any thinke that by the name of Hiſtories, all ſhould be true, he
may knowe Hiſtoriographers confeſſe they may write as they
liſt. And *Lucian* entitles his moſt fabulous narrations a true Hiſ-
torie : And if theſe be but tales, yet either hee is Maiſter, or he
cites you his tales-maiſter, (more then moſt men will do) And
very tales are heard or read by moſt of vs with good delight.
Theſe from good authors to good purpoſe are in good ſort ſet
downe. Then ſit thee downe and make thy good of them: for
haue thou a good memory and they will prooue memorable:
that nor thou repent reading, nor he writing, nor we tranſla-
ting and Imprinting. This is all, and of this make thy beſt.

ABOVE: John Cotta: A Short Discoverie of the unobserved dangers of…
severall sorts of ignorant and unconsiderate practisers of physicke, *1612
(EEBO & OBL) and BELOW: George Eld* To the Reader *in Simon Goulart's*
Admirable and Memorable Histories, *1607. (EEBO & HL)*

143

VVitches Apprehended, Ex

amined and Executed, for notable
villanies by them committed both by
Lan d and Water.

With a ſtrange and moſt true triall how to know
whether a woman be a Witch
or not.

Printed at London or *Edward Marchant*, and are to
be ſold at his ſhop ouer againſt the Croſſe in Paul's
ch-yard. 1 6 1 3.

Swimming witches; the account of the Bedford witches from Witches Apprehended,
1613. (EEBO & HL)

144

Sixthly, that man in his frailty muft not prefume of profperity, but prepare a kind of ftooping under the hand of God, when it pleafeth him to ftrike or punifh us. Seventhly, that there is no murmuring nor repining againft God , but quietly to tolerate his inflictings, whenfoever they chance, of which this worthy Earle is a memorable example to all men and ages. Eightly, that the punifhments of the wicked are fo many warnings to all irregular finners to amend their lives, and avoid the judgement to come, by penitency, and newneffe of life. Ninthly, that though man could bee content to paffe over blafphemies and offences againft the Statutes of Princes, yet God will overtake them in their owne walkes, and pull them backe by the fleeve into a flaughter-houfe, as here you know the evidences againft thefe people tooke life and power from their owne Confeffions. Tenthly, and laft of all, that private opinion cannot prevaile againft publike cenfures : for here you fee the learned and religious Judges cried out with our Saviour, *Ex ore tuo*. Therefore though it were fo, that neither Witch nor Devill could doe thefe things, yet *Let not a Witch live*, faith God, and *Let them die* (faith the Law of *England*) *that have converfation with fpirits, and prefume to blafpheme the Name of God with fpels and incantations*. O then you fonnes of men, take warning by thefe examples ; and either divert your fteps from the broad way of deftruction, and irrecoverable gulfe of damnation, or with *Iofuahs* counfell to *Achan*, Bleffe God for the difcovery of wickedneffe, and take thy death patiently, as the prevention of thy future judgement, and faving innocents from punifhment, who otherwife may be fufpected without a caufe.

Vtinam tam facile vera invenire poffem, quam falfa convincere.

The triall of a Witch.

Now as touching the triall and difcovery of a Witch (then which there cannot be any prefident more neceffary and behoovefull

hooveull for us) there are divers opinions holden; As fome by the pricking of a fharpe knife, naule, or other pointed inftrument under the ftoole or feate on which the Witch fitteth (for thereon fhee is not able to fit or abide) others by fcratching, or drawing of blood from the Witch, by either party that is grieved, or the next of blood to the fame, and others by fire ; as by burning any relique or principall ornament belonging to the fufpected Witch, which fhall no fooner bee on fire, but the Witch will prefently come running to behold it ; and of thefe, trials have beene made both in Hartfordfhire, Northamptonfhire, and Huntingtonfhire; But the onely affured and abfolute perfect way to finde her out, is to take the Witch or party fufpected either to fome Mildam, Pond, Lake or deepe River, and ftripping her to her fmocke, tie her armes acroffe, onely let her legs have free liberty ; then faftening a rope about her middle which with the helpe of by ftanders may be ever ready to fave her from drowning (in cafe fhe finke) throw her into the water, and if fhee fwimme aloft and not fincke, then draw her foorth, and have fome honeft and difcreet women neere, which may prefently fearch her for the fecret marke of Witches, as Teates, blood-moales, moift warts, and the like, which found, then the fecond time (binding her right thumbe to her left toe, and her left thumbe to her right toe) throw her into the water againe (with the affiftance of the former rope to fave her, if fhee fhould chance to fincke) and if then fhee fwim againe and doe not fincke you may moft affuredly refolve fhe is a Witch : and of this many pregnant and true proofes have beene made, as namely by one Mafter Enger of Bedfordfhire, upon the perfon of Mary Sutton (a notable Witch) whom he caft into his Mildam at Milton Mills, and found the effect as hath beene declared, and for her Witchcraft was there condemned and executed, and as this fo I could recite a world of others in the fame nature. But the trueth is fo manifeft that it needeth no flourifh to adorne it.

FINIS.

The Triall of a witch from the 1635 edition of the Belvoir Pamphlet.
(EEBO & GUL)

1632, December 15.—" It pleased my Lord to call my Lady Dutchess, my sister of Rutland, my Lord Savidge, and myselfe, and to use theise speeches unto us.

Sweete hart give mee your hand, now I pray God blisse you and your children. It greeves me I shall see none of them before I die, but I leave them my blessinge. You know there was a match wished by your housband betweene my Lord Chamberline's sonn and Mall, which I desier may go on.

That hee gave his best heroners to his Majestie and that Mr. Robert Terrett the Kinges Querey might goe to his Lordship's stable and chewes either his best huntinge horsse for the hare or his best buck hunter, which his Majestie showld make choyce of, and that I showld present them unto his Majestie.

That my Lord Savidge wowld present his humble service to his Majestie leting him know that never Kinge had a more faithfull servant or a more loyall subject then myselfe nor never subjecte had a more gracious Soveraigne, acknowledginge himselfe infinightly bound to his Majesty for his ever gracious favoures unto him.

That his Lordshippe desiered there might bee no difference betwixt my sister of Rutland and myselfe in the execution of his will; and I desier you my Lord Savidge, if there bee any, to deside it; but if you cannot, then I pray you to commend my love unto my Lord Keeper, and my desier is that your two Lordshippes showld deside it.

That there was a thowsand pounds in his iron chest at London and five hundred pounds in his servant Robert Cooks custody, and desiered us his executors to put to it five hundred pounds more, and pay it to Sir John Ayres whome he ought two thousand pounds.

His Lordshipp is pleased to give to Mr. Doctor Litster fifty pounds for the care he hath taken of him in this his sicknesse.

For my funerall I wowld have it such as my auncestors have had which will bee no greate charge, for that my toombe is allreddy made and I wowld have my bodie, so soone as it is embalmed, to bee removed forth of the Inn.

Theise directions weare by his Lordship delivered unto us, hee beeing in perfitt memory after his will was made. This 15th day of Decembe 1632." *Endorsed in Sir George Manners's hand, " My brother' speache to my Lady Rutland and myself att Storford."*

The dying testimony of Francis Manners, sixth Earl of Rutland, December, 1632. (BCA)

TO
THE MOST ILLVSTRIOVS,
RIGHT HONOVRABLE, AND VERTVOVS
L A D I E S,

THE LADIE CATHERINE DVTCHESSE,
AND DOVVAGER OF BVCKINGHAM,
SOLE DAVGHTER AND HEIRE TO THE RIGHT
HONOVRABLE FRANCIS LATE EARLE OF RVTLAND,

AND
THE LADIE CECILIE
C O V N T E S S E,
AND DOWAGER OF RVTLAND.

EEM it not I befeech you (Most Illv-striovs Noble Ladies) any the leafte dif-paragement to your Nobilities, or ble-mish to your Vertves, that your humble feruant, and Secretarie, hath prefumed to ioyne you, within the narrowe ftraites, and precincts of one, and that fo short an Epiftle, whom both terrene Dignities and heauenly Bleffings haue fo happily vnited in one moft Noble Stocke and Li-nage. He is not ignorant that the Splendor of a Dvtchesse cannot commonly be paraleld by the Dignitie and Title of a Covntesse: yet when he cófidereth the Renowne of a Covntesse defcended from moft antient and Noble Families, Daughter to the Noble, and by Name and Difcent moft antient S. Iohn Tufton of Tufton, and before shee was wifeto her mofte Noble Father, wife to the noble heyr of the greate and antient L. Hungerford should any whitt eclipfe, shadowe, or obfcure the Radiant Bea mes of a Dvtchesse. but rather by adding Splendor to Splendor,

† 2 make

First of three pages of dedication by Richard Broughton of his book, The Ecclesiasticall Historie of Great Britaine, *1633 to Cecilia Manners, recently the widow of Francis Manners, sixth Earl of Rutland and to Catherine Villiers, widow of George Villiers, Duke of Buckingham and daughter of the sixth Earl. This dedication is probably the best evidence for the belief in the 'holy CATHOLIC RELIGION' of the Manners family. (EEBO & CUL)*

147

make both more GLORIOVS and RESPLENDENT.

Moreouer he apprehendeth a mutuall and long AFFEC-
TION euen from the yonge yeares of the one betwixt MOTHER
and DAVGHTER, as also the vnited hearts of WIFE and
DAVGHTER, both embracing the moſt Noble Earle of Rutland of famous Memorie, the one with the LOVE of a WIFE
towards her HVSBAND, the other with the AFFECTION of a
DAVGHTER to her deare FATHER: Whoſe LOVE to requite,
he with his owne hands ſtiled your GRACE, his DEARE
DAVGHTER; and your HONOVR, his DEARE WIFE
of whome he further gaue his moſt ample Teſtimonie and in theſe
words: I WILL SAYE THAT THERE WAS NEVER
MAN HAD A MORE LOVING AND VERTVOVS
WIFE THEN SHE HATH BEENE TO MEE. And
as your LOVE hath beene GREAT to this moſt honourable Earle,
who was Diſcreet in his words, Prudent and iuſt in all his Actions,
Charitable to the Poore, Affable to all, Faithfull to his Countrie,
Gratious to his Soueraigne, Conſtant in his Faith and Religion,
moſt beloued and honoured of all, and then whome noe Noble
man of England was more affected, or more Generally honoured
in his life, or more Bewayled and lamented after his death; So your
VERTVES doe ſhine in this world with a moſt reſplendent LIGHT,
and are the DIAMONDS and PEARLES which adorne the RING
of your Auncient NOBILITIE. And theſe his, and your Heroicall VERTVES, being grounded on the ROCK of a true FAITH,
as they haue made the Earle, ſo they will make you CONSTANT
SVPPORTERS of holy CATHOLIKE RELIGION; Theſe being fixed
to the ANCHOR of HOPE, as they haue guided him, ſo will they direct you to the quiet HAVEN of eternall FELICITIE. Yea it is verily
to be hoped that he by theſe VERTVES, is there alreadie arriued,
whilſt the one of you like a PHAROS, and the other like the CYNO-
SVRE with the FLAMES of CHARITIE, doe giue LIGHT vnto
others, in this time of DARKNES.

Wherefore (MOST VERTVOVS LADIES) to whome after
the moſt Noble Earle (to whome this WORKE was firſt deſigned,
and for whome before his death was ſett on the PRESSE) can
I more worthilie dedicate theſe, CENTVRIES OF OVR
ECCLESIASTICALL HISTORIE, then to theſe, in
whome the Noble Earle ſtill in renowme SVRVIVES? If you eſteeme
NOBILITIE ioyned with SANCTITIE. behold here LVCIVS,
HELENA, and CONSTANTINE, three great SAINCTS,

three

three great PRINCES, and all great PROMOTORS and ESTA-
BLISHERS of the RELIGION, which you imbrace. If you take
pleaſure to ſee the DAMASKE ROSES of MARTYRDOME, here is an
ALBAN our PROTOMARTYR, here is an AMPHIBALVS
with many more, all ſtout and valiant CHAMPIONS, Who haue
ſealed the TRVETH of our FAITH with there deareſt BLOOD:
They all were once PILGRIMS in this VALE of TEARES, as
you both now are, but now they are glorious COVRTIOVRS in
the Triumphant HIERARCHIE. If you followe theire STEPS,
and imitate theire VERTVES and CONSTANCIE in FAITH,
you may haue great CONFIDENCE to be Partakers of the like
GLORIE: and in the meane time, your NAMES being prefixed
before their HEROICALL ACTIONS, may impetrate
theire PATRONAGE in all your corporall and Spirituall NECES-
SITIES; and I ſhall pray to THEM, and to all the SAINCTS, and
by THEM to the SAINCTE of SAINCTS to beſtowe on you
here all TEMPORALL, and in HEAVEN all ETERNALL FE-
LICITIE.

MADAMS

YOVR GRACES

AND

YOVR HONOVRS

Moſt humble and deuoted Seruant

R. B.

† 3   THE

Ouid. lib. de
remedio a-
moris. 1.

*Viderit Aemoniæ ſi quis mala pabula terræ,
Et magicas artes poſſe iuuare putat.*

Ab. Fleming.

If any thinke that euill herbs
in Hæmon land which be,
Or witchcraft able is to helpe,
let him make proofe and ſee.

Theſe verſes precedent do ſhew, that Ouid knew that thoſe
beggerlie ſorceries might rather kill one, or make him ſtarke
mad, than do him good towards the atteinement of his pleaſure or loue; and therefore he giueth this counſell to them that
are amorous in ſuch hot maner, that either they muſt enioy their
loue, or elſe needs die; ſaieng:

ABOVE: *The remainder of the dedication by Richard Broughton. (EEBO & CUL)*
BELOW: *Abraham Fleming's translation of Ovid for Reginald Scot's* Discoverie of
Witchcraft, *1584. (EEBO & HL)*

148

ABOVE: The Fleming Almshouses in Bottesford, probably built as a result of Fleming's will c1620, (MH) INSET: the recently renovated inscription on the Fleming Almshouses and BELOW: the Abraham Fleming memorial brass in St Mary's Church, Bottesford. (Both HER)

149

A ſtraunge,

and terrible Wunder wrought
verp late in the .pariſh Church
of Bongay , a Tovvn of no great di-
ſtance from the citie of Norwich, name-
ly the fourth of this Auguſt, in ẏ yeere of
our Lord 1577, in a great tempeſt of vi-
olent raine, lightning ,and thunder, the
like wherof hath bẻn ſel-
dome ſẻne.
With the appẻrance of an horrible ſha-
ped thing,ſenſibly perceiurd of the
people then and there
aſſembled.
Drawen into a plain method ac-
coding to the written copye.
by Abraham Fleming.

Title page of Abraham Fleming's A Straunge and Terrible Wunder, *1577.*
(EEBO & BL)

TWO
SERMONS,

lately preached at L A N-
G A R in the Valley of
Belvoir.

By C. O

I. C O R. 13. 2.

*Though I haue the gift of prophecying, and vnderstand all
mysteries and all knowledge, yea, if I haue all faith, so
that I could remoue Mountaynes, and haue no charitie,
I am nothing.*

LONDON

Printed by *W. Stansby,* and are to be
sold by *Iohn Parker* at the signe
of the three Pidgeons in
Pauls Churchyard.

1 6 2 0.

Title page of Charles Odingsell's Two Sermons... preached in the Valley of Belvoir in
1620. (EEBO & BL)

151

Ee it enacted by the King our Souereigne Lord, the Lords Spirituall and Temporall, and the Commons
in this preſent Parliament aſſembled , and by the authoritie of theſame: That the Statute made in the
fifth yeere of the reigne of our late Soueraigne Lady of moſt famous and happy memory Queene Elizabeth,
intituled, An Act againſt Coniurations, Incantments, and Witchcrafts, be from the feaſt of Saint Michael the Archangell next comming, for and concerning all offences to bee committed after the ſame feaſt, vtterly repealed. And for the better reſtraining the ſayd offences, and more ſeuere puniſhing the ſame: Bee it further enacted by the authoritie aforeſayd, that if any perſon or perſons , after the ſaid Feaſt of S. Michael the Archangell next
comming, ſhall vſe, practiſe, or exerciſe any Inuocation , or Coniuration, of any euill and wicked Spirit, or ſhall con-
ſult, couenant with, entertaine, employ, feede, or reward, any euill and wicked Spirit , to , or for any intent or purpoſe,
or take vp any dead man , woman, or childe , out of his, her, or their graue , or any other place , where the dead body
reſteth, or the ſkinne, bone, or any other part of any dead perſon, to be imployed or vſed in any manner of Witchcraft,
Sorcery, Charme, or Incantment, or ſhall vſe , practiſe, or exerciſe any Witchcraft, Inchantment, Charme, or Sorcery, whereby any perſon ſhall be killed, deſtroyed, waſted , conſumed, pined, or lamed in his or her body, or any parte
thereof: That then euery ſuch offendour or offendours, their aydors, abettors, and counſellours, being of any the ſayd
offences duely and lawfully conuicted, and attainted, ſhall ſuffer paines of death, as a Felon, or Felons, and ſhall loſe
the priuiledge and benefite of Clergie, and Sanctuary.

And further, to the intent that all manner of practiſe, vſe or exerciſe of Witchcraft, Encantement, Charme,
or Sorcerie, ſhould be from henceforth vtterly auoyded, aboliſhed, and taken away : Bee it enacted by the authoritie of this preſent Parliament, That if any perſon or perſons, ſhall from and after the ſayd Feaſt of Saint Michael
the Archangel next com━━━━ ━━━ ━━━ ━━━ ━━ ━━━ ━━━━━━━ ━━━━━ ━ ━━━━━, to tell, or de-
clare in what place any t ...... other ſecret pla-
ces, or where goods or th ...... perſon to vnlawfull Loue, or whereby a ...... to hurt or deſtroy
any perſon in his, her ...... ſuch perſon or perſons ſo offending, and be ...... by the ſpace of
one whole yeere, without ...... Market Towne
vpon the Market day, or ...... e by the ſpace of
ſixe houres , and there ſ ...... l being once conuicted of the ſame offenc ...... then euery ſuch
offendour being of any o ...... as is aforeſaid,
ſhall ſuffer paines of dea ...... rie, and Sanctuary. Sauing to the wi ...... Dower, and alſo
to the heire, and ſucceſſo ...... ights, as though
no ſuch attaindour of th ......
Prouided alwayes, t ...... Realme, then his
erpall therein to be had b ......

*James I: 1603/4 Act of Parliament against conjuration and witchcraft and dealing with
evil and wicked spirits and INSET: map of the major areas of witchcraft persecution in
Europe in the sixteenth and seventeenth centuries. (RB)*

152

THE TRIAL

The increasing concern of the Earl and Countess over their remaining son's worsening health, coupled with the growing build-up of rumours against the Flower family, finally came to a head in late 1618 and resulted in drastic legal action. After his long description of the Flowers' alleged evil-doing and the sufferings of the Manners family, the Belvoir pamphlet's author dealt with this briefly in his narrative, in a couple of paragraphs. He stated that

> Margaret and Philippa Flower were 'apprehended about Christmas [1618] and carried to Lincolne Jayle, after due examination before sufficient Justices of the Peace and discreet Majestrates' (*page 11*).

Only the two daughters stood trial; Joan did not survive to reach Lincoln. She had apparently chosen a much older form of attempting to prove her innocence, that of trial by ordeal. It is worthwhile to repeat here the account of her death according to the pamphlet: she

> 'called for Bread and Butter, and wished it might never goe through if she were guilty of that, whereupon she was examined: so mumbling it in her mouth, never spake more words after, but fell donne and dyed as she was carryed to Lincolne Goale, with a horrible excruciation of soule and body, and was buried at Ancaster.' (*page 11*)

The method of ordeal allegedly chosen by Joan Flower was based on a traditional belief similar to that behind the ordeal by water which led to the 'swimming' of an accused witch, where the 'pure' water would accept or reject her, as was explained earlier. In theory the bread was first blessed by a priest; in pre-Reformation times it could even be the bread of the Mass. There was a popular story, though it is not recorded in the *Anglo-Saxon Chronicle*, relating to the death in 1052 of Earl Godwine, father of King Harold; he is alleged to have choked on a piece of bread in an attempt to prove his innocence of accusations made against him, having first asked that the bread should choke him if he were guilty.

Joan presumably died on the way to Lincoln as she did not reach the city to face examination there. This story of how she met her death may have some basis in truth or it may be an embellishment added by the Belvoir pamphlet's author. However, it could have added to the weight of suspicion against her daughters by the time that they reached Lincoln and came to trial. There is no sign or record of any such burial at Ancaster as that claimed in the pamphlet, but not all graves, especially those of poor people, were marked and if she was an accused witch she would not have been offered burial in the churchyard. This statement indicates the route by which the party travelled from Bottesford or Belvoir to Lincoln, using the old Roman road, known as Ermine Street or the High Dyke, more easily passable in a Jacobean winter than the muddier lowland roads.

'When the Judges of the Assize came down to Lincoln about the first weeke in March' the two Flower sisters 'were convicted of Murther and executed accordingly, about the 11 of March [1619]' (*page 24*). The Belvoir author does not give the details of their actual trial; the form that it took would be familiar to his readers at the time, as a modern trial is to us. In any case, one of his main intentions in writing the pamphlet was to vindicate the Earl's family by presenting them as the innocent victims, and to undercut any claims that the Flowers had any cause for grievance against them which drove them to these extreme methods of seeking revenge. The Belvoir pamphlet's version tends to reinforce the view that the legal system was being used by the Earl to overcome his problems about his heir. He needed to make the accused women appear to be the cause of his problems through their contract with the Devil; when they were removed he hoped that his second son would be enabled to survive.

However, the pamphlet's author considered that these bald sentences needed to be expanded and so he 'thought it both meete and convenient to lay open their onne [own] Examinations and Evidences against one another' (*page 12*). As a result, we can reconstruct the legal process prior to the trial of the Flower sisters and the trial itself from these judicial examinations and by comparison with other more fully-documented contemporary trials of people accused of witchcraft, especially the well-known Lancashire case of 1612.

154

What becomes immediately apparent is that the legal system which culminated in the Lincoln murder trial in 1619 was totally different from that which prevails in England in the twenty-first century.

Before we analyse the process whereby accused people were tried for witchcraft, it is useful to discuss the range of possible reactions to rumours of witchcraft in Jacobean England. Sometimes a story flared up only to disappear as ephemeral gossip. If, however, the story persisted, community safeguards came into action, which were either secular or religious. Both safeguards could be accessed by rich or poor. For secular justice, gentry would apply direct to justices of the peace who were their social equals; ordinary men and women would talk to the village constable who was in regular communication with the local justices. In both cases the magistrates could act immediately and summon people to be examined. It was also possible for spiritual justice to be sought *via* the parish priest or his representative, the churchwarden. Therefore there were two avenues of redress if one felt threatened by witchcraft: either by applying to the local magistrates appointed by the King to uphold the laws of the Crown, derived from custom, case law or parliamentary statute or by appealing to the local church courts.

Church Courts

Church courts were responsible for legal questions arising from the administration of church property, the discipline of the clergy, the probate of wills and spiritual offences against canon law. Canon law, the law of the church, should be distinguished from secular law, which dealt with civil and criminal offences. Church canon law had developed in the thousand years following the end of the Roman Empire around the year 500 AD. In most parts of western Europe, Roman law, established from the Code of the Emperor Justinian in the sixth century, continued to provide much of the basis of civil and criminal law from 500 to 1500 AD; canon law covered those legal problems which the establishment of Christianity had created, issues deriving from wills, christening, penitence, ecclesiastical ownership and other purely ecclesiastical problems. In England there is a further area of law to consider: the common law, which was derived from what local people asserted to be the custom from earlier times, from Anglo-Saxon precedents and from the judgements of legal cases since the arrival of the Normans. The Church attempted to reconcile itself to these areas of law by its *ius commune*, the combination of Roman and Canon law which prevailed across Europe.

Ultimately the Church failed to reconcile the two sets of laws and gradually statute law, still in use elsewhere in Europe in the form of Roman law, prevailed. This is certainly what happened in England and eventually by the end of the seventeenth century local church courts were losing credibility. The reason for the diminution in the perceived validity of church courts was simple. The worst punishment to be handed down by any church court was excommunication, which as church scholar R. H. Helmholz points out, 'cut the sinner off from God... it was a "medicinal" sanction. Its primary purpose was to restore the person excommunicated to spiritual health, not to punish him'. Ideally, as we shall see, accusations of witchcraft naturally went to church courts as they were perceived to be actions against the community, which would best be treated by spiritual and moral exhortation from the Church.

Church courts were presided over by the diocesan bishop's Vicar-General. He was legally trained and, before the Reformation, he would have studied canon law at the Universities of Oxford or Cambridge. However, as part of his destruction of papal influence on the English church, Henry VIII had forbidden the study of canon law at the two universities. In consequence, post-Reformation vicars-general might have a qualification in civil law, but gradually expertise in purely church law diminished. A typical pre-Reformation church court case of an accusation of devil-worship in 1518 was that of Elizabeth Sculthorpe who lived in Bisbrooke, Rutland, south-east of Belvoir Castle: 'synce Candilmasse last she hath betaken hir self and all hir children to the devill and clerely forsaken god and the churche... this false bileve was put into hir mynde she knoweth not how but oonly by the devill'. The Vicar-General ordered her to attend church at Stamford and do a complex series of penitential acts, which mainly centred on the repetition of prayers. After the Reformation such minor accusations were still sometimes dealt with by the church courts, provided that the alleged actions did not come within the new post-Reformation statute law.

A good example of another local church court case was the accusation against a licensed curate, Thomas Johnson, who held the living of Cranwell in Lincolnshire, from approximately 1573 to 1607. The Vicar-General of Lincoln diocese, Dr John Belley, proposed eight charges against the Cranwell minister. He was accused of practising 'the worthie science of Phisicke' without a licence from the bishop. Apparently Johnson did 'administer Phisicke unto div[erse] sicke p[er]sons and didest take uppon the[e] to be a wise ma[n] to tell wome[n] they shulde hav[e] a male childe or female childe'. Johnson was accused that he 'did use exercis[e] and practise Invocans or calleinge of spirites'. Johnson was also charged with carrying out 'Inchauntem[en]ts and witchecraftes in telleinge what is become of stolne goodes you are thought to have a familiar'. Clearly Johnson's work as a curate or minister responsible for Cranwell was being investigated by the Lincoln diocesan authorities. His attempt to help his parishioners by medical means was, strictly speaking, illegal as he had not obtained a physician's licence from the Bishop.

It is possible to investigate the career of Thomas Johnson to discover reasons why he should have been investigated by the diocesan church court for witchcraft. He was not a university graduate, having been appointed only as a reader in the Cranwell living in the 1570s by its patron, the Bishop of Lincoln. This position of reader was necessary in the Elizabethan Church of England as there were simply not enough men 'bred in the schools' with a university degree, to administer the 1,271 livings in the diocese of Lincoln at the time. By 1594 Johnson had become the licensed curate, or as the French church put it 'le curé' of Cranwell. In effect he was now the established minister of the parish of Cranwell, for and on behalf of the patron, the Bishop.

In 1603, the apparent date of some of his alleged misdemeanours, he was the official incumbent, living in the vicarage which was worth £3 6s 8d a year and he had a flock of 60 communicants. In 1604 the Church of England issued a new set of canons, the laws of the Church, to which all clergy were to conform by 30 November 1604. All the clergy in Lincoln diocese now had to submit to an official visitation during the summer of 1604, but this coincided with a virulent outbreak of plague. We can only assume that Johnson was involved in helping his parishioners by applying the medical skills he had learned over the thirty years he was responsible for Cranwell. We do not know the result of his accusations, but Johnson still continued in his post at Cranwell until the 1607 visitation, when we find his name was removed and replaced by that of Richard Fleir, though this was not an unusual happening, as several other names were crossed out and replaced with others at the same time.

These two local cases related to witchcraft are typical of church courts and their dealings. The worst punishment in the case of lay people was excommunication, which could be reversed if the individual repented and performed a penance or, in the case of clerics, excommunication and deprivation of their post. It seems as though this did not happen in either of these cases. Clearly the Church acted 'lovingly' (as they termed it) towards its perceived miscreants in a way that Royal judges could not do, as secular judges had no alternative but to apply the punishments laid down by statute law if the accused either confessed or was found guilty. Gradually, church courts diminished in significance, becoming during the seventeenth century disciplinary sessions for spiritual offences, where lay people and clergy were instructed to keep canon law. If any spiritual accusation came up which could be perceived as contrary to statute law it was passed on to magistrates.

Royal Justice

During the sixteenth century both the secular law and the church law in England were increasingly brought under the control of the Crown by parliamentary statute. Roman law, common across Europe, did not prevail in England because of the considerable significance in England of common or customary law. As far as witchcraft was concerned this meant that the situation in England developed somewhat in contrast to those states which preferred Roman law. Perhaps the biggest difference was that both Roman law and canon law allowed torture as part of the process of normal accusation, as it derived from classical Roman morality. In England torture could only be applied in cases of high treason, so people accused of witchcraft in England were not tortured to obtain confessions. The death penalty was reserved in England for treason, felony or serious crime and witchcraft only effectively became a felony in 1563. Also, for reasons that are still not fully understood, the courts of inquisition established across much of Europe, with their use of torture and burning, were never set up in medieval England. For these reasons, witches were not burnt in England, as burning was reserved for heresy and for the two kinds of treason, high treason against the monarch and petty treason when a wife was found guilty of murdering her husband, who was her master in the eyes of the law.

Having made these reservations, it is important to stress that, following the Elizabethan witchcraft law of 1563, several hundred men and women in England were executed for witchcraft between 1563 and 1682. In this respect England differed little from the majority of European countries. Severe outbreaks of plague and intermittent food shortages, following population increase in the sixteenth century, caused a sense of insecurity and contributed to a combination of intense religious belief in the approaching millennium or end of the world. To these were added the tenacious survival of deep rooted folk beliefs and the omnipresence for the first time of cheap reading material, which spread the fictions of sabbaths, creating a virtual reality that led people across Europe to accuse witches. The strengthening of secular legal systems and a new, relatively short-lived focus on witchcraft as a cause of all ills contributed to the number of witchcraft trials.

The survival of documentation has been too haphazard for modern historians to be sure of the number of cases but recent historians suggest that a maximum of 40,000 people were executed in Europe following trials for witchcraft in the sixteenth and seventeenth centuries. Figures such as this do not necessarily help us understand the phenomenon; one is tempted to work out averages such as that one in five hundred people, or two hundred and fifty every year were executed, which would be completely inaccurate since it was a spasmodic rather than a regular happening. What is, however, crucial and central to an understanding is that outbreaks of witchcraft persecution were localised, and that most parts of most European countries had few, if any trials.

In England, if a problem appeared which the church courts could not deal with, local magistrates known as Justices of the Peace (JPs), assisted by petty constables, heard complaints. JPs were appointed by the Crown and were selected either from the county gentry or from borough officials. They oversaw the ever-increasing range of regulations associated with agriculture, apprenticeship, wage rates, food prices, poor law, beggars and vagabonds and laws against Catholics and nonconformists. They swore on oath to

'do equal right to the poor and to the rich after your cunning, wit and power, and after the laws and customs of the realm and statutes thereof made;... and that ye hold your sessions after the form of statutes thereof made and the

159

issues, fines and amercements that shall happen to be made and all forfeitures which shall fall before you ye shall cause to be entered without any concealment or embezzling and truly send them to the Queen's exchequer.'

During Elizabeth's reign the considerable number of new statute laws hugely increased the task of JPs, who were unpaid. They examined all accused people and dealt with them immediately if the offence was a minor misdemeanour. If, however, the offence was serious, the accused were either bound over to appear at the quarter sessions held four times a year before groups of magistrates, or put in prison to await gaol delivery to the county assizes held twice yearly in the county town. Accordingly, Margaret and Philippa Flower were examined and imprisoned by magistrates in Lincoln Jail because they were accused under the 1604 statute law of a serious felony: that they did 'consult, covenant with, entertain, employ, feed or reward any evil and wicked spirit'.

Three statute laws were passed in turn in England by Parliament and the Crown, making witchcraft a felony, *ie:* punishable by death. During the last years of Henry VIII in 1542, a short-lived but harsh act was passed against persons who 'unlawfully have devised and practised invocations and conjurations of spirits... to find treasure... to the destruction of their neighbours' persons and goods... to tell where things lost or stolen should be become... or to provoke any person to unlawful love'. When Edward VI came to the throne as a minor in 1547, his Council was well aware of the extent of threatening legislation passed during Henry's reign. In order to make a fresh start for the new youthful King, and to establish a new spirit in the country where 'subjects... should obey rather for love, and for the necessity and love of a King and prince, than for fear of his straight and severe laws', Parliament was encouraged to repeal a considerable number of Henry's laws which had established new felonies. As a result the law of 1542 making witchcraft a felony was repealed and there was no further legislation until the reign of Elizabeth I. The significant laws against witchcraft were passed by Elizabeth I in 1563 and by her second cousin James I in 1604. Can we understand why these two monarchs decided at the beginning of their reigns to pass new laws against witchcraft?

It was claimed in 1563 that since the repeal of Henry VIII's act:

'many fantastical and devilish persons have devised and practised invocations and conjurations of evil and wicked

160

spirits, and have used and practised witchcrafts, enchantments, charms and sorceries, to the destruction of the persons and goods of their neighbours and other subjects of this realm.'

Almost as soon as Elizabeth became queen a statute against witchcraft was prepared and was, indeed, successfully passed by the House of Commons. The 1559 bill 'whereby the use and practice of Enchantments, Witchcraft and Sorcery is made Felony' went to the House of Lords in April 1559 where it received two out of the necessary three readings. But the bill disappeared among the huge number of bills being discussed; the Parliament lasted from January to May 1559, passing forty Acts, relating especially to the Queen's title, supremacy, Royal income and the uniformity of common prayer.

At Elizabeth's next Parliament in 1563 it was recognised that there was no 'condigne Punishement provided against the Practisers of the wicked offences of Conjuracons and invocacons of evill spirites, and of Sorceries, Enchauntementes Charmes and Witchecrafts'. Accordingly a new bill was prepared and presented to Parliament in 15 February 1563; it was passed by both Houses by 20 March. The final Act was much less harsh than the 1542 Act of Henry VIII, punishing by death only witchcraft which resulted in death, whereas Henry's Act had imposed the death penalty for magic, treasure-hunting [by magic], making images and telling 'where things lost or stollen should become'. Elizabeth's Act punished other acts of witchcraft not resulting in death by

'Imprisonment for the Space of one whole Yere ... and once in every Quarter of the said Yere, shall in some Market Towne, upon the Market Daye or at such tyme as any Fayer shallbee kept there, stande openly upon the Pillorie, by the space of Syxe Houres, and there shall openly confesse his or her Erroure and Offence; and for the Seconde offence, being as ys aforesayd lawfully convicted or attainted, shall suffer Deathe as a Felon, and shall lose the Privilege of Clergie and Sanctuary.'

Marion Gibson points out that the emphasis of this Act was on the nature of the physical harm accused witches caused to their victims and it did not punish by death the notion of keeping familiar spirits. This Elizabethan statute was certainly aimed at halting any kind of witchcraft, but the limitation of Henrician harshness demonstrates an approach to punishment of

161

witchcraft which was milder than that developing on the mainland of Europe, especially in the lands of the Holy Roman Emperor. Consultation or covenanting with wicked spirits was not made an offence in law in itself unless it resulted in actions 'wherby any p[er]son shall happen to be killed or destroyed'.

Following Elizabeth's Act, there were several outbreaks of witchcraft prosecution. However, we will never know how many witches were accused and sent for trial, as most of the records of regional assize courts of England for this period have disappeared. The best set of records to survive relate to the county of Essex where, it is suggested, between 1560 and 1672, 291 persons were tried for witchcraft, 180 of them during Elizabeth's reign. Of these known accused witches 74, that is 24% of them, were executed. It is impossible to state exactly how many accused witches were executed in Elizabeth's and James's reigns. James Sharpe cites a figure of 574 accused witches in the south-eastern assizes of England in the late sixteenth and the seventeenth centuries. Of these, perhaps 200 derived from the period 1580–1600. What these figures indicate is that the first extensive prosecutions for witchcraft in English history took place during the reign of Queen Elizabeth. Alan Macfarlane pointed out that in Essex 'between 1560 and 1680 there are 496 surviving Assize Court prosecutions against supposed black witches. A further 230 men and women from Essex are known to have been presented at ecclesiastical courts for offences related to witchcraft'. Of all these accusations around 25% led to conviction and execution.

Elizabeth, a highly educated woman, was keenly interested in magic like many educated people of her time. She encouraged the Hermetic magician, the Rev Dr John Dee as her court astrologer, to whom she 'vouchsafeth the name of hyr philosopher' for his work in investigating the natural effect of heavenly bodies upon earthly affairs. Dee was commonly looked on as a conjurer. He had two church livings in England, his main one being in Lincolnshire at Long Leadenham, not far from Belvoir Castle, though he would rarely have been in residence there.

> 'Dee's services at court were many and varied. As court astrologer he selected the most propitious date for Elizabeth's coronation. Once, when an image of the Queen with a pin stuck in its heart was found in Lincoln's Inn

Field, a thoroughly alarmed Privy Council asked Dee to counteract any harm intended to her.'

In connection with this kind of witchcraft worry, an Act of Parliament in Elizabeth's reign was passed in 1581, including among other treasonable actions:

'setting or erecting any figure or by casting of nativities or by calculation or by any prophesying, witchcraft, conjurations, or other like unlawful means whatsoever, seek to know, and shall set forth by express words, deeds or writing, how long her Majesty shall live, or who shall reign as a king or queen of this realm of England after her Highness' decease, or else shall advisedly and with a malicious intent against her Highness, utter any manner of direct prophecies to any such intent... that then every such offence shall be felony... and shall suffer pains of death and forfeit as in case of felony is used, without any benefit of clergy or sanctuary.'

Clearly, the Queen, John Dee, the Privy Council and Parliament were all concerned about the possibilities of witchcraft, sorcery and conjuration, particularly if it might be used against the Queen. If the rulers of the country held these opinions, it is little wonder that the belief in witchcraft in the countryside was so strong. In these closing decades of the sixteenth century, witchcraft accusations were at their most widespread.

Soon after this statute law was passed, a case of image magic, 'setting or erecting a figure' *ie:* making an image to bewitch someone, was recorded in the Belvoir Castle records for 1583. A Nottingham magistrate, Sir William Holles, examined Samuel Haslabye, a husbandman who claimed that a surgeon Richard Bate 'did make a picture of waxe wherby he would consume his wyfe's mother and all the rest of her children'. Haslabye 'went to the Constable of that parish and chardged him to go and take it [the image]... before Mr Meare [Mayor] of Nottingham. And within three or four days after that there came the said Bate to Nottingham and ther was apprehended. And then this Examinant was sent for and ther he put in his bound to prosequite the lawe ageanst the said Bate'. We do not know the outcome of this case but it illustrates for us both the process and the social context of most witchcraft accusations. They were local accusations normally arising from intimate family disputes and they were generally implemented by determined family members. Samuel Haslabye, an agricultural smallholder, was able to accuse a medical practitioner and have him arrested.

When James I came to the throne in 1603 London printers, well aware of his work on witchcraft, hastened to reprint his famous text *Daemonologie*. In addition to this popularisation of his notions of sorcery, James gave his Royal assent to a new 'Act concerning Conjuration, Witchcraft and dealing with Evil and Wicked Spirits' which had its first reading in the House of Lords on 27 March 1604 and which was finally printed with the Royal assent on 7 July 1604. As far as one can judge from the Journals of the Houses of Lords and Commons there was considerable interest in this bill and great argument. The original Committee of the Lords appointed to consider the bill turned it down outright and 'thought meet to frame a new Bill instead bearing the same title'.

Twenty-two lords and twelve bishops, assisted by the Justice of the Common Pleas and the Attorney General, sat on the new Committee on 31 March. The Lord Chief Justice of Common Pleas at the time was Sir Edmund Anderson, from Lincolnshire, who was well known for his strong feelings against accused witches. Under Anderson's leadership, the Lords' committee rapidly brought in the new bill on 2 April, when it received its new first reading. The House then gave it a second reading and referred it to the same committee on 11 April. On 7 May the bill passed its third reading and was sent down to the House of Commons where it was considerably amended during its passage through the house. One of the 19 Commons committee members was Henry Hobart, a future Attorney General and Lord Chief Justice of Common Pleas, who was to be one of the Judges of Assize at Lincoln in March 1619.

In what way did this new statute law differ from the 1563 Act? Witchcraft student Gregory Durston answers this question most effectively by referring to a later Chief Justice of the Kings Bench, writing in 1678:

> 'As Mathew Hale was to observe, the Statute of 1604 (I Jac. c. 12., the only Law "now in force against it", replacing the two previous statutes and any common law decisions) separated it into "two degrees". First degree Witchcraft included the conjuration of an evil spirit, charm or sorcery. Second degree witchcraft, passed with a view to ensuring that any use of witchcraft should be "utterly avoided", made offering to find buried treasure or stolen goods, and

164

providing potions or charms that might "provoke any person to unlawful Love" an offence.'

This was the statute according to which the Flower sisters were prosecuted. To find an accused person guilty under the 1604 act for what Hale called first degree witchcraft, the jury had to be satisfied that the accused did 'consult covenant with entertain employ feede or rewarde any evill and wicked Spirit to or for any intent or purpose'. This introduced a new element into capital English witchcraft judgements: the necessity of proving a compact with the Devil. By 1619 the new statute had been in operation for approaching fifteen years and James had watched its operation intently. The well known case of the Lancashire witches had happened in 1612; Sir Edward Bromley presided over the trial and eventual execution of ten witches and, as Stephen Pumfrey states, it was then that 'the demonic pacts and witches'sabbats made their first appearance in England'.

James had become wary of hysteria entering into witchcraft trials and in 1616 he insisted, as a King by divine right with the final responsibility before God for judgement on earth, on intervening in a Leicester witchcraft trial after nine witches had been executed. The climax of the Leicester trial in July 1616 had come when a number of accused women were hanged on the evidence of 'a young gentellman of the adge of 12 or 13 years old'. It was said that the boy 'hath dyvars wonderfull straung fyts in the sight of all the greatest parsons [persons] here, as dyvers knights and ladies and many othars of the bettar sort, most tereble to be tolld'. The author of a letter about the trial, Robert Heyricke, wrote that 'Sir Henry Hastings hath doon wht he cold to hold him in his fit; but he and another as strong as he could not hold him'.

The boy, when examined by the magistrate Sir Henry Hastings, claimed the witches had '6 severall sperits, one in the lykness of a hors, another like a dog, another a cat, another a pullemar, another a fishe, another a code, with whom evary one of them tormented him'. Kittredge has explained the mysterious 'pullemar' as a misprint for 'fullemar' or polecat, and 'code' as a misprint for 'tode' an earlier spelling of 'toad'. There is an account of associated events in the Belvoir Archives, partly taken from the deposition of Sir Henry Hastings of the bewitching of John Smith by Randall and other witches. Hastings was Sheriff of Leicester in 1619 and was a religious man with a strong Protestant bias, and as such was clearly interested in examining people accused of witchcraft.

A month later, when six more women were accused of witchcraft by the same boy and condemned, it was too much for James. He had been on a Royal progress through Leicester and he commanded that the witches who had not yet been executed be reprieved; the boy was sent to the Archbishop of Canterbury, where his behaviour was shown to be merely hysterical. The witches were exonerated, although too late for one who died in prison. What is interesting is that James had stayed at Belvoir Castle on 28 August 1616 and that it was on 24 August 1616 that Dr Ridgley had prescribed 'phisicq to my lord Rosse at Belvoir'. It seems the Flower sisters from Belvoir were accused towards the end of a decade of intense interest in witchcraft and indeed, their case became something of a *cause célèbre*, with three editions of the Belvoir pamphlet in the twenty years following.

Before considering the processes leading up to the Flowers' trial it is important to summarise the Jacobean circumstances relating to witchcraft. New laws had been promulgated in response to the dangers arising from perceived political, social and religious instability. This perception of crisis was nothing new: it is difficult to find any era which does not feel that it is experiencing unique disasters against which action must be taken. What was new under Elizabeth and James was the effective existence of nation-wide secular legislation specifically aimed to overcome the problem of evil deriving from the Devil; this arose during the long reign of Elizabeth and led to the increase in harsh statute law in the place of the rather soft-hearted church law.

But perhaps as important was the nature of access to the law: anybody could ask the village constable to apply the law and as a result of popular printing the law was well known. In addition to this, people often felt that witchcraft was at the heart of problems of the Crown; a good example was the main English Royal scandal of the second decade of the seventeenth century, resulting in the trial of James's favourite Robert Carr, Earl of Somerset, for murder. In fact the huge public interest in this case was as much related to religion as to witchcraft. The Earl of Somerset was known to be keen on a Spanish marriage for Prince Charles, the heir to the throne and antagonism was easily worked up by Protestant preachers on these grounds.

166

Carr was tried for his life in May 1616, found guilty and sentenced to death, although eventually pardoned by James.

It was in July 1616 that the nine Leicester witches had been hanged. The events at Belvoir which came to a head in 1619 reflected this combination of the availability of access to the law, of widespread hysteria regarding the spread of witchcraft and of considerable religious controversy. The Bottesford villagers had recourse to action when gossip about the Flower family became widespread and this coincided with the Earl of Rutland's understandable concern for his children. It is now clear that he was prepared to use any method to keep his heir alive; strangely in 1619 the Earl offered to cure people of the stone by the use of mistletoe. This combination of the villagers' animosity and of the Earl's beliefs was to prove fatal to the Flowers.

The Examinations

As soon as a serious accusation was laid against members of the Flower family, a constable would have drawn this to the attention of the local Leicestershire magistrates. The two sisters were examined in January and February 1619 and this evidence was presented in March 1619 to the Grand Jury of Lincolnshire gentlemen, who found that there was a *billa vera* or true case for them to answer at the trial before a petty jury at the County Assize Court held in Lincoln. The Belvoir witchcraft accusations were further bolstered by examination of three other Vale of Belvoir women, Joan Willimot of Goadby Marwood, Ellen Greene of Stathern and Anne Baker of Bottesford.

A detailed study of the ten examinations (reproduced in the Belvoir pamphlet in the Appendix) puts us today into the same position as the Lincolnshire gentlemen of the Grand Jury who, by presenting Margaret and Philippa to the Assize Judges, virtually sealed their fate. It was the meeting of the Grand Jury which decided exactly which imprisoned, accused prisoners should be put on trial. We know that the Earl of Rutland, as Lord Lieutenant, went to Lincoln in March 1619, so presumably he headed the Grand Jury which represented the landed gentry of Lindsey, Kesteven and Holland, the three Parts of the County of Lincolnshire. The assizes were significant meeting times for the gentry, held twice yearly; at this period they always began with a sermon and an official statement of legal policy from the Crown.

In between the sermon and the actual trial, the Grand Jury considered the examinations of the accused, which had been 'taken and charily preserved for the continuing of sufficient evidence against [the accused]' (*page 24*). Bailey's Dictionary defines 'charily' as 'with a great deal of care and regard'. Can the examination be considered to be a true record of what the accused and the witnesses actually said and believed? Eleven pages of evidence are bound to contain some error, if only printing errors. A careful study of the original text of the three seventeenth-century editions of the pamphlet show that such errors exist. Two names are misspelt or incorrect – 'Peate' for 'Peake' and 'Francis Lord Willoughby of Ersby' for 'Robert Lord Willoughby of Eresby', presumably by confusion with Francis Earl of Rutland. In the time before the mid-eighteenth century standardisation of spelling, varied spellings are to be expected. The early eighteenth century version of the pamphlet is, however, different from these three earlier versions, in that the religious intensity of the Jacobean period disappears, to be replaced by a blander version. The 1619 Belvoir pamphlet account of Joan Willimot's examination on 2 March 1619 specified that a 'Spirit did aske of her her soule' (*page 17*) whereas the 1715 version reads that a spirit 'enquired about her soul', a completely different understanding.

Such apparent changes of meaning should not detract from the intensity of theological depth revealed in the 1619 chapbook. Rather, it reveals for us the reality of Jacobean beliefs and the manner in which they led to outcomes which were increasingly perceived as unlikely by the eighteenth century. What the examination by the nine magistrates indicates is the seriousness with which they applied themselves to clarifying witchcraft accusations. Undoubtedy the fact that the presumed victims were the children of the Lord Lieutenant of Lincolnshire would encourage them to apply themselves with assiduity to the case. The nine magistrates apparently examined five women from the area surrounding Belvoir Castle. It is difficult to work out the exact sequence of events, even though all examinations are dated. The examinations are not printed in the order in which they occurred; two of them were apparently inadvertently dated 17th March – a week after the execution of Margaret and Philippa – and they were undertaken by magistrates from Leicester and Bottesford, both in the county of Leicestershire, and from Belvoir, Aisthorpe, Market Deeping, Grimsthorpe and Brocklesby, all in Lincolnshire. In order to try to understand this complicated sequence of examinations it is essential to establish the area in which these accused women lived.

It is fairly easy to do this in the case of the women examined. Margaret and Philippa Flower lived near Belvoir Castle, possibly close to Blackberry Hill, which was earlier called Black Borrow Hill in the examination of Joan Willimot on 17 March (*page 19*). Anne Baker, who knew so many of the significant Bottesford families, was herself from Bottesford. Joan Willimot was a widow from Goadby Marwood, a few miles south of Belvoir. Her associate Ellen Greene lived in Stathern, just to the north of Goadby Marwood and a similar distance south-west of Belvoir. All the women involved came from a compact area centred on Belvoir Castle and they knew one another before the trial.

Anne Baker and Joan Willimot were examined at the very end of February and the beginning of March 1619. The dating is interesting as Joan Willimot was examined on a Sunday, 28 February and again two days later on 2 March. Meanwhile, Anne Baker was examined on Monday, Tuesday and Wednesday, 1, 2 and 3 March. These examinations post-dated the main examinations of the Flower sisters and were recorded at the same time as the Lincolnshire gentry were collecting in Lincoln for the Assizes. It appears that the Flower sisters were accused some time at the end of 1618 or the beginning of 1619 and were sent to Lincoln Castle prison to be held for examination, pending the Spring or Lent Assizes. Whether the three other witnesses were incarcerated in Lincoln is unknown. The examination reports do not state where the interviews took place, but it is possible to hazard guesses from the residences and locations of the justices who carried out the examination.

To modern eyes, one of the most extraordinary elements of the legal process was the direct intercommunication between accused, witnesses and socially high-ranking men responsible for justice in the counties of Lincolnshire and Leicestershire. The Earl of Rutland and his brother Sir George Manners, Lord Willoughby d'Eresby and Sir William Pelham were the most socially distinguished members of the Lincolnshire aristocracy and gentry. In 1623 the Earl was the Lord 'Lieutenant in the County of Lincoln and a commissioner of the Peace and Custos Rotulorum in the County of Northampton and a commissioner of the Peace and of Oyer and Terminer in Yorkshire', and in other counties. He was constable of Nottingham Castle, Keeper of Sherwood Forest, a Privy Councillor and a Knight of the Garter and close to James I, with whom he hunted.

Lord Willoughby d'Eresby (1582–1642) was a close friend of the Earl; he was, in fact, Robert Bertie, not Francis as the Belvoir pamphlet calls him, and he was the Lord of Grimsthorpe and Deputy Lord Lieutenant of Lincolnshire. Like the Earl of Rutland, he was a member of the House of Lords, becoming Lord High Chamberlain and Earl of Lindsey in 1626. Both noblemen held high office in the navy on occasions: Francis Earl of Rutland became Lord High Admiral, sent to bring Prince Charles (later Charles I) back from Spain, but without his hoped-for Spanish Catholic bride. Lord Willoughby became the vice-admiral of the fleet which took the Duke of Buckingham to France in 1626.

If these two great aristocrats were not enough, on 25 February the Flower sisters also had to face Sir George Manners and Sir William Pelham. Sir George, who lived at Fulbeck in Lincolnshire, was the final surviving brother of Francis, sixth Earl of Rutland; he was to become the seventh Earl on his brother's death in 1632. He was a Member of Parliament for Lincolnshire in 1614 and during the 1620s, when as an active parliamentarian he was involved in the reform of laws. He had been knighted by the Earl of Essex in Ireland in 1599 and had always been politically active. The fourth examiner of the two sisters was Sir William Pelham, son of the earlier Sir William who had been Chief Justice in Ireland and who was himself Sheriff of Lincoln in 1602/3. When James staged his great progress through England to claim the throne, William Pelham had been knighted by him at Belvoir, on the first of James's many visits there.

Belvoir, where they frequently met socially, was the connecting link between these four magistrates. The Castle itself, although surrounded on three sides by Leicestershire, is strictly speaking in Lincolnshire. The four were connected by even closer links than their official positions as Lord Lieutenants, Knights of the Shire and Sheriffs for that county: they were actually related, by blood or marriage. They called each other 'brother' or 'cousin': the senior Sir William Pelham had married the grand-daughter of the first Earl of Rutland. The Manners and Berties, whose seats at Belvoir and Grimsthorpe were close to each other, were interconnected by marriage with each other and with the Nevilles, Sidneys and Harringtons.

This extraordinary consanguinity between aristocratic and gentry families was the basis of both local and national government in Jacobean times. Once the Flower sisters had totally alienated the Manners family, the power of the English state could be used against them. All that seemed necessary to end the threat to the heirs of the Earls of Rutland was the application of the force of law, locally dominated by the kindred of the Rutlands. Nonetheless, the actual process of law had to be seen to be applied, and for this intelligent magistrates with legal training were required.

The sisters were examined in particular by Sir William Pelham, who had a strong legal background. Having been Sheriff in 1602–3, he was a Deputy Lieutenant of Lincolnshire to the Lieutenancies of both Roger the fifth Earl and Francis the sixth Earl of Rutland. Pelham had been legally trained at Gray's Inn, following study at New College, Oxford; he had been a JP for many years and was Knight of the Shire for Lincolnshire. Pelham had been a soldier in the continental wars during the first decade of the seventeenth century, after making a grand tour of the universities of Europe, including Strasbourg, Heidelberg, Wittenberg, Leipzig, Paris and perhaps Geneva according to Anthony à Wood. Wood expressed this youthful activity: 'Mars distracted him from the studies of Minerva as he himself used to say'.

Having brought up a huge family of twenty children, in his old age in the 1620s Pelham devoted himself to religion and scholarship. His estate was at Brocklesby, a few miles west of Grimsby; he was able to travel regularly to Lincoln, where he carried out the first recorded examination of Philippa Flower on 2 February 1619. This was the evidence recorded in the pamphlet as being 'brought in at the Assizes as evidence against her sister Margaret' (*page 21*). William Pelham was associated in this examination by Mr Butler, who was possibly William Butler of Cotes by Stow, Lincolnshire, a fellow-student at Cambridge and then in London where he studied at Lincoln's Inn. Margaret and Philippa were interviewed by qualified lawyers, not only by gentry closely associated with the Manners family.

It is this evidence to Pelham and Butler given by Philippa on 4 February and that given by Margaret on 22 January (*pages 21– 3*), presumably to the same magistrates, that fully opened up the story of apparent witchcraft. The examinations must have taken

171

place in Lincoln Jail as they were carried out by local Lincolnshire magistrates. What these magistrates were looking for, if they were to present evidence for the felony of witchcraft, was confession to the capital crime of making a compact with the Devil. It does not appear from the confessions of 22 January and 4 February 1619 that the two sisters then specifically confessed to a compact with the Devil. They told their story of how they tried to harm the children of the Earl by sympathetic magic. This involved taking materials associated with the children, notably gloves, wool from their mattresses and 'a peece of handkercher of the Lady Katherine the Earles daughter' (*page 23*). These materials were heated up, burned or buried, in the expectation that the same effects would happen to the children. These confessions were not enough for accusations of felonious compact with the Devil.

Both Pelham and Butler lived to the north of Lincoln and were frequent attenders at the county assizes. Another magistrate from close to Lincoln was Alexander Amcotts of Wickenby. Amcotts was a Lincolnshire JP, well acquainted with the law through his nephew, also called Alexander Amcotts (1593–1635), who was a counsellor at law and Deputy Recorder of Lincoln. Amcotts was the justice who interviewed Joan Willimot just before the March Lincoln assizes. The stories she told him involved the same kind of magic as did the Flowers' stories: the use of items of clothing to achieve magical aims of harm. Joan also talked at length about spirits and it was this which began to reinforce the evidence from the end of February.

It appears that the crucial examinations were those taking place on 25 February before the Earl, his brother Sir George, Robert Bertie Lord Willoughby d'Eresby and Sir William Pelham (*pages 23–4*). Philippa confessed that she 'hath a Spirit sucking on her in the forme of a white Rat' and that there was an 'agreement betwixt her Spirit and hir selfe'. She claimed that she was still in contact with this spirit as 'the last time it suckt was on Tuesday at night the 23 of February [1619]'. Margaret's confession was even more precise and it would have been these words which condemned her. She specified two familiar spirits and 'when shee first entertained them she promised them her soule, and they [the spirits] covenanted to doe all things which she commanded them'. She, too, admitted that on 'the 30 of January last past being Saturday, foure Divells appeared unto her in Lincolne Jayle'.

Using the precise dates of these examinations, in particular the correct relationship of the dates and days of the week as specified for 1619, we can reconstruct the full process of examination. The three members of the Flower family were arrested in the Belvoir area in January 1619 and sent to await judicial examination in Lincoln Prison. On the way, Mistress Joan Flower died, clearly terrified by her ordeal. Her two daughters were imprisoned in Lincoln Prison, certainly from 22 January, in the depth of winter. As they awaited examination, so they would have had limited food, being reliant on the charity of the prison-keepers. At no stage would they have had the possibility of legal defence, as this did not exist for anyone who was an accused felon. The legal theory of the Jacobean period was straightforward. The object was to discover the truth; the whole legal process was posited around the concept of confrontation between the accuser and the accused.

It seems strange to us today that it was the family of the victim who actually carried out the investigation in this case. This was not a problem in Jacobean times; it was assumed that the truth would emerge out of the confrontation. The only help the accused would have had would have been from the prison chaplain, whose role was to reconcile the accused with their likely fate. If they had, as they claimed, been dealing in sympathetic magic with the aim of causing harm, this would prey on their minds. The nightmares of the two girls in prison can only be imagined; it is not at all surprising that they gave complex accounts of visits from spirits. On 25 February Margaret described the four devils appearing 'at eleven or twelve o'clock at midnight: The one stood at her bedsfeete, with a black head like an Ape, and spake unto her, but what, shee cannot well remember, at which shee was very angry because he would speak no plainer, or let her understand his meaning: the other three were Rutterkin, Little Robin, and Spirit, but shee never mistrusted them, nor suspected herself till then' (*page 24*). The sisters' confessions of talking with spirits and having familiar spirits condemned them.

The Trial

A Jacobean trial was generally a short process which was, as David Lemmings explains, 'organised around the principle that judges and jurors had to make their discretionary decisions about verdict and (especially) sentence on the basis of an unmediated exchange between the defendant and the prosecutors'. This exchange was normally brief; trials lasted generally no more than half an hour as it was assumed that the pre-trial examinations had processed and created all necessary evidence. The central way in which Jacobean criminal trials differed from modern trials was the total absence of defence lawyers. Certainly, people accused of witchcraft were not allowed defending advocates; the Devil's power to influence intermediaries was such a concern at the heart of the Jacobean understanding of witchcraft that no opportunity for this had to be given. James I felt strongly, that 'by the Devils means can never the Divil be cast out', quoting Mark chapter 3 verse 23. So a trial must be a straightforward confrontation between the accused and the accusers, to be mediated by judge and jury.

A trial at the assizes, then, had four elements: the accused, the accusation, the jury and the judge. Another possible element of the legal process almost completely absent in common law trials for felony in England was torture. The accused by common law could not be tortured in England; torture in law could only be allowed by Privy Council warrants and all those warrants issued between 1540 and 1640 applied only to Star Chamber cases, normally associated with charges of treason. Gregory Durston points out that the 'last case in which torture was used in England for an ordinary felony [i.e. not treason] occurred in 1597'.

An important element of the treatment of the accused was that they were not put on oath when they were being examined. It was thought that this would ensure that they were not inhibited in any way during examinations and therefore they were likely to be speaking from the heart. The accused were not told of the nature of the accusation against them until the day of the trial. This circumstance clarifies the relationship of the accused with Justices of the Peace and with the judge. As there had been so much new legislation passed in Elizabeth's reign, the magistrates felt overwhelmed with work. Accordingly, they carried out their role as examiners if a person was accused; they wrote up the examination and having made the initial judgement that the accused should answer a felonious charge, the magistrates then washed their hands of the case until the assize, leaving its preparation in the hands of the clerks of the assize. Meanwhile, the accused remained in prison until the Royal judges of assize were due to appear.

The accusers were generally put on oath when they made their accusation to the magistrate. A side-effect of this would be a restriction on the numbers of accusations made. This implies that the accusers of the Flower sisters felt strongly that there was a case to answer. Quite how many accusations of witchcraft actually went to assize in the Jacobean period is impossible to say. Alan Macfarlane's suggestion that witchcraft accounted for 5% of all criminal assize indictments between 1558 and 1680 is helpful in indicating its relative rarity. The duty of the examining magistrate was to attend the assize trial to certify that the accusations were in order.

In the case of the accusations against the Flower sisters prior to the trial, the only direct evidence we have is the examinations of Margaret and Philippa themselves and of the two peripheral women Anne Baker and Joan Willimot. The dates of their evidence lead to the conclusion that all four examinations were treated as part of the testimony against them. Clearly, Margaret and Philippa were held in Lincoln Prison and each of them accused her sister of being involved in witchcraft. The rambling evidence of Anne Baker was taken on 1, 2 and 3 March 1619, only days before the trial, and this examination must have taken place in Lincoln, as we know that the magistrates involved (the Earl, his brother and the Rev Samuel Fleming) all went to Lincoln for the trial. Joan Willimot was examined on 28 February and 2 March by Alexander Amcotts, the magistrate from just north of Lincoln and he was supported by a Lincolnshire rector Thomas Robinson. Presumably, then, these four women could have had the role of accusation witnesses at the trial; in effect, the evidence given by Margaret and Philippa, self-incriminating as it was, was what ensured their conviction.

Was the Earl the chief accuser? According to the pamphlet, 'when the Earle [of Rutland] heard of their apprehension he hasted doune with his brother Sr. George, and sometimes examining them himself, and sometimes sending them to other, at last left them to the trial at Law, before the Judges of Assise at Lincolne' (*page 11*). This implies that he was not involved in the actual trial, although as Lord Lieutenant he was inevitably concerned with the assembling of gentry, magistrates, clerics and Royal judges before the actual trial process. It is possible that he or his family made accusations, as the pamphlet does state that some other examinations were made which were not printed in the pamphlet itself. Apparently the Earl 'urged nothing against [the Flower sisters] more that their onne confessions, and so quietly left them to judicial triall' (*page 25*). The evidence once collected was held by the county sheriff to be made available to the clerks of the circuit of Royal judges who came twice a year to Lincoln.

As soon as the assizes opened, following the assize sermon and the judge's charge to the jury, the evidence was presented by constables to the Grand Jury. Each criminal accusation had to be presented initially to the Grand Jury to see if there was a case to answer. This process was generally somewhat rushed as the judges clearly wanted to get through the cases as soon as possible, but they had to wait for the judgement of the local gentry, called together to see if the evidence warranted trial. We do not know the names of the local gentlemen summoned by the Sheriff of Lincoln to attend the Grand Jury, but they would have been 'gentlemen of the best figure in the county' as Blackstone explained in his eighteenth-century Commentaries. The judge of assize at York in Lent 1620 explained in his charge to the grand jury exactly what was happening:

> 'In the visitacyons of justice the course hath ever beene to begin the service with a charge to the jurors of the grand inquest of every countye, putting them in mynde of all the offences against the lawe whereof they are to enquire, to the end that they who live in the countye and have an interest in the country and are sencyble of the mischeyfs which these offences doe breede may present the offenders to the judges, who thereupon are to precede according to the terms of theyre commissyon'.

These words place the responsibility for finding out who were genuine offenders squarely on the shoulders of the Grand Jury.

Again, this seems strange to twenty-first century ears. This indeterminate number of local gentry, some JPs, some learned in the law, but the majority simply gentlemen, had to decide whether the evidence was such that the case should go forward to trial. They did not see the accused, having to make their judgement from the examinations and always being aware of the judges breathing down their necks, insisting that they find *vera billa* or true bills to indict people accused of breaking the Royal law. On the whole the grand juries did not bring in findings of *'ignoramus'*, the judgement which dismissed the case. Certainly in the case of the Flower sisters, we know that the grand jury brought in a response of *'vera billa'*.

When enough *vera billa* cases were ready, the accused were all brought before the judge and told to plead 'guilty' or 'not

176

guilty'. As soon as enough of them had pleaded 'not guilty' a petty jury was empanelled. The difference between a petty jury and the grand jury was twofold. The petty jury was twelve in number whereas a Grand Jury could be double that number. Secondly, the petty jury was frequently of a lower social rank. This was deliberate. The task of the Grand Jury was an intellectual duty: they were presumed to be well-educated men who could understand the law and thus judge if a person had seriously offended against the law of the land. The task of the petty jury was different. They were expected to judge whether a person was guilty or not from their intimate knowledge of the social circumstances of the local community and of local custom and practice. The only qualification for membership of a petty jury was to be a freeholder, similar to the forty shilling freehold right to vote at parliamentary elections.

This jury had local knowledge of which the judge was not aware; this was seen as central to their role. They were expected to devote to the case all their local awareness and understanding, especially of the honesty of local witnesses. The petty jury in effect represented the community which was affected by crime and which needed to be purged by a full investigation which laid blame on the proper culprits. The task, then, of the petty jury was to listen to the Crown witnesses and to question the accused. Ideally the case was presented and the accused could question the evidence by speaking at any stage. In practice, all depended on the judge who was absolute master of the proceedings. This circumstance somewhat militated against the intention of a Jacobean felony trial which was to allow all four parties, accused, accusers, jury and judge, full inter-communication. In reality all depended on the nature of the presiding judge. The jury decided their verdict and the prisoners were held till the end of the trials to hear their sentence or to be freed if found not guilty.

The judges of assize were absolute masters of the proceedings and the fate of the accused was ultimately in their hands. Although the documentation of the actual Lincoln trial itself has been lost, it is possible to understand a little more of it in two ways. One is by a study of the two judges involved and the second is by a study of parallel cases. The two Flower sisters were 'specially arraigned & condemned before Sir Henry Hobart and Sir Edward Bromley, Judges of Assize, for confessing themselves actors in the destruction of Henry, Lord Rosse, with their damnable practises against others the Children of the Right Honourable Francis Earle of Rutland' (*page 1*). Both these judges were well-known. Sir Henry Hobart (c.1554–1625) was the Lord Chief Justice of the Common Pleas, that is the Royal judge with overall national responsibility for the civil law. The other judge in the 1619 Lincoln Lent Assizes held during the first week of March was Sir Edward Bromley (1563–1626), Baron of the Exchequer in 1610–12, a member of the principal court of equity in England. These two judges, significant Royal servants, represented two of the highest law courts of England, the Common Pleas which was concerned with the civil law, that is, cases between individuals, and the Exchequer, the court which applied equity, *ie:* judgements based on equal hearing of all the evidence in financial cases.

Sir Henry Hobart and Sir Edward Bromley were the two judges appointed by the Crown to oversee cases in the county assize courts of the Midland Circuit in Lent 1619. King James called all his judges together before they left London to go on circuit across the country, so they were well aware of James's concerns and above all they were anxious to apply the law as he interpreted it. James believed fervently that it was 'necessary that a King should deliver his thoughts to his people'. This was one purpose of the Assize Circuits: the King told his judges what they were to do and say as they travelled his country and met his subjects. The judges' task was to 'declare and establish the will of God' through their judgements. James stresses that 'As Kings borrow their power from God, so Judges from Kings: And as Kings are to accompt to God, so Judges unto God and Kings.'

Every judge knew that James had written about witchcraft and that he insisted on the verse from the Book of Exodus, newly translated in his Authorised Version of the Bible as 'Thou shalt not suffer a witch to live'. But they also knew from his *Dæmonologie* that 'Judges ought to beware to condemne any, but such as they are sure are guiltie, neither should the clattering reporte of a carling [an old woman, a witch] serve in so weightie a case. Judges ought indeede to beware whome they condemne: For it is as great a Crime (as Solomon sayeth) *to condemne the innocent, as to let the guiltie escape free*; neither ought the report of any one infamous person, be admitted for a sufficient proofe, which can stand of no law'. The judges would also have known that, as James Sharpe expressed it, that 'James, at least as monarch of England, seems to have been

178

more likely to intervene to save witches than to secure their conviction'.

Both Hobart and Bromley would have been aware of the famous case in Leicester in 1616, when ultimately James had intervened to free witches accused by a child. This case, discussed earlier, had originally been before the two Midland Circuit judges Sir Randolf Crewe and Sir Humphrey Winch, the former a Speaker of the Commons in 1614 and the latter a judge of the Court of the Common Pleas. Winch 'fell into considerable disgrace for [his] conduct of the trial'. We do not know for certain which of the two Lincoln Assize judges, Hobart or Bromley, actually presided at the trial of the Flower sisters. The normal rule at Assizes was for one judge to oversee the criminal cases and the other the civil cases, generally known then as the *nisi prius* cases. We can, however, guess that Hobart as Lord Chief Justice of the Common Pleas, the civil law court, would preside over civil actions. After all, he was the senior judge and there was considerable money to be made from the fees payable by both parties in civil actions. Also it is more likely that Bromley would have to take responsibility for the witchcraft case as he was well known as the judge responsible for the execution of up to ten witches in the famous Lancashire trial of the Pendle witches in 1612.

The story of the Lancashire witches is by far the best known and best studied of all English witchcraft accounts, and so it is useful to use it as a model for how the Flowers' trial could have progressed, since the accounts of their Lincoln trial have not survived. In particular, the part played by Sir Edward Bromley, the judge in the Pendle case, has been thoughtfully analysed by Stephen Pumfrey, who suggests that the account of the Lancaster trial, written immediately after the event by Thomas Potts, was deliberately designed to present Bromley as dedicated to applying King James's view of witchcraft.

What is intriguing to us is that Potts' long study, *The Wonderful Discoverie of the Witches in the County of Lancaster,* was printed in 1613 by William Stansby for John Barnes, foreshadowing the printing of the Belvoir pamphlet by George Eld for John Barnes in 1619. Potts's volume is by far the longest of the English sixteenth- and seventeenth-century accounts of witchcraft accusations, at 188 pages. It was authorised by the circuit judges Sir James Altham and Sir Edward Bromley and written at their request by the clerk of the circuit 'Thomas Potts Esquier'.

It also appears that Bromley actually revised the text of the pamphlet as he wrote 'I tooke upon mee to revise and correct it, that nothing might passe but matter of Fact, apparent against them by record'.

Thomas Potts' work began with the main examinations of the suspects by one justice of the peace, Roger Nowell. In general, they are like the Belvoir examinations: familiar spirits are specified by name, such as Tibbe and Fancie; 'one spirit appeared in the likeness of a browne Dogge'. A picture was made 'to take a mans life away by witchcraft' and burned. One 'wicked Spirit moved [Anne Whittle alias Chattox] that she would become his Subject and give her Soule unto him'. Alison Device 'sayth, that two years agon, her Graundmother (called Elizabeth Sowthern, alias old Demdike) did sundry times in going or walking together as they went begging, perswade and advise this Examinate to let a Devill or Familiar appeare unto her; and that shee this Examinate, would let him sucke at some part of her'.

In this respect the examinations are similar to those in the Belvoir pamphlet, but at the end of the initial collection of examinations two extraordinary suggestions were made. The first was that plans were made by the accused 'Children and Friends being abroad at libertie' for a 'speciall meeting at Malking Tower in the Forrest of Pendle, upon Good-fryday, within a weeke after they were committed, of all the most dangerous, wicked and damnable witches in the County farre and neere. Upon Good-fryday they met, according to solemne appoyntment, solemnized this great Feastivall day according to their former order, with great cheare, merry company and much conference'. In other words, this was an account of a witches' Sabbath – the first recorded one in the stories of English witchcraft.

But more ominous for the prospect of a fair trial was the alleged plans made at this meeting. Potts claimed that 'In the end, in this great Assemblie, it was decreed M Covell [the County Coroner] by reason of his Office, shall be slaine before the next Assises. The Castle of Lancaster to be blown up, and ayde and assistance be sent to kill M Lister [junior]'. With such accusations swirling around, it is little wonder that an extensive trial for witchcraft got under way. A week prior to the Lancaster trial, the Judges of Assize at York had hanged Jennet Preston for the bewitching of Mr Lister senior and Potts included an account of this in the pamphlet on the Lancaster case.

180

The events of 1612 in Lancashire were associated with family disputes and troubles in exactly the same way as in the Belvoir case. The accused witches mainly belonged to two families. The first was the family of 'Old Demdike', a very old widow, and her daughter Elizabeth Device, who had three grandchildren, Alizon, James and Jennet. The second family was that of Anne Whittle, known as Chattox, who had a daughter Anne Redfearne. The animosity between these families reflects that between the Flower family and other local Belvoir families, particularly the Fairbairns. But such interfamilial disputes were quite common and did not in themselves usually lead to trials for witchcraft.

The actual event which triggered the accusation in the Lancashire case happened on 18 March 1612: Alizon Device was accused of bewitching a 'poore Pedler by name John Law'. Potts gives a complete record of Alizon Device's trial, and this is the closest that we can get to understanding the trial of the Flower sisters. Even though the account by Potts appears to be a minute by minute record, there are many inconsistencies which appear simply to have been ignored. There was no defence lawyer to pick up the discrepancies and the demeanour of the accused girl was such that she seems to have been overwrought:

'This Alizon Device, Prisoner in the Castle of Lancaster, being brought to the barre before the great Seat of Justice, was there according to the former order and course indicted and arraigned, for that shee feloniously had practised, exercised, and used her Devillish and wicked Arts, called Witch-crafes [sic], Inchantments, Charmes and Sorceries in, and upon one John Law, a Petti-chapman and him had lamed, so that his bodie wasted and consumed etc Contra formam Statuti etc et contra pacem dicti Domini Regis, Coronam et Dignitatem etc'.

The two Flower sisters would each have been tried in this manner, being accused that they 'fellioniously... practised... witchcraft against the form of the statute etc. And against the peace of the Crown and the Dignity of the said Lord King'.

There are three versions of Alizon Device's encounter with the pedlar in Potts's pamphlet: Alizon's, the pedlar's and that of the pedlar's son. In her version, he would not open his pack when she 'demanded of the said Pedler to buy some pinnes of him'. The pedlar said she 'was very earnest with him for pinnes, but he would give her none'. The pedlar's son said 'she had no money to pay for them withal; but... he gave her some pinnes'. The son went on to claim that 'by this Devillish art of Witchcraft his head is drawn awrie, his Eyes and face deformed, His speech not well to be understood, his Thighes and Legges starcke lame: his Armes lame especially the left side, his handes lame and turned out of their course'. Modern medical practitioners would tend to look on this as evidence of a stroke.

What is of interest to the Belvoir trial is twofold: firstly the continued references to animals as familiar spirits who could help in witchcraft and secondly the direct participation of Sir Edward Bromley. There are references to a 'Black-Dogge' providing yet another example of an ubiquitous familiar spirit, the equivalent of Abraham Fleming's Black Dog who caused mayhem in Elizabethan Bungay and Blythburgh in East Anglia, according to his 1577 pamphlet. If cats appear to be involved in the Belvoir story, dogs dominate the Pendle account, particularly brown and black dogs.

This account of Alizon Device's trial showed how prisoners were treated by the judge during a trial. Witnesses waited outside the Moot-Hall where Sir Edward Bromley presided. A local magistrate, Sir Thomas Gerard, 'moved the Court to call the poore Pedlar, who was there readie, and had attended all the Assizes, to give evidence for the Kings Majestie, against the said Alizon Device, Prisoner at the Barre, even now upon her Triall'. Gerard was the brother of John Gerard, a Catholic priest recently escaped from England and he had recently been made one of King James's first baronets. On the arrival of the pedlar, Alizon went 'humbly upon her knees at the Barre with weeping teares, prayed the Court to heare her'. At this stage Sir Edward Bromley 'commanded shee should bee brought out from the Prisoners neare unto the Court' and that she should confess. After her confession, Bromley 'beholding also the poore distressed Pedlar, standing by, commanded him upon his oath to declare the manner how, and in what sort he was handled'. This prosecution evidence and her confession condemned Alizon 'whereupon she was carried away, untill she should come to the Barre to receive her judgement of death'.

Thus was 'Alizon Device convicted upon her owne Confession'. This was exactly what happened to Margaret and Philippa Flower, and the final event similar to theirs was that Alizon was witnessed against by her sibling, James Device who, like the two Flower sisters, was also executed for witchcraft. The Lincoln trial must go alongside the Lancaster events as part of a deliberate attack by local society on a particular family which had over the years been regarded as troublemakers and had gained the reputation of being witches.

The Lincoln trial is not documented at all apart from the Belvoir pamphlet and the ballad. We can, however, conclude that what led to the hanging of Margaret and Philippa Flower was their confession and their mutual accusations. The examinations by local magistrates were the origins of their confessions. As at Lancaster, it was the confessions involving communication with spirits which were 'brought in at the Assizes as evidence' (*page 21*). In both trials, Catholic magistrates were involved. Sir Thomas Gerard and the Earl of Rutland were closet Catholics; both were close to King James who had knighted Sir Thomas on his arrival in England in 1603. It is partly this association between traditional Catholic understanding of spirit and the apparent wish to support James that led to the determination to bring these quarrelling families to trial.

Aftermath
There is no evidence regarding the execution of the Flower sisters other than the date given precisely as 11 March 1619 in the Belvoir pamphlet. Clearly, this was immediately after the end of the Lincoln Assizes which took place during the first week of March. The earliest day on which the Lincoln trial could have taken place was Thursday 4 March 1619 as the last dated piece of evidence was 3 March. Within a week of the first hearings, Margaret and Philippa were hanged. This was not unusual. At Lancaster in 1612 the trials had taken place on 18 to 19 August and the ten guilty offenders were hanged on Thursday 20 August, the following day.

The question then arises of what happened to the other three witnesses in the Belvoir trial, Anne Baker of Bottesford, Joan Willimot of Goadby Marwood and Ellen Greene of Stathern. It is tempting to consider whether the judges went on to Leicester to deal with them, but this was not a possible scenario. The route of the Midland Circuit was clearly laid down, and it was Warwick, Coventry, Leicester, Derby, Nottingham, Lincoln, Oakham and Northampton. One possibility is that they were tried at the City of Leicester court, but as the records for 1619 are lost we cannot verify that. It is strange, however, that the third examination of Joan Willimot and the only examination of Ellen Greene are dated clearly as 17 March 1619; these two examinations were carried out by Sir Henry Hastings and by the Rev Samuel Fleming, both Leicestershire justices and Hastings had been deeply involved in the Leicester trial of July 1616.

If we have no knowledge of the fates of Anne Baker, Joan Willimot and Ellen Greene, we are able to establish in great detail exactly what happened to the Earl and his family. Francis the sixth Earl maintained a delicately balanced existence, as a 'church Catholic', implying occasional attendance at Church of England services while remaining at heart a Roman Catholic. On occasions there were attempts to certify him as a Catholic recusant, but he avoided penalties by judicious movements of residence from one county to another when he was accused. The great tragedy of his life, and of his wife's, must have been the eventual death of his second and only surviving son Francis. The boy was never strong and at the beginning of March 1620 he died. He suffered from epilepsy or the 'falling sickness' as it was known then. This second of the two sons of Francis and Cecily, sixth Earl and Countess of Rutland, was buried in a 'chappell at Westminster' on 7 March 1620, exactly a year after the trial of the Flower sisters. His funeral cost £50. The Earl had spent a similar sum, £60, on the prosecution of the accused witches, but it had not saved his remaining son.

The death of the Earl's heir left the way open for George Villiers, the Royal favourite, to negotiate a huge dowry in order to marry Katherine, the Earl's daughter by his first marriage, his only surviving child and now his heir. Katherine had to renounce her Catholic faith in order to marry Villiers, but eventually she returned to the Catholic Church. The connection with Villiers, who became the Duke of Buckingham in 1623, put the Earl at the heart of English and European politics. Working with King James, Buckingham, aided by Rutland, attempted to undertake the complex process of reconciling Protestant and Catholic Europe by marrying Charles, Prince of Wales, James's only surviving son, to the Infanta of Spain, eldest daughter of the King of Spain. After Charles and Buckingham had travelled to Spain to finalise the marriage, the Earl was appointed Lord High Admiral in 1623 to sail in triumph to Spain, to bring back the betrothed pair and with them the apotheosis of James's dream of a peaceful and tolerant Europe.

Unfortunately, all went wrong: the Spanish refused to back the English attempts to force the Holy Roman Emperor to return the Palatinate state on the Rhine to James's son-in-law

Frederick, Elector Palatine and a militant Protestant. Charles could not desert his brother-in-law. The marriage negotiations collapsed and Charles, Buckingham and Rutland returned to England. They were actually given a wildly enthusiastic welcome on their return as the attitude of the majority of English people was extremely anti-Spanish. Thereafter, James's attempts at reconciliation between Protestants and Catholics became more and more unsuccessful and the Earl of Rutland drifted away from his brief role at the centre of English politics. When Buckingham was assassinated in 1628, Rutland, having lost two sons and a son-in-law, moved into the quieter role of country aristocrat, giving up his task as Lord Lieutenant of Lincolnshire to Lord Willoughby d'Eresby, newly created Lord Chamberlain and Earl of Lindsey.

Gradually the extent of anti-witch feelings which had been strong in the second decade of the seventeenth century diminished. In the 1620s and 1630s there were few witchcraft trials. It is interesting that no further cases were reported in the Vale of Belvoir. The only one major outbreak was again in Lancashire. Sir William Pelham had died in 1629 and his son, the third Sir William, commented in May1635, 'The greatest news from the country is of a huge pack of witches which are lately discovered in Lancashire'. This third Sir William was himself legally trained at Gray's Inn and married the daughter of the Secretary of State, Edward Conway, a friend and relative of his father. His reaction to the new Lancashire witchcraft affair was typical of county gentlemen, but no longer that of the intellectuals. The new case of 1634 had at its origin yet another child witness, Edmund Robinson, aged ten. In Alison Findlay's account he played the same role as the nine-year-old sister of Alizon Device: he described how the accused witch 'bridled her companion who stood up a white horse' and then rode with Robinson to a witches' congregation at Hoarestone House'. Eventually up to twenty people were accused and 'condemned at the Lancashire Assizes on 24th March 1634'.

At this stage a significant development happened. The two Royal judges found the accused guilty but would not pass death sentences and referred the case directly to the Crown. Charles I's reaction to a mass condemnation for witchcraft was only a little different from that of his father to the 1616 Leicester case. Charles ordered the medical profession to examine some of the surviving accused. Charles's physician-extraordinary was William Harvey, the discoverer of the circulation of the blood, who was a personal friend of Charles and had been one of King James's Royal physicians. Together with two other doctors and midwives, Harvey carried out physical examinations. The point at issue was largely to determine whether they had 'supernumerary nipples to feed their familiars'. Harvey and his colleagues could find no physical abnormality and the accused were pardoned by Charles. It is important to add that the Bishop of Chester was also instructed to carry out a vocal examination of the suspects before they left Lancashire to go to London, and he found that there were 'inconsistencies and evidence of bribery' in the case. This Royal scepticism about the accuracy of witchcraft accusations helped in the move towards seeing belief in witchcraft as superstition.

As this second Lancashire case was dragging through both legal courts and the Royal court, it became enormously well known and was the inspiration for a successful play. *The Late Lancashire Witches* by Thomas Heywood and Richard Brome was written and performed in London. This play concentrated almost entirely on the fabulous stories of transformation and familiar spirits, so becoming an important element in the gradual process by which witchcraft became less a significant religious, social and legal problem and more an exciting story, in other words a supernatural entertainment.

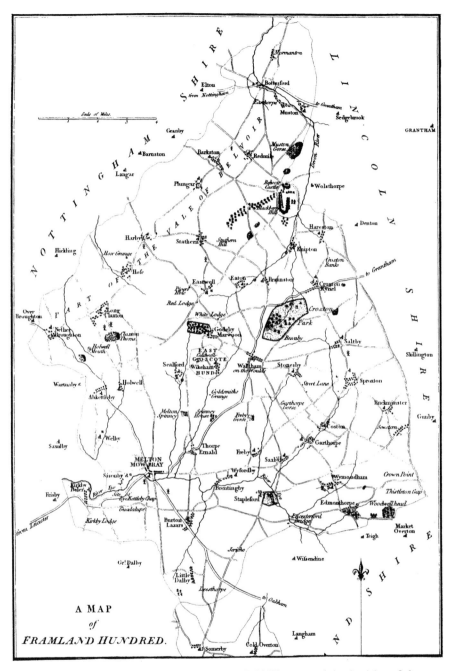

Map of north-east Leicestershire from John Nichols' History and Antiquities of the County of Leicester, *volume ii part i, c1800. (JN)*

THE ARRAIGNEMENT
AND TRIALL OF
IENNET PRESTON, Of

GISBORNE IN CRAVEN,
in the Countie of Yorke.

At the Afsifes and Generall Gaole-
Deliuerie holden at the Caftle of Yorke
in the Countie of Yorke, the xxvij. day of
Iuly laft paft, *Anno Regni Regis* IACOB
*Angliæ, &c. Decimo, & Scotiæ
quadragefimo quinto.*

Before

Sir IAMES ALTHAM *Knig*
of the Barons of his Maiefties Court of Ex
and Sir EDVVARD BROMLEY Knight, an
the Barons of his Maiefties Court of Exch
his Maiefties Iuftices of Affife, Oyer and Termi
*and generall Gaole-Deliuerie, in the Circuit
of the North-parts.*

[INSET:]

VPon the Arraignement and
triall of thefe VVitches at the
laft Afsizes and Generall
Gaole-deliuerie, holden at
Lancafter, wee found fuch apparent
matters againft them, that we thought
it neceffarie to publifh them to the
VVorld, and thereupon impofed the
labour of this VVorke vpon this Gentleman, by reafon of his place, being a
Clerke at that time in Court, imploied in the Arraignement and triall of
them.

Ja. Altham.

Edw. Bromley.

LONDON,
Printed by W. STANSBY for IOHN BARNES, and
are to be fold at his Shoppe neere Hol-
borne Conduit. 1612.

*Second title page in Thomas Potts' account of the Lancashire witches. Note the printer:
W.Stansby for John Barnes and INSET: Instructions to Thomas Potts to publish his
Wonderfull Discoverie of Witches, 1613. (Both EEBO & UI)*

The late Lancashire

VVITCHES

A well received Comedy, lately
Acted at the *Globe* on the *Banke-fide*,
by the Kings Majefties
Actors.

WRITTEN,

By THOM. HEYVVOOD,

AND

RICHARD BROOME.

Aut prodeffe folent, aut deleɛtare.

LONDON,

Printed by *Thomas Harper* for *Benjamin Fifher*,
and are to be fold at his Shop at the Signe of the
Talbot, without *Alderfgate*.
1634.

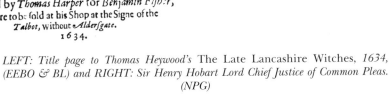

LEFT: Title page to Thomas Heywood's The Late Lancashire Witches, *1634,
(EEBO & BL) and RIGHT: Sir Henry Hobart Lord Chief Justice of Common Pleas.
(NPG)*

189

THE
Lancashire - Witches,

AND

Tegue o Divelly

THE

Irish - PRIEST

A

COMEDY

Acted at the

DUKE's Theater.

Written by *THO. SHADWELL.*

*—Nihilo quæ funt metuenda magis quam
Quæ pueri in tenebris pavitant, fingunty; futura.*

LONDON:

Printed for *John Starkey* at the *Miter* in *Fleetstreet* near
Temple-Barr. MDCLXXXII.

Title page to Thomas Shadwell's The Lancashire Witches, *1682. (EEBO & BL)*

190

EPILOGUE

The story of the Belvoir witchcraft accusations became a part of local folk-lore during the seventeenth century. The sixth Earl would have approved the inscription on his own tomb, prepared during his life-time, as his statement just before his death confirms 'my tombe is allreddy made'. The inscription in St Mary's Church, Bottesford states that he had 'two sonnes, both w[hi]ch dyed in their infancy by wicked practise & sorcerye'. This extremely rare reference to witchcraft on an English church memorial was the official public start of a story which has reverberated across four centuries. Clearly, the Earl connected the illness of his second son, Francis, with witchcraft, even though Francis died a year after the trial and hanging of the Flower sisters. The modern tale of the 'witches of Belvoir' derives from the Earl's memorial inscription.

The contemporary pamphlet and the ballad both presented witchcraft as an absolute historical reality, but they were not completely accurate in their facts. The 1619 pamphlet stated that the 'Earle had sufficient greife for the losse of his children' (*page 24*) using the plural, whereas by March 1619 only one of his three children had died. Indeed, the statement on page 7 of the pamphlet regarding 'the late wofull Tragedy of the destruction of the *Right Honourable* the *Earle* of *Rutland's* children' is written in flowing literary language reminiscent of Jacobean drama. As the story was written in dramatic language, it is easy to see how it gradually moved into the realm of folklore.

The Belvoir pamphlet was reprinted twice during the first part of the seventeenth century, in 1621 and 1635. The third edition appeared in 1635, printed by M.F. for Thomas Lambert and clearly riding on the crest of the Lancashire witchcraft cases and the associated plays of 1633/4. The pamphlet had a new title in 1635 which further extended the picture of the Belvoir events, '*Witchcrafts, strange and wonderfull: discovering the damnable practices of seven witches, against the lives of certaine noble personages, and others of this kingdome, as shall appeare in this lamentable history*'. The seventh accused witch was Mary Sutton from Bedfordshire, whose story had appeared in the second edition's postscript concerning the swimming of witches. This created a notion that

191

the events in Belvoir during James I's reign were on a similar scale to the events in Lancashire in 1612 and Leicester in 1616, whereas in reality the scale was much more limited in the Belvoir case, as only two women were tried at Lincoln.

The trial was also the subject of the 1619 ballad which survived into the second part of the seventeenth century. The only surviving copy of the original ballad, as far as I am aware, is *via* Samuel Pepys, who presented his collection of ballads to Magdalene College, Cambridge, where the original print of the Belvoir ballad still exists. The ballad is reproduced in this book and was sung to a popular tune of the late Elizabethan and early Jacobean era, 'The Ladies [or Lady's] Fall', often set to mournful ballads telling tragic tales. Using this tune, familiar to seventeenth- and eighteenth-century singers and audiences the ballad can be sung today, although there is no historical record of a performance. The famous eighteenth-century engraving by Hogarth of *The Enraged Musician* shows a poverty-stricken ballad-singer displaying her wares which include 'The Ladies Fall'. This indicates that the tune was a popular, if possibly irritatingly well-known tune. Broadside ballads such as the Belvoir ballad would have had a short shelf life as they were essentially news items, soon to be replaced by the next popular crime-related ballad.

In 1688, at approximately the same time as Pepys was collecting the ballad, a popular version of the Belvoir witchcraft story was included in *The Kingdom of Darkness*, a collection of stories of 'Daemons, Spectres, Witches, Apparitions, Possessions, Disturbances... Delusions, Miscievous Feats, and Malicious Impostures of the Devil'. The story was retold from the original pamphlet but in a reader-friendly version, incorporating the judicial examinations into the body of the narrative. Author Nathaniel Crouch was a publisher of popular history books, many of which he printed under the initials RB. He was well used to telling a lively story and *The Kingdom of Darkness* proved successful, going into at least four editions.

English Enlightenment views of witchcraft

During the eighteenth century there was a shift amongst the well-educated away from what were becoming regarded as superstitious popular ideas of the Devil and witchcraft. This changing understanding is well illustrated by the contrast between the two eighteenth-century versions of the Belvoir story, one published in 1715 and the second after 1795. The major intellectual attack on diabolical witchcraft beliefs was undertaken in 1718 by Francis Hutchinson in his *Historical Essay on Witchcraft*. Hutchinson, who later became a bishop in Ireland, was concerned to understand local circumstances and he encouraged the conversion of Irish Catholic peasants to Protestantism by translating religious texts into Irish. He was anxious to apply Locke's rational philosophy to everyday affairs and he was well aware of the distaste for superstition increasingly manifested by judges and justices.

This distaste became most forcibly apparent in the 1712 witchcraft case against Jane Wenham in Hertfordshire. The judge, Sir John Powell, listened to sixteen witnesses for the prosecution when Jane was accused of talking to the Devil, who appeared in the shape of a cat. As the 1604 law stood, Powell had to find her guilty, but he ensured that she was reprieved and released by Royal pardon. During the trial there were allegations that Jane had flown through the air as a witch; Powell was reputed to have made his famous remark, 'There is no law against flying'. Jane Wenham became well known and, as part of his investigations into witchcraft, Francis Hutchinson visited Jane after her pardon.

A huge pamphlet war developed over the Wenham case. Part of this battle of words included the 1715–16 encyclopaedic work *A Compleat History of Magick, Sorcery and Witchcraft* edited by Richard Boulton, a medical writer, and this included an updated version of the 1619 Belvoir pamphlet. The new edition excluded the whole of the theological preface to the 1619 edition. The language was altered in several places from seventeenth- to eighteenth-century forms: the description of Joan Flower was changed from 'her speech fell [cruel, deadly] and envious'(*page 8*) to the weakened phrase 'her Speech fallen and altered and envious' indicating that the original language was by now open to misunderstanding. The difficult phrase 'The Divell perceived the inficious [not accepting blame] disposition of this wretch' (*page 10*) became 'The Devil perceiving the ill Disposition of this Wretch'.

The theology of the seventeenth-century version is also softened. The sufferings of the Earl and Countess are described in the earlier version: 'many times subject to sicknesse and extraordinary convulsions, which they taking as gentle corrections from the hand of God, submit with quietnesse to his mercy, and study nothing more, than to glorifie their Creator in

193

heaven, and beare his crosses on earth' (*page 10*). In the 1715–16 version this became 'the Earl and his Countess began to be subject to Sickness, and extraordinary Convulsions, which they took with Patience, as submitting to the Hand of God, glorifying their Creator in Heaven and willingly bearing his Crosses on Earth'. On p.11 of the 1619 version witchcraft was referred to as 'such like inventions of the Divell' but in 1715 the phrase was dropped altogether. In addition, the instruction from God in 1619 'to command the Divell from executing any further vengeance on Innocents' (*page 11*) disappears completely, being changed to 'God almighty would suffer them [the Flower family] no longer to go on in their Wickedness, but bring them to Shame for their wicked and villainous Practices'. But the belief in a compact with the devil is still implicit in this early eighteenth-century version. The editor of the volume, Richard Boulton, a professional medical writer, presented this updated version but did not comment on the possibilities of changes in witchcraft law. He was hoping to sell his 'encyclopedia' as a popular work and therefore he was reluctant to go against the widespread popular beliefs.

Francis Hutchinson adopted a different attitude, one of disbelief, in his book on the history of witchcraft, published eventually in 1718. In addition to attacking Richard Boulton, he wrote opposing the witchcraft statute of 1603/4:

> 'We are free... to use our own Reason in judging which Notion of Witchcraft agrees best with the Nature of Things, as we see them before our Faces: And if the more cautious Notions be the more profitable and safe, we are free to take them, tho' our Statute be grounded upon a Supposition of the Vulgar. I have heard that King James himself came off very much from these notions in his elder Years, but when Lawes and Translations are fix'd it is a difficult thing to change them'.

Until 1720, Hutchinson was a cleric in East Anglia, where he became aware of the manner in which witchcraft accusations could destroy village communities. His book certainly reinforced the move against the old beliefs.

Another cleric, White Kennett, when he was Dean of Peterborough, delivered a sermon in 1715 about the Jacobite attack on Britain in that year. He preached that 'Witchcraft, if not an immediate compact with the Devil, is all but impudent Pretence and Delusion only; a perfect Cheat and Imposition upon the credulous Part of Mankind... It is indeed so often a meer Trick and Imposture, that some wise and good People have been beginning to suspect that there is no other Witchcraft'. Both White Kennett and Francis Hutchinson made their reputations through their historical writings. Both became bishops, Kennett of Peterborough in 1718 and Hutchinson of Down and Connor in Ireland in 1720. Clearly the leaders of the Church of England were now concluding that it was impossible to prove that human beings might have a compact with the Devil and so, in English law at least, diabolic witchcraft should no longer possess legal existence.

As a result of a stream of anti-witchcraft works by members of the clerical and medical professions, Parliament repealed James I's 1604 Witchcraft Act in 1735. The new Act got rid of the harsh 1604 legislation regarding a compact with the devil but aimed new penalties at 'Pretence to such Arts and Powers' of witchcraft. One year's imprisonment and four appearances 'on the Pillory by the Space of One Hour' was the prescribed punishment for anyone who should 'pretend to exercise or use any kind of Witchcraft, Sorcery, Inchantment or Conjuration'; here 'pretend' is the new and important change from the wording of the earlier legislation. This 1735 Act remained on the statute book until it was repealed by the Fraudulent Mediums Act of 1951.

There is a view often met with in historical discussions in connection with acts of Parliament about witchcraft, that the Elizabethan and Jacobean acts were the actual creators of a phenomenon, the so-called crime of diabolic witchcraft, rather than reactions to a genuine already existing social activity. This idea is impossible to quantify or prove but in the 1990s the historian Robin Briggs expressed this notion in a different manner, suggesting that witchcraft was a fantasy. Even though it was an 'imaginary crime' he insisted that 'despite its illusory nature... witchcraft mobilized real power to cause suffering'. During the eighteenth century the concept of diabolic witchcraft became judicially untenable, following the one hundred and fifty years during which it was a felony, because judges such as Sir John Powell felt unhappy about the difficulty of absolute proof of a compact with the Devil.

The final eighteenth-century edition of the Belvoir pamphlet was published by John Nichols in his huge history of Leicestershire, which appeared at the end of the eighteenth century. During the period between the repeal of the Witchcraft Act in 1735 and the end of the century, views on witchcraft coalesced between two positions: one was a clear intellectual ridicule of superstition and the second was the more general view that witches might have a continuing existence in society, although they were no longer to be considered as felons. This latter view was held by Samuel Johnson, who was in so many ways a traditional Tory. In 1772, when Johnson was 63, his biographer Boswell asked him to explain what he understood by the concept of witches:

> 'JOHNSON: "Why, Sir, they properly mean those who make use of the aid of evil spirits". BOSWELL: "There is no doubt, Sir, a general report and belief of their having existed". JOHNSON: "Sir, you have not only the general report of belief, but you have many voluntary solemn confessions". He did not affirm anything positively upon a subject which it is the fashion of the times to laugh at as a matter of absurd credulity. He only seemed willing, as a candid enquirer after truth, however strange and inexplicable, to shew that he understood what might be urged for it.'

So when Nichols reprinted the Belvoir story it was to a sceptical readership. He put a footnote: 'The whole pamphlet is here preserved as a most striking proof of the then prevalent opinion on the subject of witchcraft'. What this indicates is a changing historiography of witchcraft. By the end of the eighteenth century the Belvoir witchcraft account had become a strange piece of evidence for the different ways of thought of people living in the past. Nichols, unlike Richard Boulton, faithfully reprinted the 1619 version, omitting the theological preface but making no attempt to update either the language or the theology in the way Boulton had done in 1715.

Witchcraft becomes a theatrical and literary diversion

The 'witches of Belvoir' were gradually changed from historical reality into entertainment. This process of course had been under way from the moment of the publication of the pamphlet and especially of the ballad in 1619. In the Elizabethan and Jacobean period, several great plays, notably Marlowe's *Dr Faustus* and Shakespeare's *Macbeth*, had created a serious theatre of witchcraft and this tradition could be drawn on by later plays of a lighter nature. Purcell's opera *Dido and Aeneas* (1680) featured witches destroying the happiness of a noble couple.

There was never a seventeenth-century play about the Belvoir witches in the manner in which the Lancaster witches provided the substance for two comedy dramas. Thomas Heywood and Richard Brome wrote *The Late Lancashire Witches*, an entertaining comedy actually written and staged during the London examination of the second group of Lancashire accused women of 1633/4.

The second play, written by Thomas Shadwell and called *The Lancashire Witches*, was written as political and social satire in 1681, demonstrating his 'somewhat costive' reaction to the 'Doctrine of Witchcraft'. 'Costive' in this sense meant stingy or niggardly in giving belief to the reality of witchcraft. Shadwell here was self-consciously echoing Ben Jonson's use of the word in *The Alchemist*, the play about duping the credulous by claims of supernatural powers, when Jonson makes his character Surly say that he is 'somewhat costive of belief' in the existence of the Philosopher's Stone. Shadwell was demonstrating the newly sceptical approach to witchcraft in this political comedy, written to entertain the Whig gentry in the early 1680s.

In the seventeenth century, Heywood, Brome and Shadwell had been using witchcraft as an element of political satire; Shadwell wrote in the prologue to his play:

> 'But true Wit seems in Magick-Fetters bound...
> When Satyr the true Medicine is declin'd
> What hope of Cure can our Corruptions find?
> If the Poet's end only to please must be,
> Juglers, Rope-dancers, are as good as he.
> Instruction is an honest Poet's aim.'

Between 1700 and 1900 the dramatic theatrical view of witchcraft had shifted into both light opera and pantomime, where it still survives today. The story of the 'Witches of Belvoir' has been the subject of a twentieth century opera, *Rutterkin*, written by Philip Spratley and Adrian Simpson and successfully performed in the Vale of Belvoir and its neighbourhood in 1972 and 1995. We find that the story of the Lancashire witches provided Charles Dibdin with the subject-matter of his 'new Pantomime called the Lancashire Witches or the Distresses of Harlequin', the songs from which were printed in 1783. Dibdin in 1783 was not offering instruction. His only concern was pure entertainment and this was to be the essence of witchcraft stories in the next century or so.

Montague Summers, writing from a standpoint of theological belief in the reality of witchcraft, described Dibdin's entertainment: 'whose tinsel, music, and mummery drew all the macaronis and cyprians in London to the Circus during the winter of 1782-3'. As witchcraft executions gradually ceased across Europe during the eighteenth century, the subject matter of diabolic witchcraft moved, for all but the least educated or the most religiously conservative, into the realm of myth.

As a result, the nineteenth and twentieth centuries saw many novels and plays on the topic. In his *Witchcraft – a History* P.G. Maxwell-Stuart draws attention to the novelists' terrifying accounts of witches. In particular, Quintin Poynet described a witch in his novel *The Wizard Priest and the Witch* (1822) as having 'hazel eyes which squinted with an expression of mischief, horrible and malignant' which recalls the Belvoir pamphlet's portrait of Joan Flower : 'her eyes were fiery and hollow' (*page 8*). Perhaps the most terrifying of all these novels about witchcraft was Harrison Ainsworth's melodramatic *The Lancashire Witches*, first published in 1848. Ainsworth is best known for totally inventing the story of Dick Turpin's ride from London to York for one of his novels. His account of the Pendle witches was equally imaginative and inventive, and it is because of this novel that the Lancashire witches regained during the nineteenth and twentieth centuries the extraordinary notoriety that they had during the first half of the seventeenth century.

Joan Flower actually appears in two novels. She was given a part to play in Mrs Chaworth Musters's romance about the seventeenth-century Vale of Belvoir *A Cavalier Stronghold* written in 1890 and set in the area around Wiverton Hall and Langar where Odingsells had preached his anti-witchcraft sermons at the time of the actual Belvoir case. Joan was the main character in Hilda Lewis's *The Witch and the Priest*, a popular novel first published in 1956. It is based on imagined conversations between Joan Flower and Samuel Fleming, the Rector of Bottesford, one of the original JPs who conducted the examinations and who died in 1620, leaving money for an almshouse for women in the village. Hilda Lewis invented the details of Fleming's will for her book, making this bequest an act of remorse: his will has not, in fact, survived. Her book was, interestingly, dedicated to Canon Alfred Blackmore who was Rector of Bottesford at the time and it had a considerable success.

The changing historiography of witchcraft

Fortunately for our understanding of what might have really happened in the Vale of Belvoir in Jacobean times, alongside the imaginative pantomimes and novels there came a significant literary development: that of the new scientific history. In the eighteenth century Giambattista Vico had insisted on proof when writing history: in *The New Science*, he offered two sources for the historian: legend and surviving artefacts. Of the first, Vico wrote: 'Truth is sifted from everything that has been preserved for us through long centuries by those vulgar traditions which, since they have been preserved for so long a time and by entire peoples, must have had a public ground of truth'. Of the artefacts, amongst which we would today include documentary evidence, he wrote: 'The great fragments of antiquity, hitherto useless to science because they lay begrimed, broken and scattered, shed great light when cleaned, pieced together and restored'. He concluded that by careful study of the language in myths and documents it is possible to understand 'human social institutions' and their necessary causes.

Gradually documents were located, sites were studied in detail and historical study became differentiated from the re-telling of legends. As Rosemary Sweet explained, eighteenth-century antiquarians began to bring 'far more detail to the period [studied] than had any previous historian[s], not through supposition and conjecture, but through a careful reading and analysis of charters, wills, chronicles and poetry'. The British government began to publish national records at the beginning of the nineteenth century beginning with the Master of the Rolls' series, and many local record societies printed their local source documents. The national body responsible for documents in England, the Historical Manuscripts Commission, published in four volumes between 1888 and 1905 a calendar of the manuscripts held by the Duke of Rutland and thus provided much of the evidence on which this book is based.

An example of an early version of this new history was that which the Rev Irvin Eller published as his *History of Belvoir Castle* in 1841. In addition to having access to original documents in the Castle, he was possibly aware of the new Victorian reprint of the Belvoir pamphlet, printed in London by J.R. Smith in 1838. Eller slightly altered the syntax of the pamphlet's account and intensified the language of the original, saying of Joan Flower: 'her eyes very fiery and hollow', adding a 'very' to the 1619 and 1838 versions which read 'her eyes were fiery and hollow' (*page 8*). Eller

199

reprinted the whole of the narrative as given in the original pamphlet. In his reprint he does not repeat an alteration or misprint in the Victorian edition which says, incorrectly, that the accused witches 'might only be confounded' (*page 11*) whereas all other editions say 'might not only be confounded'.

Eller was being as scientific as possible, particularly in citing the original 1619 pamphlet at length. He dated the execution correctly as 11 March 1618/9 and offered a thoughtful discussion, suggesting 'that, whatever might be the belief of the common people in this particular instance, respecting the 'sorcery' employed, their superiors might have discerned evident tokens of 'wicked practice' only'. He demonstrated a nineteenth-century intellectual's scientific disbelief in sorcery. However, he then went beyond the evidence, arguing 'that these women were guilty of the murder of two noble children; and attempting the lives of the Earl and Countess, and their daughter Catherine, can be little doubted: by the means probably of some vegetable poison'. Eller could be expected to side with the nobility against the Flower family, since he had privileged entry to Belvoir Castle. It is interesting that he looked for a material explanation, somewhat different to the seventeenth-century view.

By the twentieth century historians were becoming more circumspect, hesitating to go beyond the evidence in Eller's way because they were now part of a full-scale profession, in many cases backed by state investment in university training. One further development associated with historical studies brought the whole subject-matter of witchcraft to the forefront of the academic study of history. This was the development of social anthropology, which originally arose out of the determination to describe and explain the origins and structure of national cultures. This underpinned what Karl Popper was to call 'historicism', an approach to the social sciences which believes that historical prediction is their principal aim, and which assumes that this aim is attainable by discovering the 'rhythm' or the 'pattern', the 'laws' or the 'trends' that underlie the evolution of history.

The difficulty with social anthropology was that it tended to create and reinforce stereotypes. The historical studies of witchcraft were much influenced by Margaret Murray. Using anthropological themes, some derived from her work on Egyptian culture, Murray published *The Witch-cult in Western*

Europe in 1921. She claimed that the witches' sabbath was a widespread standard feature in English witchcraft, whereas it was rarely mentioned in evidence or confessions, especially in the earlier cases. She developed the theory that there was a great witch-persecution led by the Church to defeat and repress a universal, Europe-wide ancient pagan religion, worshipping the horned god who represented nature, even pre-agricultural nature. In other words, witches were innocent followers of this faith, which she represented as joyful and which the Church was attempting to destroy.

Unfortunately, it is clear from *The Witch-cult in Western Europe* that Murray was selective in her evidence. She refers to the three witnesses in the Belvoir case to point out that they had animal-shaped familiars but does not mention the Flower family at all, or any other features of this case. Most of her evidence comes from continental European or Scottish cases. This was certainly the intellectual background which encouraged Hilda Lewis to write *The Witch and the Priest*; she included Margaret Murray's book in her 'List of books consulted'.

This approach to historical study sought to use ideas and theories from the writers' own time to explain events in the past. Christina Larner exposed the difficulties this entailed: 'because the Europe of the witch-hunt had features characteristic both of primitive, small-scale societies and of literate, stratified, large-scale societies, there are problems concerning… how the modern interpreter should view remote belief systems, and the role of ideology in a stratified society'. In other words, historians with a social-anthropological bent might be inclined to explain specific events in Jacobean England by reference to social conditions in a recently-studied African or Pacific 'primitive' society, on the assumption that similar patterns, laws and trends might exist and explain both societies.

In the 1960s an influential historical educator, W.H. Burston, wrote of the practising historian as essentially an explainer of events: 'he has the enormous advantage of knowing what came after the event which he is dealing with'. This perhaps 'gives him a decisive advantage in arriving at a correct interpretation of the intentions' of people in the past. In effect, it was the historian's desire to explain the past which gave to so much historical writing a focus coloured by modern preoccupations unknown to the people of the time that was being studied. Some over-arching studies of witchcraft suggested that misogyny lay at the heart of the attack on witches in Jacobean times, but today this is perceived as too single-track to be a sufficient explanation of the whole phenomenon. Indeed, post-modern historians would suggest that it is impossible even to consider offering a full explanation.

The work of Christina Larner in particular has brought our attention to the minute details of accusation and trials in a beneficial manner. She focused on three themes which have direct relevance to the Belvoir case. 'The first is that witch-hunting was an activity fostered by the ruling class... The second theme is that the ideas of witchcraft... encompass a variety of alleged activities, possible and impossible, probable and improbable, and attribute to the performers of these activities a variety of characteristics, all of which serve to highlight local social values'. She was critical of 'A third and subordinate theme... that of the extent to which witch-hunting is to some degree a synonym for woman-hunting'. As Alan Macfarlane explained, 'One of the striking features of Dr Larner's work is a sceptical attitude towards simple and universal explanations'.

It was during the 1970s, then, that the older anthropological explanations began to give way to our present understanding of witchcraft. In addition to Christina Larner's Edinburgh PhD in the 1960s, there were two remarkable studies prepared at the beginning of the following decade, Keith Thomas's *Religion and the Decline of Magic* in 1971 and Alan Macfarlane's *Witchcraft in Tudor and Stuart England* in 1970. These three scholars presented evidence that, whatever we may think today, Jacobean people were sure that witchcraft was real. Keith Thomas in particular was influenced by the Belvoir case, mentioning it six times and citing it as an example of an important element of witchcraft practices called 'image magic'. He wrote 'The eldest son of the Earl of Rutland was thought in 1619 to have died because his glove had been malevolently buried and allowed to rot in the earth'. My study of the Belvoir case indicates a strong probability that the Flower family did indeed engage in this activity. This is suggested by the fact that the glove is mentioned ten times in the evidence reported in the pamphlet, sometimes with telling circumstantial details such as where it was found at Belvoir Castle.

Thomas studied a huge range of witchcraft accusations, suggesting that 'the overwhelming majority of fully-documented

202

witch cases fall into this simple pattern... the victim (or, if he were an infant, the victim's parents) had been guilty of a breach of charity'. He explained that 'the task of adequately presenting this pattern in statistical form has defeated me'. His valuable conclusion was that 'the history of witchcraft *accusations*... can only be explained in terms of the immediate social environment of the witch and her accuser'. It is my view that full explanation is impossible, but by local studies we can begin to understand how people were reacting in Jacobean times. The Belvoir case should be treated as a unique story, not as a series of events to be explained by reference to other witchcraft episodes, though it can be illuminated by comparison with other cases, and can throw light on them in its turn.

At the same time as Keith Thomas insisted that witchcraft accusations are 'essentially a local phenomenon', Alan Macfarlane analysed the Essex accusations in order to come to terms with what he later called the apparently widespread belief in early modern times that there was a 'vast conspiracy of Evil abroad'. However what became clear to him, certainly when he studied the surviving ten thousand pages of the records of one Essex parish, Earl's Colne, between 1380 and 1750, was that diabolic witchcraft was almost completely unknown in that locality. There was only one accusation recorded, and that was dealt with by excommunication in a Church court. His opinion was that 'witches were the enemies of specific individuals, not of society as a whole' and his conclusion was clear: 'The English witch was in popular thought a curiously tame and homely creature. Unpleasant, vindictive, a criminal even, but not a member of a deep and concerted attack on society, a terrifying intrusion of evil into this world'. In other words, the English witch was simply a local pain in the neck! As a result of the work of Larner, Thomas and Macfarlane, this study of the Belvoir witchcraft accusation in Jacobean times is unrelentingly local; hopefully it offers some understanding of the case but it is in no way a final explanation.

This book on the Belvoir case is typical of the great number of studies of witchcraft written over the past forty years. It is an attempt to illustrate an example of a witchcraft accusation which was not mentioned in the two outstanding general discussions of witchcraft in the 1990s, the books of Stuart Clark and Robin Briggs. Along with Alan Macfarlane, these recent books have introduced us to what Briggs called the illusory nature of witchcraft, 'the crime which never happened'.

The analysis of the manner in which this illusion was turned into an intellectual movement of extraordinary proportions was given by Stuart Clark in his remarkable study, appropriately called *Thinking with Demons: the idea of witchcraft in early modern Europe*. Clark has clarified the nature of witchcraft beliefs, as opposed to the actions of witches. In addition, Robin Briggs argued that 'historical witchcraft was really more humdrum than occult, however [it was] an integral part of everyday life'. James Sharpe in his study of specifically English witchcraft, *Instruments of Darkness*, concluded that 'most people in Britain around 1600 believed in witches'. Consequently for about one hundred and fifty years in early modern England these beliefs were incorporated into statute law.

Conclusion

Like many unfortunate happenings, both in the past and today, the Belvoir case seems to have arisen over a period of years and come to a tragic climax because of an unusual and complex combination of factors. Disagreements which flare into long-lasting feuds with the taking of sides and the exchange of insults and accusations are well-known, even in closely-knit communities and workplaces. In the Belvoir case, the inevitable small frictions of community life seem to have been exacerbated by rivalries among the Castle servants for the favour and support of the Earl and Countess. Most local families either worked at the Castle or were tenants of the Earl. Margaret and Philippa Flower appropriated for their own use domestic items from the Castle and in most cases the Earl and Countess would have turned a blind eye to this. But on this occasion it appears to have reached too high a level and the Belvoir pamphlet states that Margaret was dismissed. It also seems that Mrs Flower became involved in a serious confrontation with Mr Peake, another long-term servant of the Earl. This was exactly the combination of happenings which might have led Mrs Flower and her daughters to threaten some form of malicious action when the Earl took Mr Peake's side rather than the Flowers'. Coupled with this were hints of an unacceptable level of behaviour between the Flower sisters and village men, and local resentment resulting from it.

In all probability, these events would have simply flared up and been forgotten, like most local disagreements, had it not been for the Manners family's crucial need for a male heir. First one boy, Henry, died, then the remaining boy, Francis, began to show signs of serious and long-term illness. I have listed in detail the many and varied medical attempts by the Earl and Countess to overcome this threat to the survival of their immediate family and inheritance. We do not know when the possibility of witchcraft as the cause of the family's misfortunes was first suggested. However, it is difficult to imagine that such a possibility was never mentioned when King James 'yea our owne learned and most judicious king' (*page 3*) visited Belvoir Castle. The 1616 Leicester case could have contributed to an atmosphere in which witchcraft emerged in the Vale of Belvoir as a possible cause of the Manners children's illnesses.

The associated gossip or 'newes, tales, reports' as the Belvoir author expressed it, 'by degrees gave light to their understanding to apprehend their complaints' (*page 8*) and 'some of [Joan Flower's] neighbours dared to affirme that she dealt with familiar spirits' (*page 8*). As soon as this accusation reached the ears of the constables and magistrates, examinations had to take place. Even then, the legal investigation would in most cases have come to nothing in Jacobean England, with an increasingly sceptical monarch and magistracy. In the Netherlands by this date there were to be no more executions for witchcraft and there were relatively few in England by the end of James I's reign.

Sadly for the fate of the Flower sisters, the combination of intense gossip, minor fraud, local quarrels and the fact that all the magistrates dealing with the case were closely associated with the Manners family by ties of blood, marriage or employment, proved too much. After undergoing the terrors of winter weeks in Lincoln Jail, the sisters confessed to making a compact with the Devil. With that confession, there was no escape from condemnation under the Witchcraft Act of 1604. The Earl and Countess call forth our sympathy for the loss of their son; we must also remember that it was the universal belief in witchcraft which brought about the death of the Flower sisters, deaths for which we can feel remorse and sadness four hundred years later.

Frontispiece to The Kingdom of Darkness, *1688, by RB, pseudonym of Nathaniel Crouch. (EEBO & FSL)*

THE
KINGDOM
OF
Darknels :
OR

The Hiſtory of Dæmons, Specters,
Witches, Apparitions, Poſſeſſions,
Diſturbances, and other wonderful
and ſupernatural Deluſions, Miſchie-
vous Feats, and Malicious Impoſtures
of the Devil.

Containing near Fourſcore memorable
Relations, Forreign and Domeſtick, both Anti-
ent and Modern.

Collected from Authentick Records,
Real Atteſtations, Credible Evidences, and aſ-
ſerted by Authors of Undoubted Verity.

Together with a Preface obviating the
common Objections and Allegations of the
Sadduces and Atheiſts of the Age, who deny the
Being of Spirits, Witches, &c.

With Pictures of ſeveral memorable Accidents.

By R. B.

Licenſed and Entred accozding to Ozder.

LONDON, Printed for Nath. Crouch at the Bell
in the Poultrey near Cheapſide. 1688.

Title page of The Kingdom of Darkness *by RB (Nathaniel Crouch), 1688.*
EEBO & FSL)

THE LADY'S FALL or IN PEASCOD TIME

This tune has to be sung twice for each verse of the Belvoir balla

Of dam-ned deeds and deadly dole I make my mourn-ful song, By
witch-es done in Lin-colne-shire where they have liv-ed long

ABOVE: William Hogarth's The Enraged Musician *with the ballad singer selling* The Ladies Fall *to the tune of which the Belvoir ballad can be sung – in D. Bindman's* Hogarth and His Times, *1997 (BMP) and BELOW: the tune to the ballad* The Ladies Fall *or* The Lady's Fall. *(MH)*

208

Appendix I
THE BELVOIR PAMPHLET

The Belvoir Witchcraft pamphlet has been reprinted at least ten times, which indicates its significance in witchcraft studies. It appeared first in 1619: 'printed at London by G.Eld for I. Barnes, dwelling in the long Walke neere Christ-Church'. This version had 46 small printed pages and was twice illustrated by the woodcut of three witches. The second edition of 1621, also printed by George Eld, had 21 pages and unfortunately, the title page has disappeared from the only known edition; it employed black letter type, unlike Eld's first version of 1619, which used what is to us today a conventional font. The other difference was the inclusion at the end of a new paragraph on popular methods of discovering witches, called the 'triall of a witch', which used the account of the swimming of a witch from the 1613 Bedford Witchcraft pamphlet, *Witches Apprehended*.

In 1635 a third reprint of the original pamphlet appeared with the woodcut illustration, the same text as in 1621 and a revised title: *Witchcrafts, Strange and Wonderfull: Discovering the damnable practices of seven Witches against the lives of certaine Noble Personages*. In 1688 a ten-page popular version of the story was included in *The Kingdom of Darkness*, written and printed by Nathaniel Crouch under the initials R.B. In 1715 the pamphlet was reprinted, without the theological preface, by Richard Boulton in volume I of his two volume *History of Magick, Sorcery and Witchcraft*.

The sixth publication was in John Nichols' monumental *History and Antiquities of the County of Leicester*, Volume II part ii, Framland Hundred, appendix IX, p.69, which was a reprint of the 1619 edition, without the theological preface. In the nineteenth century, a full reprint of the original 1619 print was published – in 1838, the seventh edition, and this is the one reprinted here by kind permission of Vance Harvey, who reprinted it in 1970; in effect Vance Harvey's edition was the eighth telling of the story. Marion Gibson included an excellent transcription of the 1619 edition of the pamphlet in her *Early Modern Witches* of 2000. Finally a facsimile of the original edition of 1619 has recently been included in volume 2 of the six-volume collection *English Witchcraft 1560-1736*, edited by James Sharpe, thus making a total of ten known versions.

THE
WONDERFVL
DISCOVERIE OF THE
Witchcrafts of *Margaret* and *Phillip*
Flower, daughters of *Joan Flower* neere *Beuer*
Castle : executed at Lincolne, *March* ii. 1618.

Who were specially arraigned & condemned before
Sir *Henry Hobart*, and Sir *Edward Bromley*, Judges
of Assize, for confessing themselues actors in the destruction of *Henry*, Lord *Rosse*, with their damnable practises against others the Children of the Right
Honourable Francis Earle of *Rutland*.

Together with the seuerall Examinations and Confessions of *Anne
Baker*, *Ioan Willimot*, and *Ellen Greene*, Witches in *Leicestershire*.

Printed at London by *G. Eld* for *I. Barnes*, dwelling in the long Walke
neere Christ-Church. 1619.

THE WONDERFVL
DISCOVERIE OF THE

Witch-craftes of *Margaret* and *Phillip*
Flower, *Daughters* of Joan Flower,
by Beauer Castle, and executed at Lincolne the
II. *of March.*
1618.

Y meaning is not to make any conten-
tious arguments about the discourses,
distinction or definition of Witchcraft,
the power of Diuells, the nature of Spirits, the force of Charmes, the secrets of
Incantation and such like, because the
Scriptures are full of prohibitions to this
purpose, and proclaimes death to the presumptuous attempters
of the same: Besides both Princes (yea our onne learned and
most iudicious King) Philosophers, Poets, Chronologers, Historiographers, and many worthy writers, have concurred and
concluded in this; that divers impious and fascinorus mis-
chiefes have beene effectuated through the instruments of the
Diuell, by permission of God, so that the actors of the same
have carried away the opinion of the world, to doe that which
they did by Witchcraft, or at least to be esteemed Witches, for
bringing such and such things to passe: For howsoeuer the
learned haue charactred delinquents in this kind by titles of
sundry sortes, and most significant attributes, as *Pythonissæ*
dealing with artificial Charmes; *Magi* anciently reputed so,
for extraordinary wisedome and knowledge in the secrets of
simples and hearbes; *Chaldei*, famous for Astronomy and Astrology; *Necromancers* for practising to raise dead bodies,

and by them to foretell euents of the earth; *Geomantici*, for
conuersing with Spirits, and using Inchantations; *Genethliaci*,
for presuming on the calculating of Natiuities, or if you will,
assuming the credit of Figure casting; *Ventriloqui*, for speaking with hollow voyces as if they were possessed with Diuells;
Venefici, for dealing with Poyson, and either killing or curing
that way: For you must understand howeuer the Professors
aforesaid practise murther and mischeife, yet many times they
Pretend cures and preseruation; with many others, carrying
the shew of great learning and admired knowledge; yet haue
they all but one familier tearme with vs in English called
Witches. As for the conceit of wisemen or wisewomen, they
are all meerely coseners and deceiuers; so that if they make
you belieue that by their meanes you shall heare of things lost
or stolne, it is either done by Confederacy, or put off by protraction to deceiue you of your money.

Only (as I said before) there be certaine men and women
gronne in yeares, and ouer gronne with Melancholly and Athe-
isme, who out of a malitious disposition against their betters,
or others thriuing by them; but most times from a heart-burn-
ing desire of reuenge, hauing entertained some impression of
displeasure, and vnkindnesse, study nothing but mischeife, and
exoticke practises of loathsome Artes and Sciences: yet I must
needes say, that sometimes the fained reputation of wisedome,
cunning, to be reputed a dangerous and skilfull person, hath so
preuailed with diuers, that they haue taken vpon them indeed
to know more than God euer afforded any creature, and to per-
forme no lesse than the Creator both of Heauen and Earth;
making you beleeue with *Medea*, that they can raise tempests,
turne the Sunne into blood, pull the Moone out of her Speare,
and saile ouer the Sea in a cockle shell, according to the Poet.
Flectere si nequeam Superos, Acheronta monebo.

> If Art doe faile to moue the Gods
> consent vnto my minde:
> I will the Diuells raise, to doe
> what they can in their kinde.

But howsoeuer special persons are transported with an opinion
of their onne worth, and preuailing in this kinde, yet by lament-

able experience we know too well, what monstrous effects haue
bene produced, and euen to the horror of the hearers, and
damnation of their onn soules by such kind of people: For as
it is in the tale of the enuious man, that put out one of his eyes
to haue his companion loose both; so fareth it with them and
worse, to giue away their soules to be reuenged of their aduer-
saries bodies wherein the monstrous subtility of the Diuell is
so apparant, that it is wonderfull one way to relate, and lamentable another way to obserue the same. For no sooner shall
such motiues poyson the inward conceite or apprehension of
such damnable Caitiffes: But then steppeth forth the Diuell, and
not only sheweth them the way, but prescribeth the manner
of effecting the same, with facility and easinesse, assuring that
hee himself will attend them in some familiar shape of Rat,
Cat, Toade, Birde, Cricket, &c.: yea effectuate whatsoeuer they
shall demaund or desire, and for their better assurance and
corroboration of their credulity, they shall haue palpable and
forcible touches of sucking, pinching, kissing, closing, colling
and such like: Wherevpon without any feare of God or Man,
knowledge of Christ, hope of redemption, confidence of mercy,
or true beleefe that their is any other thing to bee looked after
but this present world; according to that Atheisticall position
of *Epicurus.*

Ede, bibe, lude, post mortem nulla voluptas.

Eat, drink, sport, play and take thy pleasures rest:
For after death, who knows what shall be best.

They admit of those execrable conditions of commutation of
soules for the entertaining of the spirits, and so fall to their
abominable practises, continuing in the same till God laugh
them to scorne, and will by no meanes suffer them to abuse
his holy name nor deceiue others by their prophane liues any
longer: Witnesses for the generall those infinite Treatises of
many of them conuinced by Law, and condemned to death, to
the fearefull example of all carnall and hypocriticall Christians:
but more especially you may ouerlooke (if you please) that
learned Discource of *Dæmonologie,* composed in forme of a
Dialogue, by the High and Mighty Prince, IAMES by the grace of
God, King of *England, Scotland, France* and *Ireland,* &c. and

printed (as I take it) according to the coppy of Edenburgh 1603.
As also a Treatise of Witch-craft made by that learned Mr.
Alexander Roberts Preacher at Kings-Line in Norfolke, 1615.
vpon the discouery of the Witch-crafts of *Mary Smith*, wife of
Henry Smith Glouer, with her vocall contract betweene the
Diuell and herselfe, in solemne tearmes, and such like impos-
turing filthinesse: with many hurts and mischeifes which
thereby she procured: As also a Certaine discouery 1611. made
by *John Cottu* Docter of Phisicke in Northampton, of Empericks, woemen about sicke persons: Quacksaluers, and fugitiues,
which seeme to worke iuggling wonders, Surgeons, Apothecaries, practisers by Spells, the true discouery of Witch-craft,
especially in the Sicke with many instances in that kind,
Wisards, and seruants, of Phisitions, who may be called Min-
istring helpers: To this hee hath added the *Methodian* learned
deceiuer, or hereticke Phisitions, Astrologers, *Ephemerides-*
maisters, Coniecters by vrine, Trauellers, and last of all, the
true Artist his right description and election. As also a Dialogue concerning Witches and Witchcraft, composed by *George
Gifford*, Minister of Gods word in Maldon, 1603. Wherein
the cunning of the Diuell is discouered, both concerning the
deceiuing of Witches, and the seducing of others into many
great errors: As also an ancient discourse of the fearefull practises of foure notorious French Witches, with the manner of
their strange execution. As also the several and damnable
practises of Mother *Sutton* of Milton Miles in the County of
Bedford, and *Mary Sutton* her daughter who were arraigned,
and condemned, and executed for the same: As also 1612. the
wonderfull discouery of Witches in Lancashire, being 19. in
number, notorious for many infamed actions, and conuicted
before Sr. *James Altham*, and S. *Edward Bromley*, Barons
of the Exchequer together with the arraignment and triall of
Iennet Preston, at *Yorke*, with her fearefull execution for the
murthering of Mr. Lisker by Witchcraft, with infinite other
relations concerning the generall conuiction of Witches, and
their practises, and condemnation of the particular opinion of
some men, who suppose there bee none at all, or at least that
they do not personally or truely effect such things as are
imputed vnto them, and which out of some dangerous impres-

sion of melancholly, vaineglory, or some other diseased operation, they assume to themselues by reason of a former contract
with the Diuell. And so much for the certainty of a Story,
and fearefullnesse of the truth concerning the damnable practises of Witches and cunning of the Diuell to deceiue them.

But yet because the mind of man may be carried away with
many idle coniectures, either that woemen confessed these
things by extreamity of Torture, or that ancient examples are
by this time forgotten (although the particulars are upon record, for the benefit of all posterity:) Or that they were besides
themselues, or subject to some weake deuise or other, rather to
bring in question the integrity of *Iustice;* then to make odious
the liues of such horrible offendors. I haue preseumed to present on the *Stage* of verity for the good of my Country and the
loue of truth, the late wofull Tragedy of the destruction of the
Right Honourable the *Earle* of *Rutlands* Children, who to
his eternall praise proceeded yet both religiously and charitably
against the Offenders, leauing their prosecution to the law and
submitting himselfe, and deplorable case to the prouidence of
God, who afflicteth his best Seruant with punishments, and many
times, sendeth extraordinary vengeance as well on the innocent
as the bad deseruer, to manifest his glory: Therefore by way
of Caution I aduise thee (gentle Reader) whosoeuer thou art,
to take heede how thou doest either despise the power of God
in his Creatures, or vilipend the subtilty and fury of the Diuell,
as Gods instrument of vengeance, considering that truth in
despight of gaine sayers will preuaile, according to that principle: *Magna est veritas & prevalebit.*

The Story followes.

After the Right Honourable Sr. *Francis Manners* succeeded
his Brother in the Earledome of Rutland: and so not only tooke
possession of Beauer Castle, but of all other his demeanes,
Lordships, Tonnes, Mannors, Lands, and Revennues appropriate to the same Earledome: he proceeded so honourably in
the course of his life, as neither displacing Tenants, discharg-

ing seruants, denying the accesse of the poore, welcoming of strangers, and performing all the duties of a noble Lord, that hee fastened as it were vnto himself the loue and good opinion of the Country wherein he walked the more cheerefully and remarkable, because his honourable Countesse marched arme and arme with him in the same race; so that Beauer Castle was a continuall Pallace of entertainment, and a daily reception for all sorts both rich and poore, especially such auncient people as neighboured the same; amongst whom one *Ioane Flower*, with her Daughters *Margaret* and *Phillip* were not only relieued at first from thence, but quickly entertained as Chair-women, and *Margaret* admitted as a continual dweller in the Castle, looking both to the poultrey abroad and the wash-house within dores : In which life they continued with equal correspondency, till something was discouered to the Noble Lady, which concerned the misdemeanour of these women. And although such honourable persons shall not want of all sorts of people, either to bring the newes, tales, reports, or to serue their turne in all offices whatsoeuer ; so that it may well be said of them, as it is of Great Kings and Princes, that they haue large hands, wide eares, and piercing sights to discouer the vnswept corners of their remotest confines, to reach euen to their furthermost borders, and to vnderstand the secrets of their meanest subjects : yet in this matter were they busie-bodies, flatterers, malicious politicians, vnderminers, nor supplanters one of anothers good fortune ; but went simply to worke, as regarding the honor of the Earle and his Lady, and so by degrees gaue light to their understanding to apprehend their complaints. First that *Ioane Flower* the Mother was a monstrous malicious woman, full of oathes, curses, and imprecations irreligious, and for any thing they saw by her, a plaine Atheist; besides of late days her very countenance was estranged, her eyes were fiery and hollow, her speech fell and enuious, her demeanour strange and exoticke, and her conuersation sequestered ; so that the whole course of her life gaue great suspition that she was a notorious Witch, yea some of her neighbours dared to affirme that she dealt with familiar Spirits, and terrified them all with curses and threatning of reuenge, if there were neuer so little cause of displeasure and vnkindnesse.

Concerning *Margaret* that she often resorted from the Castle to her Mother, bringing such provision as they thought was vnbefitting for a seruant to purloyne, and coming at such unseasonable houres, that they could not but coniecture some mischeife between them, and that their extraordinary ryot and expences tended both to rob the Lady, and to maintaine certaine deboist and base company which frequented this *Ioane Flowers* house the mother, and especially her youngest Daughter. Concerning *Phillip* that she was lewdly transported with the loue of one *Th: Simpson*, who presumed to say, that she had bewitched him : for hee had no power to leaue, and was as he supposed maruellously altered both in minde and body, since her acquainted company : these complaints began many years before either their conuiction, or publique apprehension : Notwithstanding such was the honour of this Earle and his Lady; such was the cunning of this monstrous woman in obseruation towards them ; such was the subtilty of the Diuell to bring his purposes to passe; such was the pleasure of God to make tryall of his seruants ; and such was the effect of a damnable womans wit and malitious enuy, that all things were carried away in the smooth Channell of liking and good entertainment on euery side, untill the Earle by degrees conceiued some mislike against; and, so peradventure estranged himself from that familiarity and accustomed conferences he was wont to haue with her : untill one Peate offered her some wrong ; against whom she complained, but found that my Lord did affect her clamours, and malicious information, vntill one Mr. *Vauasor* abandoned her company, as either suspicious of her lewd life, or distasted with his onn misliking of such base and poore Creatures, whom nobody loued but the Earles houshold : vntill the Countesse misconceiuing of her daughter *Margaret* and discouering some vndecencies both in her life and neglect of her businesse, discharged her from lying any more in the Castle, yet gaue her 40s. a bolster, and a mattresse of wooll : commanding her to go home, vntill the slacknesse of her repayring to the Castle, as she was wont, did turne her loue and liking toward this honourable Earle and his family into hate and rancor : wherevpon despighted to bee so neglected, and exprobated by her neighbours for her Daughters casting out of doores, and other conceiued displeasures, she grew past all shame and woman-hood, and many times cursed them all that were the cause of this discontentment, and made her so loathsome to her former familiar friends and beneficial acquaintance.

When the Diuell perceiued the inficious disposition of this wretch, and that she and her Daughters might easily bee made instruments to enlarge his Kingdome, and bee as it were the executioners of his vengeance; not caring whether it lighted vpon innocents or no, he came more neerer vnto them, and in plaine tearmes to come quickly to the purpose, offered them his seruice, and that in such a manner, as they might command what they pleased: for he would attend you in such prety formes of Dog, Cat or Rat, that they should neither be terrified nor any body else suspicious of the matter. Vpon this they agree, and (as it should seeme) giue away their soules for the seruice of such Spirits, as he had promised them; which filthy conditions were ratified with abominable kisses, and an odious sacrifice of blood, not leauing out certaine charmes and coniurations with which the Diuell deceiued them, as though nothing could bee done without ceremony, and a solemnity of orderly ratification. By this time doth Sathan triumph, and goeth away satisfied to haue caught such fish in the net of his illusions: By this time are those women Diuels incarnate, and grow proud again in their cunning and artificiall power, to doe what mischeife they listed: By this time they haue learnt the manner of incantations, Spells and Charmes: By this they will kill what Cattle they list; and vnder the couert of flattery and familiar entertainment, keepe hidden the stinging serpent of mallice, and a venomous inclination to mischeife: By this time is the Earle and his family threatened, and must feele the burthen of a terrible tempest, which from these womens Diuellish deuises fell vppon him, he neither suspecting nor vnderstanding the same: By this time both himself and his honourable Countesse, are many times subiect to sicknesse and extraordinary convulsions, which they taking as gentle corrections from the hand of God, submit with quietnesse to his mercy, and study nothing more, then to glorifie their Creator in heauen, and beare his crosses on earth.

At last, as mallice increased in these damnable Women; so his family felt the smart of their reuenge and inficious disposition, For his eldest Sonne *Henry* Lord *Rosse* sickened very strangely, and after awhile died: his next named *Francis* Lord *Rosse* accordingly, was seuerely tormented by them; and most barbarously and inhumanely tortured by a strange sicknesse; not long after the Lady *Katherine* was set vpon by their dangerous and ·diuellish practises, and many times in great danger of life, through extreame maladies and vnusuall fits, nay (as it should seeme, and they afterwards confessed) both the Earle and his Countesse were brought into their snares as they imagined, and indeed determined to keepe them from hauing any more Children. Oh vnheard of wickednesse and mischievous damnation? Notwithstanding all this did the noble Earle attend his Majesty, both at Newmarket before Christmas, and at Christmas at Whitehall; bearing the losse of his Children most nobly, and little suspecting they had miscarried by witchcraft, or such like inuentions of the Diuell, vntill it pleased God to discouer the villanous practises, of these Woemen, and to command the Diuell from executing any further vengeance on Innocents, but leaue them to their Shames, and the hands of Iustice, that they might only be confounded for their villanous practises, but remaine as a notorious example to all ages of iudgement and fury. Thus were they apprehended about Christmas and carried to Lincolne Jayle, after due examination, before sufficient Iustices of the Peace, and discreete Maiestrates, who wondered at their audacious wickednes, but *Ioane Flower* the Mother before conuiction, (as they say) called for Bread and Butter, and wished it might neuer goe through if she were guilty of that, wherevpon she was examined: so mumbling it in her mouth, neuer spake more wordes after, but fell donne and dyed as she was carryed to Lincolne Goale, with a horrible excruciation of soule and body, and was buried at Ancaster.

When the Earle heard of their apprehension he hasted donne with his brother Sr. *George*, and sometimes examining them himself, and sometimes sending them to others; at last left them to the triall at Law, before the Iudges of Assise at *Lincolne*; and so they were conuicted of Murther and executed accordingly, about the 11. of March, to the terror of all beholders, and example of such dissolute and abominable Creatures, and because you shall haue both cause to glorifie God for this discouery, and occasion to apprehend the strangenesse of their liues, and truth of their proceedings : I thought it both meete and conuenient to lay open their onne Examinations and Euidences against one another, with such apparant circumstances, as doe not only shew the cause of their mislike and distasting against the Earle and his family; but the manner of their proceedings and reuenges, with other particulars belonging to the true and plaine discouery of their Villany and Witch-craft.

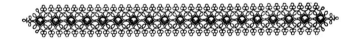

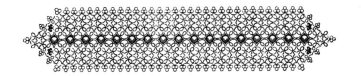

The Examinations of
Anne Baker, Ioane Willimot,
and *Ellen Greene;* as

followeth, &c.

Anne Baker.   *Ioane Willimot.*   *Ellen Greene.*

THE EXAMINATION

of *Anne Baker* of *Bottesford* in the County of *Leicester Spinster,* taken *March* 1. 1618. by the Right Honourable, *Francis Earl of Rutland,* Sir *George Manners Knight,* two of his *Maiesties Iustices* of the peace for the County of *Lincolne,* and *Samuel Fleming Doctor of Diuinitie,* one of his *Maiesties Iustices* of the peace for the County of *Leicester* aforesaid.

SHE *saith that there are foure colours of* Planets, *Blacke, Yellow, Greene, and Blew, and that Blacke is alwaies death, and she saw the Blew* Plannet *strike* Thomas Fairebarne *the eldest son vnto* William Fairebarne *of* Bottesford *aforesaid by the* Pinfold *there, within the which time the said* William Fairebarne *did beat her and breake her head, wherevpon the said* Thomas Fairebarne, *did mend. And being asked who did send that Planet? answered it was not I.*

Further shee saith, that shee saw a hand appeare vnto her, and that shee heard a voyce in the ayre said vnto her : Anne Baker, *saue thy selfe, for to morrow thou and thy Maister must be slaine : and the next day her Maister and shee were in a Cart together ; and suddainly shee saw a flash of fire, and said her prayers, and the fire went away, and shortly after a Crow came and peched upon her cloathes, and she said her prayers againe, and bad the Crow to go to whom he was sent, and the Crow went vnto her Maister, and did beat him to death, and shee with her prayers recouered him to life ; but he was sicke a fortnight after, and saith, that if shee had not*

224

had more knowledge then her Maister, both he and shee and all the Cattell had beene slaine.

Being examined concerning a Childe of Anne Stannidge, *which she was suspected to haue bewitched to death; saith, the said* Anne Stannidge *did deliuer her Childe into her hands, and that she did lay it upon her skirt, but did no harme vnto it: And being charged by the Mother of the Childe, that upon the burning of the haire and the paring of the nailes of the said Childe, the said* Anne Baker *came in and set her donne, and for one houres spaces could speake nothing; confesseth she came into the house of the said* Anne Stannidge *in great paine, but did not know of the burning of the haire and nailes of the said Childe; but said she was sicke that she did not know whither she went.*

Being charged that shee bewitched Elizabeth Hough, *the wife of* William Hough *to death, for that shee angred her in giuing her almes of her second bread; confesseth that she was angry with her and said she might haue giuen her of her better bread, for she had gone too often on her errands, but more she saith not.*

This Examinat confesseth that shee came to Ioane Gylles *house, her Child being sicke, and that shee intreated this Examinat to look on the Child, and to tell her whether it was forspoken or no, and this Examinat said it was forspoken; but when the said Child died she cannot tell.*

And being asked concerning Nortley *carrying of his Child home vnto his onn house, where the said* Anne Baker *was, shee asked him, who gaue the said Child that loafe, he told her* Anthony Gill, *to whom this Examinat said, he might haue had a Child of his onne if hee would haue sought in time for it: which words shee confessed shee did speake.*

Being blamed by Henry Milles *in this sort: A fire set on you, I haue two or three ill nights; to whom shee made answere, you should haue let me alone then, which shee confesseth.*

The said Anne Baker, *March* 2. 1618. *confesseth before* Samuel Fleming *Doctor of Diuinity, that about* 3. *yeares agoe, shee went into Northamptonshire, and that at her coming back againe, one* Peakes *wife and* Dennis *his wife of Beluoyre told her that my young Lord* Henry *was dead, and that their was a gloue of the said Lord buried in the ground ; and as that gloue did rot and wast, so did the liuer of the said Lord rot and wast.*

Further she said, March 3. 1618. *before Sr.* George Manners *Knight, and* Samuel Fleming *Doctor of Diuinity, that shee hath a Spirit which hath the shape of a White Dogge, which shee calleth her good Spirit.*

Samuel Fleming *test.*

The Examination of *Ioan Willimot*, taken the 28. of *February*, in the 16. yeare of the raigne of our Soueraigne Lord, IAMES, ouer *England* King and ouer *Scotland* the 52. before *Alexander Amcotts* Esquire, one of his Maiesties Iustices of the Peace of the said parts and County.

THIS Examinat saith, that *Ioane Flower* told her that my Lord of *Rutland* had dealt badly with her and that they had put away her Daughter, and that although she could not haue her will of my Lord himselfe, yet she had spied my Lords Sonne and had striken him to the heart. And she saith that my Lords Sonne was striken with a white Spirit, and that shee can cure some that send vnto her, and that some reward her for her paines, and of some she taketh nothing.

She further saith, that vpon Fryday night last, her Spirit came to her and told her that there was a bad woman at *Deeping* who had giuen her Soule to the Diuell: and that her said Spirit did then appeare vnto her in a more ugly forme then it had formerly done, and that it urged much to giue it something, although it were but a peece of her Girdle, and told her that it had taken great paines for her, but she saith that she would giue it nothing, and told it that she had sent it to no place but onely to see how my Lord *Rosse* did, and that her Spirit told her that he should doe well.

The Examination of the *Ioan Willimott*, taken the second day of March in the year abouesaid, before the said *Alexander Amcotts*.

THIS Examinate saith, That shee hath a Spirit which shee calleth *Pretty*, which was giuen vnto her by *William Berry* of *Langholme* in *Rutlandshire*, whom she serued three yeares; and that her Master when he gaue it vnto her, willed her to open her mouth, and hee would blow into her a Fairy which should doe her good; and that shee opened her mouth, and he did blow into her mouth; and that presently after his blowing, there came out of her mouth a Spirit, which stood vpon the ground in the shape and form of a Woman, which Spirit aske of her her Soule, which shee then promised vnto it, being willed therevnto by her Master. Shee further confesseth, that shee neuer hurt any body, but did helpe diuers that sent for her, which were stricken or fore-spoken: and that her Spirit came weekly to her, and would tell her of diuers persons that were stricken and forespoken. And shee saith, that the vse which shee had of the Spirit, was to know how those did which shee had vndertaken to amend; and that shee did helpe them by certaine prayers which she vsed, and not by her onne Spirit; neyther did shee imploy her Spirit in any thing, but onely to bring word how those did which she had vndertaken to cure.

And shee further saith, that her Spirit came vnto her this last night (as she thought) in the forme of a woman, mumbling, but she could not vnderstand what it said. And being asked whether shee were not in a dreame or slumber when she thought she saw it, shee said no, and she was as waking as at this present.

Alexander Amcotts.
Thomas Robinson test.

The Examination of *Ioane Willimot* of *Goadby* in the County of *Leicester* Widdow, taken the 17. of *March* 1618. by Sir *Henry Hastings* Knight, and *Samuel Fleming* Doctor of Diuinity, two of his Maiesties Iustices of the Peace of the said County of *Leicester*.

SHE saith that she tould one *Cookes* wife of *Stathorne* in the said County Labourer, that *Iohn Patchet* might haue had his Child aliue, if he would haue sought forth for it in time, and if it were not death stricken in her wayes, and that *Patchets* wife had an euil thing within her, which should make an end of her, and that she knew by her Girdle.

She saith further, that *Gamaliel Greete* of *Waltham* in the said County Shepheard, had a Spirit like a White Mouse put into him in his swearing; and that if hee did looke vpon any thing with an intent to hurt, it should be hurt, and that he had a marke on his left arme, which was cut away; and that her onn Spirit did tell her all this before it went from her.

Further she saith that *Ioane Flower, Margaret Flower* and shee, did meet about a week before *Ioane Flowers* apprehension, in *Black-borrow-hill*, and went from thence home to the said *Ioan Flowers* house, and there she saw two Spirits one like a Rat, and the other like an Owle; and one of them did sucke vnder her right eare, as she thought: and the said *Ioan* told her, that her Spirits did say that shee should neyther be hanged or burnt. Further she saith, that the said *Ioan Flower* did take up some earth and spet vpon it, and did worke it with her finger, and put it up into her purse, and said though she could not hurt the Lord himselfe, yet shee had sped his Sonne, which is dead.

H. Hastings.
Samuel Fleming.

The Examination of *Ellen Greene* of *Stathorne* in the County of *Leicester*, taken the 17. of *March* 1618. by Sir *Henry Hastings* Knight: and *Samuel Fleming* D. of Diuinitie, two of his Maiesties Iustices of Peace of said County.

SHEE saith, that one *Ioan Willimott* of *Goadby* came about sixe yeares since to her in the Wowlds, and perswaded this Examinate to forsake God, and betake her to the diuel, and she would giue her two Spirits, to which she gaue her consent, and therevpon the said *Ioan Willimot* called two

Spirits, one in the likenesse of a Kittin, and the other of a Moldiwarp: the first the said *Willimot* called *pusse*, the other *hiffe, hiffe*, and they presently came to her, and she departing left them with this Examinate, and they leapt on her shoulder, and the Kittin suckt vnder her right eare on her neck, and the Moldiwarp on the left side in the like place. After they had suckt her, shee sent the Kittin to a Baker of that Towne, whose name shee remembers not, who had called her Witch and stricken her; and bad her said Spirit goe and bewitch him to death: the Moldiwarp shee then bad go to *Anne Dawse* of the same towne and bewitch her to death, because she had called this Examinate witch, whore, jade, &c. and within one fortnight they both dyed.

And further this Examinate saith, that she sent both her Spirits to *Stonesby*, to one *Willison*, a husbandman, and *Robert Williman* a husbandmans sonne, and bad the Kittin goe to *Willison* and bewitch him to death, and the Moldywarp to the other, and bewitch him to death which they did; and within tenne dayes they dyed. These foure were bewitched while this Examinate dwelt at *Waltham* aforesaid.

About three yeares since, this Examinate remoued thence to *Stathorne*, where she now dwelt: vpon a difference between the said *Willimot* and the wife of *Iohn Patchet* of the said *Stathorne* Yeoman, she the said *Willimot* called her this Examinate to goe and touch the said *Iohn Patchets* Wife and her Childe, which shee did, touching the said *Iohn Patchets* Wife in her bed, and the Childe in the Grace-wifes armes, and then sent her said Spirits to bewitch them to death, which they did, and so the woman lay languishing by the space of a moneth and more, for then shee dyed; the Childe dyed the next day after she touched it.

And shee further saith, that the said *Ioane Willimot* had a Spirit sucking on her, vnder the left flanke in the likenesse of a little white Dogge which this Examinate saith, that she saw the same sucking in Barley-haruest last, being then at the house of the said *Ioan Willimot*.

And for hirselfe this Examinate further saith, that she gaue her soule to the Diuell to haue the Spirits at her command; for a confirmation whereof, she suffered them to suck her always as aforesaid about the change and full of the Moone.

H. Hastings.
Samuel Fleming.

The Examination of *Philip Flower,* sister of *Margaret Flower,* and daughter of *Ioan Flower,* before Sir *William Pelham,* and Mr. *Butler,* Iustices of the Peace, *Feb.* 4. 1618. which was brought in at the Assizes as euidence against her sister *Margaret.*

SHE saith, that her mother and her sister maliced the Earle of *Rutlande,* his Countesse, and their Children, because her sister *Margaret* was put out of the Ladies seruice of Laundry, and exempted from other seruices about the house, wherevpon her said sister, by the commandement of her mother, brought from the Castle the right hand gloue of the Lord *Henry Rosse,* which she deliuered to her Mother; who presently rubd it on the backe of her Spirit *Rutterkin,* and then put it into hot boyling water, afterward shee pricked it often and buried it in the yard, wishing the Lord *Rosse* might neuer thriue, and so her sister *Margaret* continued with her mother, where she often saw the Cat *Rutterkin* leape on her shoulder, and sucke her necke.

Shee further confesseth, that shee heard her mother often curse the Earle and his Lady, and therevpon would boyle feathers and blood together, vsing many Diuellish speeches and strange gestures.

The Examination of *Margaret Flower,* sister of *Phillip Flower* &c. about the 22 of January. 1618.

SHE saith and confesseth that about foure or fiue yeare since her Mother sent her for the right hand gloue of *Henry* Lord *Rosse* afterward that her mother bade her goe againe into the Castle of *Beauer,* and bring downe the gloue or some other thing of *Henry* Lord *Rosse,* and shee askt what to doe ? Her mother replyed to hurt my Lord *Rosse:* wherevpon she brought downe a gloue, and deliuered the same to her mother, who stroked *Rutterkin* her Cat with it, after it was dipt in hot water, and so prickt it often, after which *Henry* Lord *Rosse* fell sicke within a weeke, and was much tormented with the same. She further saith, that finding a gloue about two or three yeares since of *Francis* Lord *Rosse* on a dung-hill, she deliuered it to her mother, who put it into hot water, and after tooke it out and rubd it on *Rutterkin* the Cat, and bade him goe vpwards, and after her mother buried it in the yard, and said a mischeife light on him, but he will not mend againe.

She further saith, that her Mother and shee, and her Sister agreed together to bewitch the Earle and his Lady, that they might haue no more Children : and being demanded the cause of this their malice and ill-will; she saith, that about foure yeares since the Countesse (growing into some mislike with her) gaue her forty shillings, a bolster, and a mattresse, and bad her lye at home, and come no more to dwell at the Castle ; which she not onely tooke in ill part, but grudged at it exceedingly, swearing in her heart to be reuenged. After this, her Mother complained to the Earle against one *Peake,* who had offered her some wrong, wherein she conceiued that the Earle tooke not her part, as shee expected, which dislike with the rest, exasperated her displeasure against him, and so she watched the opportunity to bee reuenged: wherevpon she tooke wooll out of the said mattresse, and a pair of gloues, which were giuen her by Mr. *Vauasor,* and put them into warm water, mingling them with some blood, and stirring it together, then shee tooke the wooll and gloues out of the water, and rubd them on the belly of *Rutterkin* her Cat, saying the Lord and the Lady should haue more Children but it should be long first.

She further confesseth, that by her Mothers commandement, she brought to her a peece of a handkercher of the Lady *Katherine* the Earles daughter, and her mother put it into hot water, and then taking it out rubd it on *Rutterkin*, bidding him flye, and go; wherevpon *Rutterkin* whined and cryed Mew: wherevpon she said, that *Rutterkin* had no power ouer the Lady *Katherine* to hurt her.

The Examination of *Phillip Flower,* the 25. of *February* 1618. before *Francis* Earl of *Rutland, Francis* Lord *Willoughby* of Ersby, Sr. *George Manners,* and Sr. *William Pelham.*

SHEE confesseth and saith, that shee hath a Spirit sucking on her in the forme of a white Rat, which keepeth her left breast, and hath so done for three or foure yeares, and concerning the agreement betwixt her Spirit and hir selfe she confesseth and saith, that when it came first vnto her, shee gaue her Soule to it, and it promised to doe her good, and cause *Thomas Simpson* to loue her, if she would suffer it to sucke her, which she agreed vnto; and so the last time it suckt was on Tuesday at night the 23 of February.

The Examination of *Margaret Flower,* at the same time, &c.

SHEE confesseth, that shee hath two familiar Spirits sucking on her, the one white, the other black spotted; the white sucked vnder her left breast, and the blacke spotted within the inward parts of her secrets. When shee first entertained them shee promised them her soule, and they couenanted to doe all things which she commanded them, &c.

Shee further saith, that about the 30. of *Ianuary*, last past being Saturday, foure Diuells appeared vnto her in *Lincolne* Jayle, at eleuen or twelue o'clock at midnight: The one stood at her beds feete, with a blacke head like an Ape, and spake vnto her, but what, shee cannot well remember, at which shee was very angry because he would speake no plainer, or let her understand his meaning: the other three were *Rutterkin, Little Robin*, and *Spirit*, but shee neuer mistrusted them, nor suspected herselfe till then.

There is another Examination of the said *Margaret Flower*, taken the fourth of *February* 1618. tending to this effect.

THAT being asked what shee knoweth concerning the bewitching of the Earle of *Rutland*, his Wife, and Children, shee saith, that it is true, that her selfe, her mother, and sister were all displeased with him, especially with the Countesse, for turning her out of service, wherevpon some four year since her mother commanded her to goe vp to the Castle, and bring her the right hand gloue of the Lord *Henry Rosse*, the Earles eldest sonne; which gloue which she found on the rushes in the Nurcery, and deliuered the same to her mother, who put it into hot water, prickt it often with her knife, then tooke it out of the water, and rubd it vpon *Rutterkin*, bidding him height and goe, and doe some hurt to *Henry* Lord *Rosse*, wherevpon hee fell sicke, and shortly after dyed, which her mother hearing of, said it was well: but after shee had rubd the gloue on the Spirit *Rutterkin*, shee threw it into the fire and burnt it, &c.

THESE Examinations and some others were taken and charily preserued for the continuing of sufficient euidences against them, and when the Iudges of the Assize came downe to *Lincolne* about the first weeke in *March*, being Sir *Henry Hobart*, Lord Cheife Iustice of the Common Pleas, and Sir *Ed: Bromley* one of the Barons of the Exchequer, they were presented vnto them, who not only wondred at the wickednesse of these persons, but were amazed at their practises and horrible contracts with the Diuell to damne their onn soules: And although the Right Honourable Earle had sufficient greife for the losse of his Children; yet no doubt it was the greater to consider the manner, and how it pleased God to inflict on him such a fashion of visitation: Besides, as it amazed the hearers to vnderstand the particulars, and the circumstances of this diuellish contract, so was it as wonderfull to see their desperate impenitency, and horrible distraction, according to the rest of that sort, exclaiming against the Diuell for deluding them, and now breaking promise with them, when they stood in most need of his helpe. Notwithstanding all these aggrauations, such was the vnparelleld magnanimity, wisedome, and patience of this generous Nobleman, that hee vrged nothing against them more then their onne confessions, and so quietly left them to iudiciall triall, desiring of God mercy for their soules, and of men charity to censure them in their condemnation: but God is not mocked, and so gaue them ouer to iudgement, nor man so reformed, but for the Earles sake, they cursed them to that place which they themselues long before had bargained for.

What now remaines (gentle Reader) but for thee to make vse of so wonderfull a Story, and remarkable an accident, out of which to draw to a conclusion, thou maist collect these particulars. First that God is the supreame Commander of all things, and permitteth wonderfull actions in the world, for the tryall of the Godly, the punishment of the wicked, and his onne glory: of which man shall neuer attaine to know the reason or occasion. Secondly, that the Diuell is the meere seruant and agent of God, to prosecute whatsoeuer hee shall command rather then giue leaue vnto; limitting him yet thus farre in his onne nature, that he can go no further then the bounds within which hee is hedged. Thirdly that this God hath punishments, *ad correctionem*, that is to say Chasticements of the Godly, and *ad ruinam*, *Videlicet*, Iudgements against the wicked, wherein yet man must disclaime any knowledge, and forsake preiudicate opinions. For the very iust shall be tried like gold, and no man exempted from castigation whom God doth loue. Fourthly, that this Diuell, though he bee Gods Instrument, yet worketh altogether by deceit: for as he was lyer from the beginning; so let no man trust him, because he aymeth at the confusion of all mankinde. Fifthly, that the wicked (howeuer they may thriue and prosper for a time) yet in the end are sure to bee payed home, either with punishment in this life or the life to come, or both, as a finall reward of monstrous impiety. Sixthly, that Man in his frailty must not presume of prosperity, but prepare a kinde of stooping vnder the hand of God, when it pleaseth him to strike or punish us. Seauenthly, that there is no murmuring or repining against God, but quietly to tolerate his inflictings, whensoeuer they chance, of which this worthy Earle is a memorable example of all men and Ages. Eighthly, that the punishments of the wicked are so many warnings to all irregular sinners to amend their liues, and auoid the iudgement to come, by penitency and newnesse of life. Ninthly, that though man could bee content to passe ouer blasphemies and offences against the Statutes of Princes, yet God will ouertake them in their onn walks, and pull them backe by the sleeue into a Slaughter-house, as here you know the euidences against these people tooke life and power from their onne Confessions. Tenthly, and last of all, that priuate opinion, cannot preuaile against publique censures : for here you see the learned and religious Iudges cryed out with our Sauiour, *Exore tuo.* Therefore though it were so, that neither Witch nor Diuell could doe these things, yet *Let not a Witch liue,* saith God, and *Let them dye* (saith the Law of England) *that haue conuersation with Spirits, and presume to blaspheme the name of God with spells and incantation.* O then you sonnes of men, take warning by these examples, and eyther diuert your steps from the broad way of destruction, and irrecouerable gulph of damnation, or with *Iosuahs* counsell to *Achan,* blesse God for the discouery of wickednesse, and take thy death patiently, as the preuention of thy future iudgement, and sauing innocents from punishment, who otherwise may be suspected without cause.

Vtinam tam facile vera inuenire possem, quam falsa conuincere.

FINIS.

Appendix II
DAMNABLE PRACTISES

Of three Lincolne-shire Witches, *Joane Flower,* and her two Daughters, *Margret* and *Phillip Flower,* against *Henry* Lord *Rosse,* with others the Children of the Right Honourable the Earle of Rutland, at Beaver Castle, who for the same were executed at Lincolne the 11. of *March* last.

To the tune of the Ladies fall.

1. Of damned deeds, and deadly dole,
   I make my mournfull song,
   By Witches done in Lincolne-shire,
   where they have lived long:
   And practisd many a wicked deed,
   within that Country there,
   Which fills my brest and bosome full,
   of sobs, and trembling feare.

2. Fine Beaver Castle is a place,
   that welcome gives to all,
   By which the Earle of Rutland gaines
   the loves of great and small:
   His Countesse of like friendlinesse,
   doth beare as free a mind:
   And so from them both rich and poore,
   do helps and succour find.

3. Amongst the rest were Witches three,
   that to this Castle came,
   Call'd Margaret and Phillip Flower,
   and Joane their Mothers name:
   which Women dayly found reliefe,
   and were contented well:
   And at the last this Margret was,
   received there to dwell.

4. She tooke unto such houshold charge,
   as unto her belongd,
   Yet she, possest with fraud and guile,
   her place and office wrongd;
   She secretly purloyned things
   unto her mother home:
   And at unlawful howers from thence,
   would nightly goe and come.

5. And when the Earle & Countesse heard,
   and of her dealings knew,
   They grieved much that she should prove,
   unto them so untrue:
   And so discharg'd her of the house,
   therein to come no more:
   For of her lewd and filching pranks
   of proofes there were some store.

6. And likewise that her Mother was,
   a woman full of wrath,
   A swearing and blaspheming wretch,
   forespeaking sodaine death:
   And how that neighbours in her lookes,
   malitious signes did see:
   And some affirm'd she dealt with Sprits,
   and so a Witch might be.

7. And that her Sister Phillip was
   well known a Strumpet lewd,
   And how she had a young mans love,
   bewitched and subdued,
   Which made the young man often say,
   he had no power to leave
   Her curst inticing company,
   that did him so deceave.

8. When to the Earle and Countesse thus
   these just complaints were made,
   Their hearts began to breed dislike,
   and greatly grew afraid:
   Commanding that she never should
   returne unto their sight,
   Nor back into the Castle come,
   but be excluded quite.

238

9. Whereat the old malitious feend,
   with these her darlings thought:
   The Earle and Countesse them disgrac't
   and their discredits wrought:
   In turning thus despightfully,
   her daughter out of dores,
   For which revengement, in her mind
   she many a mischief stores.

10. Heereat the Divell made entrance in,
   his Kingdome to inlarge.
   And puts his executing wrath,
   unto these womens charge:
   Not caring whom it lighted on,
   the Innocent or no,
   And offered them his diligence,
   to flye, to run, and goe.

11. And to attend in pretty forms,
   of Dog, or Cat, or Rat,
   To which they freely gave consent,
   and much reioyc't thereat:
   And as it seemd they sould their soules,
   for service of such Spirits,
   And sealing it with drops of blood,
   damnation so inherits.

12. These Women thus being Divels grown,
   most cunning in their Arts,
   With charmes and with inchanting spells,
   they plaid most damned parts:
   They did forespeake, and Cattle kild,
   that neighbours could not thrive,
   And oftentimes their Children young
   of life they would deprive.

13. At length the Countesse and her Lord,
   to fits of sicknesse grew:
   The which they deemd the hand of God,
   and their corrections due:
   Which crosses patiently they bore,
   misdoubting no such deeds,
   As from these wicked Witches heere,
   malitiously proceeds.

14. Yet so their malice more increast,
    that mischief set in foote,
    To blast the branches of that house
    and undermine the roote:
    Their eldest son Henry Lord Rosse,
    possest with sicknesse strange,
    Did lingring, lye tormented long,
    till death his life did change.

15. Their second sonne Lord Francis next,
    felt like continuing woe:
    Both day and night in grievous sort,
    yet none the cause did know:
    And then the Lady Katherin,
    into such torments fell:
    By these their devilish practises,
    as grieves my heart to tell.

The second Part. To the same tune.

16. Yet did this noble minded Earle,
    so patiently it beare:
    As if his childrens punishments,
    right natures troubles were:
    Suspecting little, that such meanes,
    against them should be wrought,
    Untill it please'd the Lord to have
    to light these mischiefes brought.

17. For greatly here the hand of God,
    did worke in iustice cause:
    When he for these their practises
    Ttem all in question drawes.
    And so before the Magistrates,
    when as the yongest came,
    Who being guilty of the fact
    confest and tould the same.

240

18. How that her mother and her selfe,
    and sister gave consent:
    To give the Countesse and her Lord,
    occasions to repent
    That ere they turnd her out of dores,
    in such a vile disgrace:
    For which, or them or theirs should be,
    brought into heavy case.

19. And how her sister found a time,
    Lord Rosses glove to take:
    Who gave it to her mothers hand
    consuming spels to make.
    The which she prickt all full of holes,
    and layd it deepe in ground:
    Where as it rotted, so should he,
    be quite away consum'd.

20. At which her elder sister did,
    acknowledge to be true:
    And how that she in boyling blood,
    did oft the same imbrew,
    And hereupon the yong Lord Rosse,
    such torments did abide:
    That strangely he consum'd away,
    untill the houre he died.

21. And likewise she confest how they
    together all agreed:
    Against the children of this Earle,
    to practise and prceed.
    Not leaving them a child alive,
    and never to have more:
    If witchcraft so could doe, because
    they turnd them out of dore.

22. The mother as the daughters told,
    could hardly this deny:
    For which they were attached all,
    by Justice speedily.
    And unto Lincolne Citty borne,
    therein to live in Jayle:
    Until the Judging Sizes came,
    that death might be their bayle.

23. But there his hatefull mother witch,
    these speeches did recall:
    And said that in Lord Rosses death,
    she had no hand at all.
    Whereon she bread and butter tooke,
    God let this same (quoth she)
    If I be guilty of his death,
    passe never thorough me.

24. So mumbling it within her mouth,
    she never spake more words:
    But fell downe dead, a iudgment iust,
    and wonder of the Lords.
    Her Daughters two their tryalls had,
    of which being guilty found,
    They dyed in shame, by strangling twist,
    and layd by shame in ground.

25. Have mercy Heaven, on sinners all,
    and grant that never like
    Be in this Nation knowne or done,
    but Lord in vengeance strike:
    Or else convert their wicked lives
    which in bad wayes are spent:
    The feares of God and love of heaven,
    such courses will prevent.

FINIS

There is a booke printed of these
Witches, wherein you shall know
all their examinations and confessions
at large: As also the wicked practise
of three other most Notorious Witches in *Leceister*-shire with all their
examinations and confessions.

Printed by *G.Eld* for *Iohn Barnes* dwelling in the long Walke neere
Christ-Church   1619

*[Note: The section after 'FINIS' is not a further verse of the ballad, but a
printer's advertisement for the pamphlet, printed at the bottom right-
hand corner of the original sheet.]*

Appendix III
EARLS OF RUTLAND 1525–1703

Following the re-creation of the Earldom of Rutland in 1525, there were six generations or so of the Manners family who held the Earldom

First Generation

Thomas Manners First Earl of Rutland (c.1488-1543) was a close personal friend and distant relative of HenryVIII, as he traced his lineage from Edward IV. Thomas first married Elizabeth Lovell. On her death without children, he married Eleanor Paston and they had 11 children

Second Generation

Henry Manners Second Earl of Rutland (c. 1516-1563) married Margaret Neville (d. 1560) and they had five children, including Edward (3rd Earl) and John (4th Earl). Henry's second wife was Bridget, née Hussey, who after Henry's death married the Earl of Bedford and thereafter was known as Lady Bedford, chief mourner at the funeral of Mary Queen of Scots in 1588.One of Henry's many brothers was Sir John Manners of Haddon, (died 1611) married to Dorothy Vernon and they had four children including Sir George Manners.

Third Generation:

Edward Manners Third Earl of Rutland (1549-1587) married Isabel , née Holcroft, and they had one surviving child, Elizabeth, who became Baroness Ros in her own right on her father's death and had a son William Cecil, Lord Ros, died 1618. Edward, a significant diplomat who supported the young James VI of Scotland, was succeeded by his brother: John Manners Fourth Earl of Rutland (c.1552-1588) who was married to Elizabeth, née Charlton. Earl for less than a year and they had 4 surviving sons and three surviving daughters. Their cousin Sir George Manners of Haddon(c.1573-1623) son of Sir John Manners, married Grace Pierpont and they had 8 children

Fourth and Fifth Generation:

Roger Manners Fifth Earl of Rutland (1576-1612) became Earl when a student at Cambridge, aged 12. He married Elizabeth Sidney the daughter of Sir Philip Sidney and their marriage was childless. Both died in the year 1612, the same year as the Prince of Wales, Prince Henry. Francis Manners Sixth Earl of Rutland (1578-1632) married Frances née Knyvett, died ?1607 and they had one surviving daughter, Catherine, later the Duchess of Buckingham and Baroness Ros in her own right. In October 1608 Francis married a strong catholic Cecily née Tufton and they had two sons, Henry who died in 1613 and Francis who died in 1620. The catholic Earl Francis had his own tomb built before his death and was succeeded by his brother George Manners Seventh Earl of Rutland (1580-1641) who married Frances née Carey; they had no surviving children and as Sir Oliver Manners, a catholic gentleman, the fourth surviving brother had died in1613, George was succeeded in 1641 by his second cousin John Manners Eighth Earl of Rutland of Haddon (1604-1679) married a strong protestant Frances, daughter of Lord Montague of Boughton and they had at least ten children. Earl John was a lukewarm parliamentarian during the Civil War and so the family did not suffer, but Belvoir Castle was destroyed as a potential refuge for royalists and it was rebuilt in the 1650s, following designs by John Webb

Sixth Generation:

John Manners Ninth Earl of Rutland and First Duke (1638-1711) like his father a supporter of parliament and a strong advocate of the 1688 revolution, had a problematic first wife, Anne daughter of the Marquis of Dorchester. Having divorced her and disinherited her child by Act of Parliament, he married Diana daughter of the Earl of Aylesbury who died in childbirth. He then married Catherin Noel and had 4 children. As a result of his support of Princess Anne in 1688, he was eventually created first Duke of Rutland in 1703

Appendix IV

LETTER FROM DR HENRY ATKINS TO CECILIA, COUNTESS OF RUTLAND

Right honourable............................
I reseyved your L^r.........................
Mr Athil a physician of y^r Countrey
unknown to me I am sory that ....
hath any instance to use .... selfe
....................the matter is not great that y^r
L[adyship] rigt of because I find not by yr le^r that
the little lord hath any cōvulsions or fits that
take away his sence or .... his motions
but onely a jumping of his mouth by reason
of some physicke gathering in his mouth
& jawes or throte ....making him sometime
move his mouth some times a little more
than ordinary, yet I doe not wish that
it should be neglected but that some means
may be used [for?] pservation & prevention
I am informed by Mr Athil that some
[means?] of things with ....
in his [rages?] but he hath set down
....thinge
..............I for my part am not used to give
..............opinions of things I have not [witnessed?]
.... not trew [instruct?] therefore
I pray you pardon me yt I pass that
over for I love not to walk in the dark
And the answer I have in a peece
of paper by itself set downe
some things I wold have the
little lord use I have sent him
w^t wth the things what directions as
I .... will serve until I see
y^m at London. And for I take
my leave & rest for ever at
y^r L^y comandment   He Atkins
[?] Sept 1616

244

REFERENCES

The works used in the preparation and writing of this book are listed below as they appear chapter by chapter and page by page in the book. If a text is cited extensively, the full citation is given on the first occasion in which it is referred to, and an abbreviated reference to the author is put after this citation in square brackets. For all further citations, the abbreviated reference is used, generally with a precise page reference, especially relating to a quotation from that text.

The page references in round brackets in the body of the main text of the book, *eg*: (*page 9*), refer exclusively to the original page-numbers of the Belvoir pamphlet *The Wonderful Discoverie of the Witchcrafts of Margaret and Phillip Flower daughters of Joan Flower neere Bever Castle* 1619, reprinted around 1838, which is printed as an appendix on pages 209 to 232. My citations from the Belvoir pamphlet generally employ the spelling of the 1838 reprint.

Twenty-first century conventional page numbering was not always used in Jacobean books, which were sometimes paginated in groups of folios: *recto* means the first side and *verso* the second side of a page, so that:

A1 recto = p.1; A1 verso = p.2; A2 recto = p.3; A2 verso = p.4; A3 recto = p.5; A3 verso = p.6; A4 recto = p.7; A4 verso = p.8; B1 recto = p.9; B1 verso = p.10; etc. So Z3 verso = 102, i.e. the last page of Potts' pamphlet on the Lancashire witches (I think!).

The following abbreviations are used in the References:

CSPD = Calendar of State Papers Domestic; D of R = Duke of Rutland; ed = edited by; HMC = Historical Manuscripts Commission; LRO = Leicestershire and Rutland Record Office; LA = Lincolnshire Archives; LRS = Lincoln Record Society; MSS = manuscripts; ODNB = Oxford Dictionary of National Biography; p. = page; NA/ PRO = National Archives/Public Record Office, Kew.

Prologue

p.13: Richard Boulton *Compleat History of Magick, Sorcery, and Witchcraft* 1715–16 [Boulton] p.181.

p.13: Robin Briggs *Witches and Neighbours: The Social and Cultural Context of European Witchcraft* 1996 [Briggs] p.285.

p.14: Stuart Clark *Thinking with Demons: The Idea of Witchcraft in Early Modern Europe* 1997 [Clark i].

p.16: Historical Manuscripts Commission *The Manuscripts of his Grace the Duke of Rutland GCB preserved at Belvoir Castle* vol. i and ii 1888; vol. iv 1905 [*MSS D of R* i; *MSS D of R* ii; *MSS D of R* iv].

p.19: Marion Gibson *Reading Witchcraft: Stories of early English witches* 1999 [Gibson i].

p.19: Reginald Scot *The Discoverie of Witchcraft* 1584 pp.7, 13.

The Vale Families

p.29: *MSS D of R* iv pp.385, 452 and 505.

p.30: Bottesford Parish Register in the LRO.

p.31: Will of Thomas Fairbairn, LRO Bottesford wills.

p.32: Keith Thomas *Religion and the Decline of Magic* 1973 [Thomas] p.758.

p.32: William Perkins *The Foundation of the Christian Religion* 1600 printed in William Perkins *A Golden Chaine* 1600 p.1027 [Perkins i].

p.33: Robin Briggs *The Witches of Lorraine* 2007; personal communication.

p.33: Adam Daubney, 'The Portable Antiquities Scheme in Lincolnshire' in *Lincolnshire History and Archæology* vol. 38, 2003 p.86. For fuller details of local witch-bottles, see Bob Sparham's very useful account on the Bottesford Living History website, www.bottesfordhistory.org.uk.

p.36: Marion Gibson *Early Modern Witches: Witchcraft Cases in Contemporary Writing* 2000 [Gibson ii] index, p.325.

p.36: Alan Macfarlane *Witchcraft in Tudor and Stuart England: A Regional and Comparative Study* 1970 [Macfarlane i].

p.36: Thomas p.661.

p.36: Briggs p.142, p.147.

p.39: *MSS D of R* iv p.437.

p.40: Marion Gibson 'Accusers' Stories in Print in Early Modern England' in Marijke Gijswijt, Hilary Marland, Hans de Waardt (eds) [Gijswijt] *Illness and Healing Alternatives in Western Europe*,1997.

p.40: S.T. Coleridge *Notes on the Tragedies of Shakespeare: Othello* in *Oxford Dictionary of Quotations* 2nd edition 1953.

The Castle Family: The Earls of Rutland

p.46: William Burton *Description of Leicestershire* 1622 p.43.

p.47: *MSS D of R* iv pp.260–528.

p.38: The genealogical details are from Rev. Irvin Eller *History of Belvoir Castle* 1841 [Eller] p.1.

p.48: *MSS D of R* iv pp.185–187.

p.54: *MSS D of* R i p.366.

p.55: Eller p.43.

pp.55: *MSS D of R* iv pp.296–300.

p.56: *MSS D of R* i p.201; MSS D of R iv p.469.

p.58: *MSS D of* R iv pp.388–393.

p.60:*MSS D of R* i p.247.

p.60: HMC *Earl of Salisbury MSS* vol. xx p.37.

pp.61–62: Robert Devereux, Earl of Essex *Profitable Instructions* 1633 pp.30–31, 52, 60.

p.62: *MSS D of R* iv p.494.

p.64: *Proclamation by the Queene* 1600/1, Bodleian Library, Oxford.

p.66: *MSS D of R* i p.374.

pp.66–67: Laurence Stone *Family and Fortune: Studies in Aristocratic Finance in the Sixteenth and Seventeenth Centuries*1973 pp.181, 184.

pp.67–68: *MSS D of* R i pp.413–4.

The Physicians

p.75: Stuart Clark 'Demons and Disease' in Gijswijt et al. p.47.

p.75: The Isaac Watts quotation is taken from Samuel Johnson *Dictionary of the English Language* 1755: 'prophylactick'.

pp.75–76: Mathias Prideaux *An easy and compendious introduction* Oxford 1682 p.376.

p.76: Andrew Wear *Knowledge and Practice in English Medicine 1550–1680* Cambridge. 2000 p.156 [Wear].

p.76: Roy Porter *The Greatest Benefit to Mankind* 1997 p.202.

p.76: Unpublished letter from the Rev. Francis Curtis to Maurice Johnson, early eighteenth century undated but probably 1713, in the archives of the Spalding Gentlemen's Society, Spalding, Lincolnshire; see Diana and Michael Honeybone 'Calendar of the Letters of the Spalding Gentlemen's Society' forthcoming, LRS.

p.77: John Thorys's letter is in HMC *MSS of the Marquis of Downshire* vol. 3 p.297.

p.79: *MSS D of R* iv p.464.

p.79: See Wear p.33 for Thomas Decker.

p.79: Nathan Bailey *Dictionarium Britannicum* 1730 in George Olms' reprint 1969 [Bailey].

pp.79–80: William Clowes: in FNL Poynter (ed) *Selected Writings of William Clowes 1544–1604* 1948 p.77.

p.80: Philemon Holland *Regimen Sanitatis Salerni* English translation 1617, preface.

pp.80–81: Gervase Markham *The English House-Wife* 1649 pp.13–14.

p.82: Definition of 'bezoar': J. Bullokar *An English Expositor: Teaching the interpretation of the hardest words used in our language* 1616 [Bullokar]. For a modern usage see J.K.Rowling *Harry Potter and the Philosopher's Stone* 1997, p.103.

p.82: *MSS D of R* iv pp.415, 416, 417, 48.

pp.82–83: *MSS D of R* iv p.490, 491.

p.83: Definition of 'issue': Bailey.

p.84: *MSS D of R* ii p.353: iv p.457.

p.84: *MSS D of R* iv p.499.

p.84: Elizabeth Furdell *The Royal Doctors 1485–1714: Medical Personnel at the Tudor and Stuart Courts* p.109, p.112.

p.84: Vivian Nutton 'Dr Butler Revisited' in *Medical History* 1978, 22, pp.419, 421.

p.85: Francis Peck *Desiderata Curiosa* Liber VI 1779 edition [Peck] p.198: Dr Atkins.

p.85: Roy Strong *Henry Prince of Wales and England's Lost Renaissance* 2000 p.166. This book is a good life of Prince Henry, 'England's Hope', as Prince of Wales in 1610.

pp.85–86: Peck p.207.

pp.86–87: *MSS D of R* iv p.497, i p.449. The original letter is in the archives of Belvoir Castle. Dr Atkins' writing, like that of some doctors today, is not easy to follow. See Appendix IV, p.244.

p.88: *MSS D of R* iv pp.502, 507, 510.

p.88: William Birken 'The social problem of the English Physicians in the early seventeenth century' in *Medical History* 1987, 31: 201–216 p.213.

p.88; *MSS D of R* i p.453.

p.89: William Birken: Entry for Thomas Ridgley in *ONDB*, 2004 (source *Lansdowne MSS* 238 folio 149).

p.89: Jonathan Andrews: Entry for Richard Napier in *ODNB*, 2004.

p.89: *MSS D of R* iv pp.501, 504.

p.90: Michael MacDonald *Mystical Bedlam: Madness, anxiety and healing in seventeenth-century England* 1981 [MacDonald] p.32.

p.90: The detailed references to Dr Napier's activities are all in the Bodleian Library, Oxford: Mss Ashmole 237 especially folios 56 recto, 66 recto, 90 verso, 105 verso, 108 recto, 111 verso, 190 recto.

p.91: Porter p.116.

p.91: MacDonald p.199.

p.92: John Cotta *The Triall of Witchcrafts shewing the true and right method of the discovery* 1616 p.57 and Epistle Dedicatory.

p.93: MacDonald p.209.

p.93: Francis Anthony *Aurum-Potabile or the Receit of Dr Fr. Antonie* 1683 [Anthony i] pp.75, 78.

p.93: *MSS D of R* iv p.512.

p.94: Bullokar: Definition of 'dram'.

p.94: Francis Anthony *The Apologie* 1616 [Anthony ii] title page and p.24. He discusses his five reasons for using his *aurum potabile* on pp.5–15.

p.95: Henry Cockeram *The English Dictionarie or An Interpreter of Hard English Words* 1626, reprinted Olms 197: definition of 'experiment'.

p.95: Anthony ii pp.77–78.

Perceptions of Witchcraft

p.105: Clark i p. 249.

p.105: Gijswijt et al. p.47.

p.106: F.L. Cross and E.A. Livingstone (eds) *The Oxford Dictionary of the Christian Church* 1997 p.1530.

p.106: David Wootton 'Reginald Scot/ Abraham Fleming/the Family of Love' in Stuart Clark ed. *Languages of Witchcraft*, 2001, p.122 (the quotation from Scot) and p.124 [Clark ii].

p.106: Jean Bodin *Démonomanie des Sorciers* 1580: personal communication from Robin Briggs.

p.108: William Perkins *The Whole Treatise of the Cases of Conscience* 1606 facsimile reprint 1972 [Perkins ii] p.153.

p.108: Clark i p.246: Torreblanca discussion.

p.109: Perkins ii p.152–159.

p.110: King James I *Dæmonologie* 1597 [*Dæmonologie*] pp.4, 5, Preface.

p.110: S.R. Gardiner, *History of England from the accession of James I to the outbreak of the Civil War 1603–1642* vol. VII, 1629–1635, p.323.

p.110: *Dæmonologie* p.55.

p.110: Briggs p.284.

pp.110–111: *Dæmonologie* p.98, p.79, p.1, p.79. p.80.

p.111: Alexander Roberts *A Treatise of Witchcraft* 1616 [Roberts] p.A2 recto, p.2, p.4, p.24.

p.112: Gibson ii p.175.

p.113: Gibson i p.181.

p.113: George Gifford *A dialogue concerning witches and witchcrafts* 1593 [Gifford], folios 2 verso, A2 verso.

pp.113–114: Gifford folio A2 verso.

P.114: Roberts p.4.

p.114: Gifford folio A3 recto.

p.115: Alan Macfarlane 'A Tudor Anthropologist: George Gifford's *Discourse* and *Dialogue*' in Sidney Anglo (ed) *The Damned Art: Essays in the literature of Witchcraft* 1977 [Macfarlane ii] pp.140, 148.

p.115: Gifford folios H3 verso, D2 verso, B4 verso, all specified in Alan Macfarlane's article cited above.

p.116: Darren Oldridge 'Protestant Conceptions of the Devil in early Stuart England' *History* vol.85 April 2000, pp.236, 234.

p.116: John Cotta *A short discoverie of the unobserved dangers of severall sorts of ignorant and unconsiderate practisers of physicke in England* 1612 [Cotta i].

p.117: Cotta i contents page: 'The severall tractates'.

pp.117–118: John Cotta *The triall of witch-craft, shewing the true and right methode of the discovery: with a confutation of erroneous wayes* 1616 [Cotta ii] pp.87, 101, 113, 114, 115, 116, 126.

pp.118–9: Peter Elmer: Entry for John Cotta in *ODNB* 2004.

p.119: Cotta i p.66.

p.119: Gibson ii p.180.

p.119: Thomas Potts *The wonderfull discoverie of Witches in the countie of Lancaster* 1613 [Potts], folios A2 verso, A3 verso.

p.119: Mark Beard: Entry for William Stansby in *ODNB* 2004.

p.120: I. Goulart, translated by Edward Grimstone *Admirable and Memorable Histories containing the wonders of our time* 1607, folio A4 verso.

p.120: Anon *The wonderfull discoverie of the witch-crafts of Margaret and Phillip Flower* 2nd edition, printed by G. Eld 1621, folios D recto and D verso.

pp.125–126: Roberts pp.54–5, 55–6, 57–8.

pp. 127–128: Anon *The life and death of Lewis Gaufredy* 1612 folios B4 recto, D3 recto, D3 verso, title page.

p.128: Clark i p.425.

p.128: James Sharpe *Instruments of Darkness: Witchcraft in England 1550–1750* 1996 p.65.

pp.129–131: Anon *Witches apprehended, examined and executed, for notable villanies by them committed both by land and water With a strange and most true triall how to know whether a woman be a witch or not.* 1613, folios B verso, B recto, B3 recto, B3 verso, B4 recto, folio C1 recto, A2.

p.132: Clark i p.513.

pp.132–133: *MSS D of R* i p.492. The sixth Earl's will is in the NA/PRO.

p.133: *House of Lords Journal* vol.3 20 May 1624.

pp.133–134: Clark i p.527.

p.134: I am indebted to Clare Painting-Stubbs for her detailed and enlightening work on Abraham Fleming.

p.135: Wootton 'Reginald Scot/Abraham Fleming/the Family of Love' in Clark ii p.125.

p.135: Reginald Scot *The Discoverie of Witchcraft* 1584 Book 6 Chapter VI p.123.

pp.137–139: Charles Odingsells: *Two Sermons, lately preached at Langar in the Valley of Belvoir* 1619, 1620 printed by William Stansby, pp.10, 12, 13, 14,17, 20, 35, 38, 40–41, 50–51.

p.140: Alexandra Walsham '"Frantic Hacket": Prophecy, Sorcery, Insanity and the Elizabethan Puritan Movement' in *Historical Journal* vol.41 issue 01,1998, p.31.

248

The Trial

p.156: R.H. Helmholz *Roman Canon Law in Reformation England* 2004 p.604.

p.156: Margaret Bowker *An Episcopal Court Book for the Diocese of Lincoln 1514–1520* L R S vol.61 1967, pp.84–5.

pp.156–158: For the case re. Thomas Johnson, see LA Court Papers 58/2 170, among the Lincoln Diocesan Records.

p.159: James Sharpe *The Bewitching of Anne Gunter* 2000 [Sharpe ii] p.65 (for figure of 40,000 accusations), an excellent study of a specific witchcraft accusation.

pp.159–160: G.W. Prothero *Select Statutes and other Constitutional Documents illustrative of the Reigns of Elizabeth and James I* 1913 [Prothero] pp.149–150.

p.160: The four relevant Acts of Parliament were 33 Henry VIII c.8 (1542) repealed by 1 Edward VI c.12 (1547); 6 Elizabeth I c.16 (1563) and 1 James I c.12 (1604). The best sources for these acts are the various eighteenth- and nineteenth-century volumes of *Statutes at Large of England* and Marion Gibson *Witchcraft and Society in England and America 1550–1750* 2003, pp.1–7.

p.162: Sharpe ii p.67.

p.162: Macfarlane ii p.40.

p.162: Malcolm Gaskill *Crime and Mentalities in Early Modern England* 2000, p.29. Malcolm Gaskill's study of Matthew Hopkins: *Witchfinders A Seventeenth-Century English Tragedy* 2005 is the best study of a single witchcraft episode today.

pp.162–163: Peter French *John Dee: The World of an Elizabethan Magus* 1984, pp.6, 11.

p.163: Prothero i pp.78–9.

pp.163–164: *MSS D of R* i pp.147, 294.

p.164: The process of the 1604 bill through both Houses of Parliament can be followed through the relevant House of Lords Journal and House of Commons Journal for 1604 which can be located at www.british-history.ac.uk .

pp.164–165: Gregory Durston *Witchcraft and Witch Trials: a History of English Witchcraft and its Legal Perspective 1542–1736* 2000 p.179: a first rate study of witchcraft trials.

p.165: Stephen Pumfrey 'Potts, plots and politics: James I's *Dæmonologie* and *The Wonderfull Discoverie of Witches*' in Robert Poole (ed.) *The Lancashire Witches: Histories and Stories* 2002 p.19, another fine set of studies of a specific trial.

p.165: John Nichols *History and Antiquities of the County of Leicestershire* vol.II part i, p.471.

p.165: G.L.Kittredge 'King James I and "The Devil is an Ass"' in *Modern Philology* 1911 vol. 9 no. 2 p.198.

pp.165–166: *MSS D of R* i p.422 for Hastings.

p.166: *MSS D of R* iv p.510.

p.168: Boulton p.185.

p.169: *House of Lords Journal* vol. 3, 20 May 1624.

p.171: Anthony à Wood *Athenæ Oxonienses* 1691 vol. i p.435.

p.173: David Lemmings 'Criminal trial procedure in eighteenth-century England' in *Journal of Legal History* April 2005 vol 26 no. 1 p.66.

p.174: James I *Dæmonologie* 1597 p.49.

p.174: Durston p.290.

p.175: Macfarlane i pp.23–65.

p.176: J.S. Cockburn *A History of English Assizes* 1972 p.112 for Blackstone.

p.176: Cockburn p.311 for York Assizes.

p.178: James Sharpe 'The writings of James VI and I' in *Essays presented to G.E. Aylmer* 1993 p.89.

p.178: King James I *The Works of the most High and Mightie Prince James* 1616 p.551.

p.178: *Exodus* chapter 22 verse 18.

p.178: *Dæmonologie* p.78–9.

pp.178–179: Sharpe i pp.48–9.

p.179: Durston p.154.

p.179: Stephen Pumfrey in Poole (ed.) pp.26–7 for Bromley.

pp.179–180: Potts folio A3 verso for Bromley.

p.180: Potts folios B3 recto, B3 verso, B4 recto, C1 recto, C3 recto.

p.180: Potts folios X3 recto to Z3 verso.

p.181: Potts folios S1 verso, R3 recto.

pp.181–182: Potts folios R2 verso to S2 recto, trial of Alizon Device; see the transcription in Gibson i pp.242–246, where all quotations can be found.

p.182: Abraham Fleming *A Straunge and Terrible Wunder* 1577: account of the Black Dog of Bungay.

p.184: *MSS D of R* iv p.519.

p.185: J. Bruce (ed.) *Calendar of State Papers Domestic 1634–5* (*CSPD*) for Pelham.

p.185: Alison Findlay 'Sexual and spiritual politics in the events of 1633–34' in Poole pp.146–7 and *CSPD* reference above.

Epilogue

p.191: *MSS D of R* i p.492.

p.192: RB *The Kingdom of Darkness* 1688, printed by the actual author, Nathaniel Crouch. Crouch possibly took his pseudonym from the initials of Robert Burton, the very popular author of *The Anatomy of Melancholy* (ODNB).

pp.193–194: Boulton pp.178, 179, 180, 181.

p.194: Francis Hutchinson *An Historical Essay concerning Witchcraft* 1718 p.180.

pp.194–195: White Kennett *A sermon upon the Witchcraft of the present Rebellion* 1715 p.9.

p.195: Briggs pp.283, 409.

p.196: James Boswell *Life of Johnson* Oxford World Classics edition 1998 p.483.

p.196: John Nichols *History and Antiquities of the History of Leicestershire* c.1800 ,vol. II part i Appendix p.69.

p.197: Thomas Heywood and Richard Brome *The Late Lancashire Witches* 1634.

p.197: Thomas Shadwell *The Lancashire Witches* 1682.

p.197: Charles Dibdin *The Songs etc in a new Pantomime called the Lancashire Witches: or the Distresses of Harlequin* 1783.

p.198: Montague Summers *The History of Witchcraft and Demonology* 1992 p.309.

p.198: P.G. Maxwell-Stuart *Witchcraft a History* 2000 p.131.

p.199: Giambattista Vico *The New Science* 3rd edition of 1744 reprinted Cornell 1976 pp.103, 106.

p.199: Rosemary Sweet *Antiquaries: the Discovery of the Past in Eighteenth Century Britain* 2004 p.347.

pp,199–200: Eller pp.62, 65.

p.200: Karl Popper *The Poverty of Historicism* 1961 p.3.

pp.200–201: Margaret Murray *The Witchcult in Western Europe* 1921.

p.201: Hilda Lewis *The Witch and the Priest* 1956 p.303.

p.201: Christina Larner *Enemies of God. The Witch-hunt in Scotland 1981* p.3 [Larner].

p.201: WH Burston *Principles of History Teaching* 1963 pp.129, 131.

p.202: Larner pp.1–3.

p.202: Christina Larner in Alan Macfarlane (ed.)*Witchcraft and Religion The Politics of Popular Belief* 1984 p.vii.

pp.202–203: Thomas, pp.613, 660, 661 n. 89, 697.

p.203: Alan Macfarlane *The Culture of Capitalism* 1987 Chapter Five. pp. 98–122 for an excellent discussion of the connection between evil and witchcraft, to which I am very much indebted; see especially pp.103–112.

p.203–204: Briggs p.283, 411.

p.203: Sharpe i p.302.

In addition to all the books referred to above I have found the following fictional versions of the story, both by the Australian author Jon Elbourne, most interesting and based on sound research:

Mother Flower or the Witches of Belvoir Castle 1999 (a play) ISBN 0 646 2178 3;
The True Story of the Witches of Belvoir Castle (a short story) ISBN 978 0 9589168 9 9.

PICTURE CREDITS

I wish to acknowledge the kindness of the following people and institutions who have generously allowed me to use material for which they hold the copyright. If I have inadvertently failed to acknowledge the ownership of copyright of other illustrations I apologise and would ask the owner to contact me or the publisher.

BC	Buccleuch Collection at Boughton House
BCA	Belvoir Castle and Archives
BL	British Library
BLH	Bottesford Living History Website
BMP	British Museum Press
CU	Cornell University
CUL	Cambridge University Library
EEBO	Early English Books Online
FSL	Folger Shakespeare Library
GJ	Grantham Journal
HER	Ted Rayson
HL	Huntington Library, California
HUL	Harvard University Library
IE	Rev.Irvin Eller *Belvoir Castle*, 1841
JM	John Macdonald
JN	John Nichols *History & Antiquities of the County of Leicester* c.1800 vol. II pt. i
LLS	From the Local Studies Collection Lincoln Central Library, by courtesy Lincolnshire county Council, Culture and Adult Education Services
LRO	Leicestershire and Rutland Record Office
MCC	Magdalene College, Cambridge
MH	Michael Honeybone
NPG	National Portrait Gallery
OAM	Oxford Ashmolean Museum
OB	Oxford Bodleian Library
OUP	Oxford University Press
RB	Robin Briggs *Witches and Neighbours*, 1996
SGS	Spalding Gentlemen's Society
SNPG	Scottish National Portrait Gallery
SMCB	St Mary's Church, Bottesford
SUP	Stanford University Press
UEAL	University of East Anglia Library
UI	University of Illinois
VPE	Vaughan Evans

INDEX Figures in *italics* refer to illustrations

SUBSCRIBERS

Presentation copies

1 St Mary's Church, Bottesford
2 The Duke and Duchess of Rutland
3 Bottesford Local History Society
4 Bottesford Living History Community Heritage Project
5 Mr Robin Briggs
6 Professor Stuart Clark
7 Dr Marion Gibson
8 Mr Vance Harvey

9 Clive and Carolyn Birch
10 Michael and Diana Honeybone
11 Aileen Collinson
12 John and Jean Hammond
13 Dorothy Baines
14–15 Stephen Vogt
16 Rod and Rita Poxon of Gayton, Northants
17 Ted and Kathleen Rayson
18 T.W. Hollingworth
19 Mr and Mrs R.J. Hirst
20 Nicola and Glyn Moxham
21 Judith and Mike Bayley
22 Nataša and Patrick Honeybone
23 Alan Peterson
24 Mr B. Sullivan
25 Joan Holland
26 J.C. Morgan
27 J.W. Belsham
28–29 Nottinghamshire County Council
30 Andrew Forsyth
31 Robert Trubshaw
32 Kayte Redding
33 Norman and Celia Whiting
34 Mark Leggott
35 Clare Painting-Stubbs
36 Nigel and Caroline Webb
37 Mrs P.A. Allpress
38 Darren Wintle
39 Christine Wensley
40 Mike Sparkes
41– 45. Nottingham Central Library
46 Emily Cockayne
47 Peter and Peggy Topps
48 Betty Brammer
49 Mark Acton
50 Jean and James Honeybone
51 Alison Honeybone
52 The Morley Family
53 Vic and Mu Martin

54 Emily and Rhys Jones
55 Joseph Martin and Emily Rubython
56 Andrew Gallop
57 Lucille Chesterton
58 Ralph Wadsworth
59 Derek Booles
60 Peter Elmer
61 Myles An Dyscajor
62 Ann Hoskins
63 Leslie Staniland
64 Alice Trickett
65 Pat Riley
66 Rev. Robert Sweeney
67–68 University of East Anglia Library
69 Keith Alexander Brodie
70 Mr and Mrs P. Allen
71 Rodney and Janet Callow, Lincoln
72 Roy and Pat Palmer
73 Julian Sadowski
74 Mrs Anne Cherry
75 Helen and Lee
76 Mr M.S. Plaskitt
77 Allan and Linda Shields
78 Professor John Pearn
79 Dr John B. Manterfield
80 Mrs Enid M. Bean
81 Barbara and Alan Pizzey
82 Malcolm Withers
83 The King's School, Grantham
84 Jon Elbourne
85 Naomi Field
86 Jane Frost
87 Jackie Fish
88 George Davidson
89 Hugh Holbrook
90 Stella Goldsborough
91 Pat Hodson
92 Barbara and Bob Tristram
93 Long Field High School, Melton Mowbray
94 Peter Noon
95 The University of Nottingham
96–98 Leicester City Libraries
99 Mrs Margaret Webster
100 Kim Graham for Spalding Grammar School
101 Sarah Christopher
102 Malcolm and Jennifer Swire
103 Christopher Kimberley
104 Norwich Cathedral Library

105 Wendy Lloyd
106–107 Andrew and Sarah Wells
108 Mary Owen
109 Mrs Sheila McAlpine Stevens
110 Douglas W. Huke
111 Claire Walton
112–113 Nottinghamshire County Library
114 Nancy and Michael Snowdon
115 Fiona Torrens-Spence
116 Angela and Alan Kapellar
117 Malcolm Hook
118 A.J. Macfarlane
119 Nigel Panting
120 Mrs Ann Riddoch
121 Richard and Chrisandra D'Arcy
122 Mr A.F. Morris
123 Mr R. Bradshaw
124 Hugh Burns
125 Rhi Clark
126 John Daybell
127 Brian Howes
128 Sallyann Jackson
129 Edwina V. Johnston
130 Mariya Limerick
131 Sarah Allen
132 R. and W. Lockey
133 Rinah M.Wall
134 Mrs J. Ward
135 Mrs R. Donaldson
136 Susan Ward
137 Bill Whitaker
138 Kirsten Harrison
139 Glyn Jones FRPS
140 Abbie Shephard
141 Maureen Cubitt
142 The Merchant's House, Marlborough
143 Sara Slinn
144 Mike and Gill Frisby
145 John Lethbridge
146 Paul Anderton
147 J.C. Head
148 Mrs Constance Summers
149 Malcolm Johnson
150 Carole and Roy Wiltshire
151 Pat Atkins
152 Molly A.B. Ford
153 Michael J. Ford
154 C.R. Lyon
155 H.P. Stephens
156 Joyce Barnes, Sam Branson
157 Geoffrey Elliott
158–159 David and Sue Middleton
160 Nicolaus Copernicus University, Torun, Poland
161 Dr hab. Jaroslaw Dumanowski
162 Brenda Coulson
163 June M.T. Edwards
164 Bromley House Library, Nottingham
165 David Cozens
166 The University of Illinois
167 Mrs A. Broadbent
168 Mr and Mrs N.R. Marshall
169 Geoffrey A. Petch
170 John Dockrell
171 Brian Jones
172 Mr K. Donlan
173 Linda and Terry Donlan
174 Mary and Nigel Morley
175 Ann and Barry Donlan
176 Ivan Morrell, Audrey Morrell
177 Christine Y.L. Drew
178 Jon Dawson
179 Nigel and Sylvia Turner
180 C.F.K. Granger
181 Chris and Emily Hurn
182 Brenda Pask
183 Mrs Irene Evans
184 Rev Charles Bradshaw

Remaining subscribers' names unlisted